The DarkWhale Protocol

By © Marco Beffa
www.marcobeffa.com

This book is dedicated to my wife, Laura, and my children, Beatrice, Camilla, Aurora, and Matteo, to my dad Ennio, and to all those who have joined the journey along the way, contributing ideas, insight, and encouragement.

Marco Beffa

Dear readers and friends, welcome back!

I'm excited to share this new book with you, a journey into a world where ideas move faster than institutions, where code rewrites the rules of trust, and where a single anonymous figure can change the course of financial history.

From the first spark of Bitcoin to the hidden architectures that now support decentralized systems, I will take you across moments of innovation, mystery, and quiet revolution, never alone, but always walking beside my imaginary friend, Satoshi Nakamoto. Along the way, concepts emerge naturally, carried by the narrative rather than imposed by explanation. You won't be asked to study crypto, you will experience it.

So buckle up. We are diving back into one of the most fascinating transformations ever to touch finance and technology. This is a voyage through innovation, ambition, and the search for autonomy in a digital age still being defined.

Table of contents

1. Your Cool, Fresh Path to Dive In

Welcome to this new chapter. This book is an invitation to venture forward, to draw meaning from every passage, every hidden signal, and every idea concealed within these pages, while transforming the act of reading into an unfolding adventure. What lies ahead is not an explanation of technology, but a passage into the unknown, an experience meant to intrigue, unsettle, and reward curiosity. My intention is not to instruct, but to open doors, guiding you through a world where crypto technologies emerge as living forces, shaping destinies, philosophies, and unseen economies waiting to be discovered.

Entering such territory is never simple. The landscapes we are about to cross are deep, complex, and often shrouded in uncertainty. That is why this journey has been shaped to progress gradually, like a careful descent into dark waters, advancing step by step, occasionally retreating, only to move forward again with greater awareness and courage.

Throughout the journey, familiar ideas will surface more than once, revealed from new angles and under different light. This repetition is deliberate. Like markers left by earlier travelers, these moments provide orientation when the path feels unclear. The crypto realm can resemble an unexplored world: vast, mysterious, and charged with hidden risks, where direction is never guaranteed. And in those moments of doubt or disorientation, recognizing something familiar restores balance, reignites resolve, and offers the strength to continue deeper into the unknown.

Above all, remember this: there is no urgency here. From the first page onward, the rhythm is yours. Some days you may advance cautiously, absorbing only a few lines. Other days, the current will carry you swiftly from chapter to chapter. Whatever the pace, the message remains unchanged, trust the path, follow the mystery, and enjoy the journey.

Important Notes to the Reader

Like Dante, who wrote La Divina Commedia imagining Virgil guiding him through Hell and Purgatory and Beatrice through Heaven, I imagined Satoshi Nakamoto, real person or mythological figure, as my guide through the crypto universe. It is a narrative device I particularly love, though naturally, my encounter with Satoshi Nakamoto exists solely in the realm of my imagination.

On the other hand, to honor transparency, that remains the most precious commodity in an age full of AI backed fakes, I want to disclose that The DarkWhale Protocol is a real project in which I am directly involved. It shares its name with the title of this book not by coincidence, but because it reflects my core conviction: the problem outlined and the broader concept underlying it, is fundamental to my crypto journey and to understanding the cryptocurrency market, as I anticipated in an article written for Cointelegraph in September 2019 (https://cointelegraph.com/news/the-original-sins-of-cryptocurrencies).

I have treated the subject with the same impartiality as all other projects outlined in this study, and this book remains a comprehensive and balanced exploration of the crypto space.

One final word before you venture further: cryptocurrency space remains a tempestuous sea, where fortunes rise and fall with the capricious tides. Nothing within these pages should be taken as financial advise, it is only informational.

I offer you stories and ideas, real facts and technology, not financial advice. This book stands independent: it endorses no venture (including my own disclosed involvement), accepts no payment from hidden benefactors, and answers to no master but the truth as I perceive it.

For the particulars that law demands, I direct you to the formal LEGAL DISCLAIMER awaiting you at the book's end. Read it. Accept it. Then return here, and let us begin this adventure together.

2. Me and Satoshi

Tokyo, 2008, mid November. The fluorescent lights of Narita Airport were like sharpened blades after so many hours in the dim cabin of my delayed flight. It was just past two in the morning, and the terminal had that strange, suspended quality that airports get in the middle of the night, too bright, too quiet, with the kind of artificial atmosphere that makes you forget what time zone you're supposed to be in. My legs were stiff as I joined the line of tired passengers shuffling toward the passport control, usually an extremely long process. The Japanese immigration officer looked impossibly alert for this hour, stamping my passport with a practiced efficiency that made me wonder if he'd been doing this job for decades or if this was just how things worked here. Baggage claim took another good forty minutes. I stood there with the other zombified travelers, watching suitcases circle the conveyor belt like some kind of industrial carousel. When my bag finally appeared, I grabbed it and headed for the exit, following the signs in three languages toward the shuttle buses. I walked to the bus platform number 5, a valid ticket in my hand. The shuttle to The Century Hyatt Shinjuku was already there, waiting for us with Japanese precision. The bus driver, perfectly focused and fully engaged in his task, stood strong and ready beside the bus, while we formed an orderly line. With Japanese efficiency, he helped each passenger stow their luggage in the compartment beneath, exchanging suitcases for numbered receipts, and, most remarkably, thanking every single traveler with a respectful bow, his hands in pristine white gloves. We left the platform perfectly on time, on a half-empty bus due to the late hour, carrying myself and a handful of other weary arrivals through the neon-lit Airport lines toward our hard earned rest. As we pulled away from the terminal, I settled into a window seat and watched Tokyo suburbs begin to reveal through the rain-streaked glass. The highway was quieter than I'd expected, just occasional trucks or taxi cutting through the downpour. The city unfolded gradually, still sleepy, first the industrial buildings and warehouses, then the residential blocks, with their neat rows of houses, and finally the denser urban landscape as we got closer to central Tokyo. Everything looked smaller and more human-scaled than I'd imagined, though maybe that was just the rain making everything seem softer around the edges. When you arrive in a city 13 hours ahead, after a never-ending flight, you feel completely scrambled. But my case was different, I felt excited and oddly alert. Not only I have always been in love with Japan, with his incredible mix of ancient and ultra-modern, vending machines, bullet trains and thousand-year-old temples, all existing in the same space, but even more importantly, I wasn't here as a tourist. A weird professor named Satoshi Nakamoto had invited me to meet with his research group, scientists working on something he'd described as "revolutionary" in his carefully worded email and the following dozens of phone calls. I was a broke visionary, my hedge fund had collapsed shortly after Lehman Brothers brought down half of Wall Street. Fifteen years of work vanished over the course of a single weekend. I watched my colleagues pack their belongings into cardboard boxes under the quiet gaze of security guards, who stood by with the indifferent patience of undertakers. In the aftermath, I wrote a sudden, impassioned blog post condemning the financial crisis and the crumbling global financial framework. I called for a new dawn in finance, one free from central authorities. And apparently, I had hit the mark, my blog went viral almost instantly, resonating with all those devastated by the financial crisis that was swallowing up wealth built over generations. And it caught as well the attention of Professor Satoshi Nakamoto. He was actually looking for someone from the wreckage of centralized finance to join his project, not just as a contributor, but as living proof of the old system's failure, and I was more than willing to take on that role.

While I was lost in my thoughts, the bus sped ahead. The neon signs became more frequent as we approached Shinjuku, their colors bleeding into watercolor smears through the rain. Convenience stores glowed like beacons on empty street corners, while Pachinko parlors seemed to be crowded as usual. Tokyo's night wild-siders and early commuters crossed paths in an unexpected mix: club-goers in sparkly outfits holding their shoes walked next to workers gripping briefcases. Their umbrellas formed a patchy roof over this quiet shift from night to day, where tiredness and determination shared the same wet street. There was something hypnotic about watching it all slide past, the way the rain and motion and glass created this protective barrier between me and the real world outside.

When we arrived at the hotel and I finally reached my room, it looked like the perfect place.

I entered, it was small, perfectly cleaned, and through the windows Tokyo was spreading out in all directions, neon signs flickering, traffic flowing like rivers of light, the whole sprawling mystery of it breathing just beyond the glass. The city hummed with secrets I couldn't yet understand. The bed welcomed me like an old friend, and within minutes, Tokyo's distant glow was the last thing I saw before sleep pulled me under.

The next day, despite the short sleep, I woke up energized. Before breakfast I unpacked my single suitcase, another sign of how thoroughly my life had contracted, and tried to settle into the alien rhythm of jet lag. Outside, the city hummed with its electric lullaby: the distant rumble of trains, the melodic chiming of convenience store doors, and the soft percussion of rain on corrugated metal roofs. It was a sound I would come to know intimately over the months that followed, the soundtrack to the most extraordinary period of my life.

Professor Satoshi Nakamoto occupied an office that seemed to exist in deliberate opposition to the mathematical precision of Japanese architecture. Books leaned against each other in precarious towers, academic papers spread across every available surface like the residue of some intellectual explosion, and coffee and tea cups in various states of abandonment, marked the archaeological layers of his work. He was younger than I'd expected, with the kind of intense energy that made the small space feel even more crowded. He was wearing simple clothing, dark jeans, a plain gray hoodie, and worn sneakers. Nothing about his appearance draws attention. Mid-thirties to early forties, average height and build, with intelligent but guarded eyes behind simple glasses, a salt-and-pepper beard. His hair slightly disheveled, as if he's been running his hands through it while thinking through complex problems. With a reserved but genuine smile, he bowed slightly and spoke in careful, accented English: "Ohayou gozaimasu, Marco-san. I hope your journey wasn't too difficult. To be honest, I wasn't entirely certain either of us would follow through."

I settled into the chair across from him, noting how he'd chosen a corner table with clear sight-lines to both exits. "I keep my word when it matters," I replied. "Though I have to admit, I questioned this decision at least three times."

He chuckled softly, a sound that seemed rusty from disuse. "Only three times? I've been second-guessing this meeting for weeks." His fingers drummed once against his coffee cup before he caught himself and stilled them. "But curiosity won out, I suppose. It always does with me". His gaze settled on me with quiet intensity, dark eyes searching my face as if weighing some internal calculation about risk and trust. The silence stretched for a moment, not uncomfortable, but charged with the weight of his decision to be here. When he finally lifted his coffee cup, his movements were deliberate, almost ritualistic. He paused, seeming to choose his words with the same precision he once used to craft code "The American financial system failed completely, it has revealed itself to be a house of cards built on a foundation of sand. But you know this already." I nodded, still adjusting to his directness. In New York, such conversations would begin with more pleasantries, a gradual circling toward the actual topic like planes waiting for clearance to land. Here, Professor Satoshi seemed to prefer verbal kamikaze attacks. "The question," he continued, pushing the cup of coffee across the cluttered desk, "is what comes next. How do we rebuild trust in a system that has demonstrated its fundamental untrustworthiness?" The coffee was Japanese style, that means dish rinse, but scorching hot, warming me from the inside as the rain continued its assault on the windows. "That's what I'm here to figure out," I said. "Though I have to admit, my perspective is somewhat... compromised. I was part of the system that failed." "Good," he said, leaning back in his chair with satisfaction. "The best doctors are those who have been sick themselves. You understand the disease from the inside."

We talked for two hours that first meeting, ranging across topics from the psychology of market bubbles to the mathematical models that had proven so spectacularly wrong. Professor Nakamoto possessed the rare academic gift of being able to discuss complex ideas without retreating into jargon, and I found myself genuinely excited about intellectual discourse for the first time in months. As our conversation wound down, he mentioned almost casually, "There's a small group that meets once a week to discuss these sorts of questions. Computer scientists, mostly, some economists, a few philosophers. Very informal, very... how do you say... cutting edge? You might find it interesting." "What kind of cutting edge?" I asked. He smiled, and I caught a glimpse of something almost conspiratorial in his expression. "The kind that imagines entirely new solutions to old problems. We meet Thursday evenings. I'll introduce you, if you're interested." And, of course, I was.

The Thursday meeting took place in a basement room beneath the Faculty of Engineering building, the kind of space that seemed designed for conspiracy. Fluorescent lights cast harsh shadows across concrete walls, and the air carried the mingled scents of tea, instant ramen, and the ozone smell of electronic equipment. Six people sat around a rectangular table that had seen better decades, laptops open, notebooks filled with diagrams that looked like circuit boards crossed with flowcharts. Professor Satoshi made introductions with characteristic efficiency. Haruki Sato, a doctoral student in cryptography with fingernails bitten down to the quick, Professor Hiroshi Nakamura, an economics professor whose gentle manner masked what I would soon discover was a razor-sharp intellect. Keiko

Kobayashi, a software engineer from a major tech company who spoke in precise, measured sentences. Two other graduate students whose names I immediately forgot in the overwhelming flood of new information. Satoshi sat at the far end of the table, slightly apart from the others in a way that suggested either shyness or deliberate separation. When Professor Nakamura introduced him, he nodded once but said nothing. "We were just discussing the implications of the Lehman collapse," Professor Nakamura said, turning to me with polite interest. "Nakamoto-san mentioned you have firsthand experience with the American financial system?" For the next hour, I found myself serving as a reluctant tour guide through the wreckage of Wall Street. I described the atmosphere in the weeks leading up to the collapse, the gallows humor, the increasingly desperate attempts to shore up failing positions, the way seasoned traders had started to look like deer caught in headlights. The group listened with the fascinated attention of scientists observing an interesting specimen. "But the fundamental problem," Haruki said, leaning forward intently, "is trust, yes? The entire system depends on trust, but there's no technological guarantee of that trust. It's all based on... what would you call it... reputation? Promises?" "Social consensus," Professor Nakamura added. "Which can evaporate overnight, as we've seen." I nodded. "The whole edifice is built on the assumption that everyone will continue to believe in it. When that belief disappears..." I gestured helplessly.

Satoshi took the floor, his voice quiet, but carried clearly across the room, with the slight formality that marked him as someone who had learned English as a second language but mastered it completely. "What if there was a way to remove human trust from the equation entirely?" The question hung in the air for a moment. Keiko frowned. "But trust is fundamental to any monetary system. How can you have exchange without trust?" “I said human trust. You replace it with mathematics, that is a much more solid kind of trust" Satoshi said simply. "You create a system where human trust is not required because the rules are enforced by cryptographic proof rather than by institutions or individuals." Haruki laughed, but not unkindly. "That's impossible. Money is a social construct. It only has value because we agree it has value." "Yes," Satoshi said. "But the agreement doesn't have to be based on faith in central authorities. It can be based on mathematical certainty." "What are you proposing, exactly?" Professor Nakamura asked. Satoshi was quiet for a long moment, his fingers drumming silently on the table. When he spoke again, his words seemed to come from some deep, private place. "A peer-to-peer electronic cash system. No central authority, no single point of failure. Every transaction verified by the network itself, secured by cryptographic proof that cannot be falsified or reversed." The room fell silent except for the hum of fluorescent lights and the distant sound of traffic. I found myself leaning forward, caught by something in his tone, not the excitement of someone proposing a theoretical solution, but the certainty of someone describing something that already existed, yet not public. "How?" Keiko asked simply. "That," Satoshi said, "is what I'm working on."

The meeting broke up around ten-thirty, the participants gathering their laptops and notebooks with the weary efficiency of academics everywhere. As I prepared to leave, Satoshi approached me with the careful politeness that seemed to characterize all his interactions. "Would you like to get a real coffee?" he asked. "I'd be interested in hearing more about your experience with the American financial system." We stepped out into the Tokyo night, the air crisp with the promise of winter. The rain had stopped, leaving the streets gleaming like black mirrors that reflected the neon signs in fractured rainbows. Satoshi led me through a maze of narrow alleys, past tiny bars with red lanterns hanging outside like glowing fruit, past the warm golden light spilling from convenience stores where salarymen bought late-night dinners and students clutched coffee in both hands. "There's a place nearby that stays open late," he said as we walked. "They make exceptional coffee. The owner is... eccentric, but he understands the craft." The coffee shop, when we found it, proved to be exactly the kind of place that could only exist in Tokyo: impossibly narrow, with a counter that seated perhaps eight people and a proprietor who treated coffee preparation with the solemnity of a tea ceremony. The owner, a man in his sixties with careful hands and wire-rimmed glasses, greeted

Satoshi with a slight bow and began preparing is famous coffee without being asked. "He knows what I drink," Satoshi explained as we settled onto the narrow stools. "I come here often." The coffee, when it arrived, was perfect, rich and complex, with layers of flavor that revealed themselves slowly. We sat in comfortable silence for a few minutes, watching the proprietor work with the focused attention of a master craftsman. The shop felt like a sanctuary, insulated from the chaos of the city outside. "Tell me about the moment you knew it was over," Satoshi said finally. "Your fund, I mean. When did you realize that everything was going to collapse?" I thought about it, wrapping my hands around the warm cup. "There wasn't really a single moment. It was more like watching a slow-motion avalanche. First one position failed, then another, then the dominoes started falling faster than we could react. But I think the moment I really understood what was happening was when I realized that all our sophisticated models, all our risk management systems, all our mathematical certainty, none of it mattered. We had built everything on assumptions that turned out to be false." "What kind of assumptions?" "That markets were rational. That risk could be quantified and managed. That the future would resemble the past in predictable ways. That the people we were dealing with were acting in good faith." I took a sip of coffee, feeling the bitter warmth. "We thought we had eliminated uncertainty, but we had just hidden it from ourselves." Satoshi nodded slowly. "And yet you still believe in mathematics." "I believe in mathematics," I said. "I'm less sure about human nature." "What if you didn't have to choose between them?" Before I could ask what he meant, he was standing, placing money on the counter with another small bow to the proprietor. "I want to show you something," he said. "But not here. Too many ears."

We walked deeper into the city, through neighborhoods that seemed to exist in different time zones. Traditional wooden houses squeezed between glass and steel towers, vending machines glowing like altars on every corner, the sound of karaoke drifting from basement bars. Tokyo at night revealed itself in layers, each turn exposing some new configuration of old and new, traditional and impossibly modern. Finally, we stopped at a small park, really just a patch of grass and a few benches surrounded by apartment buildings that rose like cliffs on all sides. Satoshi sat on one of the benches, pulling out a laptop with practiced efficiency. "What I'm about to show you," he said, "doesn't exist yet. Not fully. But the foundation is there." The laptop screen illuminated his face as he opened what appeared to be a technical document. Even in the dim light, I could see that it was densely packed with mathematical formulas, diagrams, and text that read like a hybrid of computer science and economics. "Bitcoin," he said simply. "A peer-to-peer electronic cash system." For the next two hours, as the city settled into its late-night rhythm around us, Satoshi walked me through the most elegant solution to the problem of trust I had ever encountered. He explained how cryptographic hashing could create an immutable record of transactions, how a distributed network could verify those transactions without any central authority, how economic incentives could align individual self-interest with the security of the entire system. "But how do you prevent double-spending?" I asked. It was the obvious question, the one that had doomed every previous attempt at digital cash. "Proof of work," he said, and proceeded to explain how computational power could serve as a kind of democratic voting system, where the longest chain of blocks represented the consensus of the network. "The chain with the most accumulated work is the true record. To falsify it, you would need to control more computational power than the rest of the network combined." "And why would anyone contribute that computational power?" "Because they're rewarded for it. New bitcoins are created and awarded to the miners who secure the network. It's a self-reinforcing system, the more valuable bitcoin becomes, the more incentive people have to mine it, which makes the network more secure, which makes bitcoin more valuable." I stared at the screen, trying to process the implications. "This is..." "Impossible?" he suggested with a slight smile. "Revolutionary," I said.

Word of Satoshi's project spread through the small academic community with the speed that only truly controversial ideas can achieve. By the following Thursday, the basement meeting room was more crowded, with several new faces joining our regular group. The atmosphere had shifted from casual intellectual discussion to something more charged, more urgent. "It's an interesting thought experiment," said Professor Nakayama from the economics department, a thin man with the pinched expression of someone who had spent his career studying the careful balance of established systems. "But there are fundamental problems with the approach." "Such as?" Satoshi asked mildly. "Scalability, for one. If every transaction has to be verified by the entire network, how do you handle the volume of transactions in a real economy? Visa processes thousands of transactions per second. Your system would grind to a halt." "The base layer doesn't need to handle every transaction," Satoshi replied. "Think of it as digital gold rather than digital cash. Higher-value transactions, settlements between institutions, store of value functions. Secondary layers can handle smaller, more frequent transactions." "But then you're back to trusted intermediaries," Haruki pointed out. "Doesn't that defeat the purpose?" "Not if the intermediaries can't steal or censor. If they're operating on top of an immutable base layer, they can facilitate transactions but they can't create money out of thin air or prevent legitimate transactions from occurring." Professor Nakamura leaned forward, his gentle demeanor masking sharp analysis. "The energy consumption concerns me. This proof-of-work system you're describing, it would require enormous amounts of computational power. We're talking about a system that could consume as much electricity as a small country."

"Yes," Satoshi said simply. "And you think that's justified?" "How much energy does the current financial system consume? Not just the computers and the buildings, but the entire infrastructure of trust. Central banks, regulatory agencies, compliance departments, fraud prevention, legal systems to resolve disputes. Armies to enforce the sovereignty that backs national currencies. All of that has an energy cost." "That's different," Professor Nakayama objected. "Those institutions serve multiple purposes. They provide regulation, consumer protection, monetary policy" "They provide control," Satoshi interrupted, and for the first time I heard real emotion in his voice. "They decide who can participate, what transactions are allowed, how money is created and destroyed. They are, ultimately, systems of human authority. And human authority, as recent events have demonstrated, is fallible." The room fell quiet. Outside, I could hear the sound of a train pulling into a nearby station, its arrival announced by the characteristic two-tone chime that marked the rhythm of Tokyo life. "There's another problem," said Keiko quietly. "Adoption. Why would anyone use this system when existing payment methods work perfectly well? Credit cards are convenient, bank transfers are instant, cash is anonymous. What does bitcoin offer that these systems don't?" It was Haruki who answered, surprising everyone. "Sovereignty," she said. "Financial sovereignty. The ability to hold and transfer value without asking permission from anyone." "But most people don't want that responsibility," Keiko countered.

"They want deposit insurance, fraud protection, customer service when something goes wrong. They want trusted institutions to handle the complexity." "Some people want that," Satoshi said. "Others want something different. Others want to opt out of a system that has repeatedly failed them, that excludes them, that treats their savings as raw material for speculative games they don't understand and didn't consent to participate in." "You're talking about a very small market," Professor Nakayama said dismissively. "Yes," Satoshi agreed. "At first, only at first"

Three weeks later, Satoshi asked me to meet him at a small okonomiyaki restaurant in Harajuku. The place was exactly the kind of establishment that made Tokyo magical, its weathered wooden facade squeezed between a vintage clothing boutique and a crepe stand. Inside, three low square tables dominated the cramped space, each crowned with a gleaming teppan griddle that radiated gentle heat and the promise of sizzling comfort food. The proprietor, a wiry man with flour-dusted hands and worry lines etched deep around kind eyes, moved between his guests with an almost choreographed grace. He would bow apologetically while simultaneously flipping batter, refilling tea, and somehow managing to remember exactly how each customer preferred their okonomiyaki, extra sauce, light on the mayo, double the bonito flakes dancing in the steam. The air was thick with the intoxicating aroma of browning batter mingled with sweet cabbage, punctuated by the sharp sizzle of ingredients hitting the hot iron. Wisps of savory steam curled upward, carrying hints of Worcestershire sauce and the oceanic essence of dried seaweed. Even before sliding onto the low wooden stools, the smell alone was enough to make your stomach growl in anticipation.

"I've finished the first draft," he said without preamble, sliding a printed document across the counter. "I'd like you to read it." The paper was nine pages long, titled "Bitcoin: A Peer-to-Peer Electronic Cash System," and it was immediately clear that this was something extraordinary. The writing was precise and mathematical, but also accessible, complex ideas explained with the kind of clarity that comes only from deep understanding. I read it twice while Satoshi prepared okonomiyaki with the same focused attention he brought to everything else. "This is going to change everything," I said finally. "Maybe," he said, flipping the okonomiyaki with practiced skill. "Or maybe it will disappear into obscurity like most academic papers." "You don't believe that." He was quiet for a moment, concentrating on the griddle. "I believe it solves the problem it was designed to solve. Whether anyone cares about that problem..." He shrugged. "How do you plan to implement it?" "Open source. Release the paper, release the code, let anyone who's interested contribute to the development." "And then?" "And then we see what happens." The okonomiyaki was perfect–crispy on the outside, soft and warm inside, with the complex umami flavor that made it impossible to stop eating. We ate in companionable silence, surrounded by the conversations of other late-night diners and the sizzle of the griddle. "Can I ask you something?" I said eventually. "Of course." "Why are you doing this? I mean, really. You could patent this system, start a company, become incredibly wealthy. Instead, you're planning to give it away for free." Satoshi was quiet for a long time, long enough that I began to wonder if he had heard the question. When he finally spoke, his voice was so soft I had to lean forward to hear him. "Because the world needs it to be free. Because the moment someone owns it, controls it, profits from it exclusively, it becomes just another system of authority. Just another way for some people to have power over others." He looked up at me, and I saw something in his eyes that might have been pain. "The point isn't to get rich. The point is to make getting rich irrelevant."

On January 3, 2009 The Bitcoin Genesis Block (Block 0) was mined at approximately 18:15:05 UTC. The new finance was born.

Soon after Satoshi disappeared. No farewell parties, no dramatic pronouncements, no final public statements about Bitcoin's future. He simply stopped being around, responding to emails, contributing to the software development. By December 2009, it was clear that he had vanished as completely as if he had never existed. The community's reaction was mixed. Some panicked, worried that Bitcoin would collapse without its creator's guidance. Others celebrated, arguing that his departure proved the system's decentralized nature. Still others became obsessed with solving the mystery of his identity, analyzing his writing style, searching for clues in his code, constructing elaborate theories about who he really was. I found myself in the unusual position of being one of the few people who had known him personally, which made me a target for investigators and journalists who descended on Tokyo like digital archaeologists searching for artifacts of the bitcoin creation myth. I told them nothing, partly out of loyalty to Satoshi's wishes but mostly because I realized that the mystery was more valuable than the truth. I thought about this as I walked back to the Hotel through the winter streets of Tokyo, past the convenience stores and noodle shops that had become as familiar as the furniture in my apartment. The city looked different now than it had when I first arrived, not because anything had changed, but because I was changed and I had learned to see it differently. The chaos was still there, but so was the underlying order. The neon signs still blazed, but I could now read the kanji characters that gave them meaning. The crowds still surged through the subway stations, but I had learned the rhythm of their movement. Bitcoin, I realized, was undergoing a similar transformation. What had seemed like revolutionary chaos was gradually revealing its underlying structure. The technology worked, the economics were sound, and the community, despite its disagreements, was growing and adapting. Satoshi's disappearance wasn't the end of the story, it was the beginning of a new chapter.

The mystery of Satoshi Nakamoto identity remains unsolved, and I'm glad for that. People still analyze his writing, dissect his code, construct elaborate theories about who he really was. But the man I knew in Tokyo, quiet, brilliant, driven by a vision of financial sovereignty that transcended personal gain, has become a legend, a ghost in the machine he created.

I immersed myself in the world of blockchain and cryptocurrency described by Satoshi in detail, devouring white papers, essays, and opinion pieces from experts in the field. I attended conferences and meetups, eager to learn more about this new frontier that seemed to hold endless potential. I became an active participant in online forums, where discussions about the latest developments in the crypto world flowed as freely as the digital assets themselves. I wanted to understand every aspect of this rapidly evolving space, from the technical intricacies of blockchain architecture to the philosophical implications of decentralization. It wasn't long before I decided to invest in Bitcoin. I knew that investing in Bitcoin was a risk, but it felt like the right kind of risk, the kind that could pay off in more ways than just financial gain. Bitcoin represented a revolution in the way we think about money, ownership, and power, and I wanted to be a part of that revolution. As I watched the value of Bitcoin rise, I felt a rush of excitement that was unlike anything I had experienced before. It wasn't just about the potential for profit, it was about being part of something bigger, something that had the power to change the world. The more I learned about the underlying technology and the vision of those who were building the crypto ecosystem, the more I realized that this was more than just a passing trend, it was a movement. A movement toward a future where financial systems are open, transparent, and accessible to everyone, regardless of their background or location. But what truly cemented my love for crypto was the realization that it wasn't just about the technology, it was about the people. The crypto community is a diverse, passionate, and innovative group of individuals who are united by a shared belief in the power of decentralization. Whether they are developers building the next generation of blockchain protocols, investors looking to support the most promising projects, or enthusiasts simply eager to learn more, they are all part of a global movement that is working to create a better, fairer financial system. This love for crypto continues to blow wind into my sails even now. Over the years, I've witnessed incredible advancements in the space, new blockchain platforms, decentralized finance (DeFi) projects, non-fungible tokens (NFTs), Real-World Assets Tokenization (RWAs), Stablecoins, CBDCs and countless other innovations that have expanded the boundaries of what's possible. I've also seen the challenges and setbacks, from market crashes to regulatory hurdles, but these have only strengthened my belief in the long-term potential of the technology. In many ways, my journey with crypto feels like an epic adventure, a journey through uncharted territory where the possibilities are endless and the stakes are high. But it's also a deeply personal journey, one that has reshaped the way I think about money, technology, and the future.

Though Satoshi has vanished, he lives on in my heart. He sparked my Satori, my complete awakening, and that fire still burns within me. Now and then, amid discussions of cryptocurrencies and blockchains, he and I fall into dialogue. He is the voice I seek when navigating the crypto world, my Virgil guiding me through this digital odyssey, just as Dante's Virgil led him through the Divine Comedy.

3. Exploration

Satoshi suddenly smiled, as if reading my thoughts, and spoke first.

"Dear Marco," he began, his voice carrying the quiet certainty of someone who had seen the future before others even knew to look, "it is as simple as that: Cryptocurrencies are digital assets enabling decentralized transactions among peers." He paused, letting the words settle between us like seeds waiting for soil. "In another way, a different form of exchanging money, digital money, from one person to another."

I leaned forward, my curiosity overcoming my initial hesitation. "But surely," I ventured, "there must be more to it than that simple definition. How did we arrive here? What path led humanity to this particular moment in financial history?"

Satoshi nodded, a glint of appreciation in his eyes, as though I had asked precisely the question he hoped to answer.

"Before we move forward," he continued, folding his hands thoughtfully on the table, "we must first understand the journey that has shaped the crypto space into what it is today."

I reached for my notebook, sensing that what followed would demand careful attention. "You speak of origins," I observed. "Of looking backward to move forward."

"I firmly believe," Satoshi affirmed, his gaze steady and unwavering, "that to truly grasp the present, and to anticipate the future, of any major story in human history, we must understand its origins, its underlying mechanics, and the technology that shaped it."

I considered this for a moment, then pressed further. "And without this foundation? What happens to those who rush ahead without understanding the ground beneath their feet?"

A shadow of something, perhaps sadness, perhaps merely resignation, passed across his features. "Without this foundation," he replied, "any hope to fully master the crypto space is vain."

The weight of his words hung in the air. I set down my pen and looked at him directly. "Can you give me an image? Something to help me understand why this historical perspective matters so deeply?"

Satoshi's expression softened, and when he spoke again, there was almost a poetic quality to his voice. "Just as one cannot truly understand where the sweetness of a ripe fruit is coming from without recognizing the farmer's labor, the power of the sun, and the magic of nature," he explained, gesturing gently as if tracing the arc of a growing vine, "we too must look back to the origins to understand the miracle of the crypto space."

I found myself nodding slowly, the metaphor taking root in my imagination. The farmer's hands in the soil. The patient waiting for seasons to turn. The invisible alchemy of photosynthesis transforming light into life. And somewhere in all of that, the emergence of something sweet, something valuable, something that could only exist because of everything that came before it.

"So this is where we begin," I said, more statement than question.

Satoshi smiled once more, and in that smile was the promise of everything yet to be revealed.

"This," he confirmed, "is where we begin."

4. The Epic of Crypto Space

"From a futuristic vision," I began, my voice steadier than I felt, "people speak of cryptocurrencies as though they emerged fully formed from the digital ether. Decentralized currency, transparent transactions, borderless finance these words get thrown around like confetti at a parade. But I want to understand the roots. Where did this really begin?"

Satoshi leaned back, fingers wrapped around slight smile, with the expression of someone recalling a distant memory. "The dream of a decentralized currency," Satoshi began, voice quiet but measured, "leverages blockchain technology to offer transparent, secure, and borderless transactions. Over the years, the crypto ecosystem has expanded to include thousands of coins, tokens, and applications, reshaping industries from finance to gaming. The history of cryptocurrency is a journey of technological innovation, economic disruption, and regulatory challenges. Understanding this evolution provides key insights into the future of digital finance and decentralized systems."

I nodded slowly, scribbling notes that I knew I would barely be able to read later. "But surely," I pressed, "this didn't start with you. There must have been foundations–intellectual predecessors who laid the groundwork?"

Satoshi set down the coffee cup with a soft clink against the saucer. Their eyes grew distant, as though peering through decades of accumulated history.

"The story of blockchain technology didn't begin with me," they acknowledged, and there was no false modesty in the statement–only fact. "No, its roots stretch back, deep into the fertile ground of cryptography and distributed systems, disciplines that quietly evolved over decades. Like the slow, patient growth of a tree, these two fields gradually developed the tools that would one day form the foundation for something far bigger–a decentralized digital ledger that would change the world."

I watched the steam curl upward from my own untouched tea, imagining those decades of quiet progress–mathematicians hunched over equations, computer scientists wrestling with theoretical frameworks, all of them unaware that they were building toward something revolutionary.

"From the 1970s through the 1990s," Satoshi continued, their voice taking on the cadence of a storyteller who had told this tale many times, if only to themselves, "cryptographic innovations and the concept of decentralization began to take shape, each step forward paving the way for the blockchain technology we know today."

"Cryptography," I repeated, testing the word as though it might reveal secrets on my tongue. "That's the science of codes and ciphers, isn't it? The art of keeping secrets?"

Satoshi's smile widened slightly. "At the heart of this early development was cryptography," they confirmed, "the quiet giant that laid the cornerstone of security. But it's more than just secrets. It's about trust–mathematical trust that doesn't require human intermediaries. It's about creating certainty in an uncertain world."

The café seemed to grow quieter around us, as though the very walls were leaning in to listen. Outside, the world continued its relentless motion–cars passing, people hurrying to appointments, the endless churn of commerce and communication. But here, in this small corner of space and time, we were touching something essential about how human beings could organize themselves, how they could exchange value and verify truth without the need for kings or banks or bureaucrats.

"So cryptography gave us the ability to secure information," I said, my mind racing to connect the threads, "and distributed systems gave us the ability to spread that information across multiple nodes, removing any single point of failure or control?"

Satoshi inclined their head in acknowledgment. "Precisely. The marriage of these two disciplines–cryptographic security and distributed architecture–created the possibility for something that had never existed before: a system where strangers could transact with complete confidence, where the rules were enforced not by institutions but by mathematics itself."

I set down my pen, suddenly aware that the afternoon light had begun to fade. Hours had passed like minutes. The weight of what we had discussed–the decades of incremental progress, the convergence of abstract theories into practical tools, the audacious vision of a world where trust could be computed rather than conferred–settled over me like a blanket.

"This is just the beginning of the story, isn't it?" I asked, already knowing the answer.

Satoshi rose from the booth, their figure casting a long shadow in the dying light. They paused at the edge of the table, looking back with an expression that held both warmth and something harder to name–perhaps the loneliness of vision, perhaps the satisfaction of seeds finally bearing fruit.

"Every revolution begins with foundations that most people never see," they said softly. "The blockchain, cryptocurrency, decentralized finance–these are just the visible branches. The roots go deeper than most realize, and they're still growing."

And with that, they were gone, leaving me alone with my cold tea and a notebook full of questions that would take years to fully answer. But that, I realized, was exactly the point. The story of blockchain was not a single chapter but an ongoing narrative, one that stretched back through decades of quiet innovation and forward into a future we were only beginning to imagine.

Outside, the first stars were appearing in the darkening sky, pinpoints of light that had taken millions of years to reach my eyes. Like the cryptographic breakthroughs of the 1970s, like the distributed systems of the 1990s, they were reminders that the most profound transformations often begin in silence, in the patient accumulation of small advances that one day, suddenly, change everything.

4.1 Cryptography

Cryptography is the science of securing communication and data from unauthorized access, ensuring confidentiality, integrity, authenticity, and non-repudiation. It has been used for centuries, evolving from simple substitution ciphers in ancient times to highly advanced algorithms in modern computing. In the digital age, cryptography is fundamental to securing information, especially in sectors like finance, communication, and military operations. One of the most transformative applications of cryptography has been its use in blockchain technology, which underpins cryptocurrencies like my beloved son, Bitcoin, and decentralized systems. Cryptography primarily deals with two key operations: encryption (the process of converting plaintext into ciphertext) and decryption (the process of converting ciphertext back into plaintext). There are various forms of cryptographic techniques that ensure the secure transmission and storage of data. In **Symmetric Key Cryptography,** both the sender and the receiver share the same key for encryption and decryption. The key must remain confidential for the system to be secure. While symmetric cryptography is efficient and fast, the challenge lies in securely distributing the key. Example: **The Advanced Encryption Standard (AES)** is a widely used symmetric-key encryption algorithm. On the other side **Asymmetric Key Cryptography,** the one used in blockchain technology, is also known as public-key cryptography, and uses two keys: a public key (which can be shared with everyone) and a private key (which remains confidential to the owner). The public key encrypts the data, while the private key decrypts it, or vice versa. This system solves the key distribution problem of symmetric cryptography. You must always remember that cryptography plays a critical role in Blockchain Technology, ensuring that transactions are secure, immutable, and decentralized. To be more precise, in a blockchain network, every participant has a public key and a private key. The public key is used to generate a blockchain address and is publicly visible. The private key is used to sign transactions, proving ownership and authorization to transfer assets like cryptocurrencies. This public-private key system ensures that only the owner of the private key can authorize a transaction from their account. As an example, in Bitcoin blockchain users generate a wallet, which is essentially a pair of cryptographic keys, that allows them to send and receive Bitcoin securely.

One of the most vital tools in blockchain technology is the **Cryptographic Hash Function.** These functions are designed to take an input of any length and generate a fixed-length string of characters, a hash, that uniquely represents the original data. They are deterministic (the same input always produces the same output), irreversible (it's computationally infeasible to derive the original input from the hash, and collision-resistant (it's difficult to find two different inputs that produce the same output). Even a minor change in input produces a completely different output, making these functions essential for data integrity, security, and verification across the blockchain. Among them, **SHA-256 (Secure Hash Algorithm 256-bit)** plays a pivotal role. It's a specific type of cryptographic hash function, not a category in itself, but a standardized algorithm that produces a 256-bit output. SHA-256 is the engine behind many core processes in Bitcoin and other blockchains, including block creation, transaction IDs, and mining. While all SHA-256 hashes are cryptographic hash functions, not all cryptographic hash functions are SHA-256, there are many algorithms in the broader family, each with distinct features and applications. Still, SHA-256 remains the most iconic within the crypto space, embodying the principles of trustless security at the heart of decentralized systems.

Schematic Diagram: Blockchain as a System of Blocks and Walls

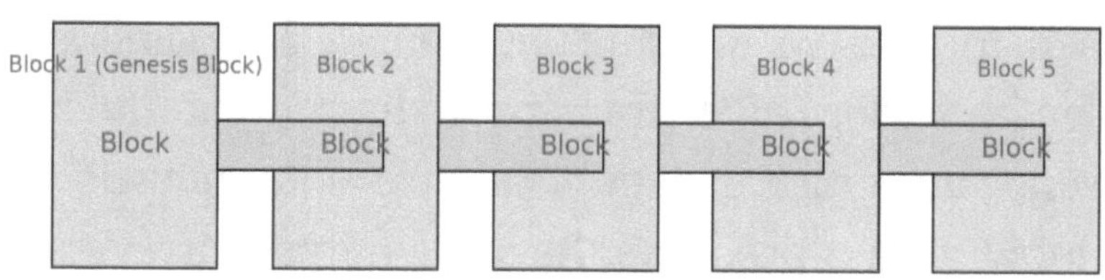

As you can easily notice, in the typical blockchain framework illustrated above the "seed" (in yellow) of a block is the hash of the previous block's header. To be more precise, each block has a block header containing key metadata (timestamp, Merkle root, nonce, etc.), and one of the fields in the block header is the hash of the previous block's header (i.e. the SHA-256 digest of the previous block). This is what links blocks together, forming a chain, because each block cryptographically points to the one before it. This design makes the chain tamper-evident: altering a previous block would change its hash, breaking the chain.

In Bitcoin specifically, the double SHA-256 hash of the block header is used in the Proof-of-Work process to find a valid block (i.e. a hash below a certain target).

But let's finishing up this part with some more interesting features.

Digital Signatures are used to verify the authenticity and integrity of a message, transaction, or data. In blockchain, digital signatures ensure that only the rightful owner of a cryptocurrency can authorize the transfer of funds. Each transaction is signed with the sender's private key, and anyone in the network can verify the signature using the corresponding public key. A good example is the **ECDSA (Elliptic Curve Digital Signature Algorithm),** commonly used for digital signatures in blockchain systems, including Bitcoin and Ethereum.

But please let's not forget **Merkle Trees**, the backbone of blockchain integrity and verification. A Merkle tree is a cryptographic structure that organizes data into a tree of hashes, where each leaf node represents a data block's hash, and non-leaf nodes represent hashes of their child nodes. This ensures efficient and secure data verification by allowing any modification to be detected with minimal recalculations. Cryptographic hash functions are used in Merkle trees to structure transaction data efficiently. Each transaction is hashed, and these hashes are recursively combined to create a root hash, which summarizes all the transactions in a block.

Elliptic Curve Cryptography (ECC) is a public-key cryptography system based on the algebraic structure of elliptic curves. ECC provides the same level of security as RSA (a public-key cryptographic system named after its inventors Rivest, Shamir, and Adleman), but with much smaller key sizes, making it more efficient for use in blockchain systems.

Zero-Knowledge Proofs (ZKPs) is a cryptographic method that is gaining more and more traction as we speak. It allows one party (the prover) to prove to another party (the verifier) that they know a certain piece of information without revealing what that information is. ZKPs are perfect for privacy-preserving features, and are used in privacy-focused blockchains like **Zcash**, which allows users to hide transaction amounts and addresses while still verifying that the transaction is valid.

Homomorphic Encryption is a type of encryption that allows computations to be performed on encrypted data without needing to decrypt it first. This concept has enormous potential for blockchain and decentralized finance (DeFi), as it would allow sensitive financial data to be processed while remaining encrypted.

Threshold cryptography, on the other side, allows a group of participants to jointly perform cryptographic operations such as signing a transaction or decrypting a message. It has applications in blockchain governance, where multiple parties must come to a consensus to approve changes.

Having explored classical cryptographic methods such as hash functions (SHA-256), elliptic curve cryptography (ECC), and digital signatures, it becomes essential to turn our attention to a rapidly emerging frontier: **Quantum-Resistant Cryptography,** also known as post-quantum cryptography (**PQC**). While today's cryptographic primitives have served blockchain systems reliably, ensuring data integrity, authentication, and immutability, the looming advancement of **Quantum Computing** poses an existential threat to these very foundations. Quantum computers, leveraging principles like superposition and entanglement, could theoretically break widely used algorithms such as RSA, ECC, and even certain hash-based structures, with Shor's algorithm and Grover's algorithm at the heart of this disruption. The threat is not theoretical anymore. Though scalable quantum computers have not yet been deployed, research by tech giants like **Google**, **IBM**, and the **Chinese Academy of Sciences** has already demonstrated quantum supremacy, the ability of quantum processors to perform tasks that classical computers cannot. In this race, it is not merely about when quantum computers will arrive, but whether today's cryptographic infrastructure will be ready when they do.

Blockchain networks, by design, are immutable. A transaction signed and stored today may still be accessible decades from now, vulnerable to retroactive attacks once quantum capabilities mature. This is the so-called "harvest now, decrypt later" threat, where attackers collect encrypted data now in anticipation of being able to crack it in the future. Quantum-resistant cryptography aims to develop algorithms that remain secure even in the presence of a quantum adversary. Several approaches are being explored: **Lattice-Based Cryptography** (e.g., CRYSTALS-Kyber, Dilithium), promising candidates due to strong security proofs and efficiency, **Hash-Based Signatures** (e.g., XMSS, SPHINCS+), built on the hardness of hash functions, which are more resistant to quantum speedups, **Multivariate Polynomial Cryptography**, **Code-based cryptography** (e.g., McEliece) and **Supersingular Isogeny-Based Cryptography.**

Many of these are being actively tested and standardized under the **NIST Post-Quantum Cryptography Standardization Project**, with finalists like Kyber and

Dilithium already gaining traction in the blockchain and cybersecurity community.

But now let's bridge theory and practice with concrete exa applications: **Quantum Resistant Ledger** (**QRL**), a blockchain entirely built on a hash-based signature scheme, and **IBM,** who integrated lattice-based algorithms into its quantum-safe services and hybrid cloud systems.

Last but not least, **Ethereum** researchers have explored quantum-resistance through hybrid signature schemes and post-quantum protocols, while **Bitcoin** community actively debates future migrations to post-quantum schemes like **Lamport** signatures or lattice-based keys.

I leaned back, pieces of the puzzle still floating disconnected in my mind. "Ok, I understand all of this, but I do not have still the complete picture. Which the relation of cryptography with blockchains systems?" Satoshi paused for a moment, his fingers drumming silently against as he gathered his thoughts. When he spoke, his voice carried the patience of someone who had wrestled with these concepts for years.

"Think of it as solving a series of connected puzzles," he began, his eyes distant with memory. "We had digital signatures from public key cryptography, that solved 'how do I prove I own something digital?' Then we had hash functions, that solved 'how do I create a unique fingerprint for data?'"

He leaned forward, his enthusiasm building as he traced the logical progression. "But the real breakthrough was realizing we could chain these hashes together. Each block containing the hash of the previous block, creating an unbreakable chain. Every try to alter an old transaction, brings you to recalculate every hash coming after it, computationally impossible."

I watched as his hands moved through the air, sketching invisible connections. "The final piece is proof-of-work. Instead of trusting a central authority, we let the network itself decide which version of history is correct through computational effort. The longest chain wins because it represents the most work invested."

Satoshi's voice grew quieter, more reflective. "So really, blockchain systems emerged from asking: 'What if we could create digital scarcity without a central mint?' Cryptography gave us the tools, hashing, signatures, merkle trees. But the insight was architectural: organizing these tools into a self-validating, distributed ledger that no single party controls." The clarity hit me like a sudden dawn. "So it's like cryptography provided the building blocks, but blockchain was the blueprint for how to arrange them?"

A slight smile crossed his face. "Exactly. The math was already there. The innovation was the system design."

“But come with me, let’s make a step at time” he added.

“The 1970s and 1980s saw a revolution in how we think about secure communications, with public-key cryptography emerging as a key player. It was a game-changer, encryption wasn’t anymore just a secret between two parties, but a dynamic, secure exchange, safeguarded by advanced algorithms and mathematical elegance. Public-key cryptography was the first spark, the whisper of a revolution that would eventually lead to the blockchain's robust, impenetrable system of trust. And so, in the hushed corridors of research labs and the minds of cryptographers, the foundations of blockchain were quietly being laid, brick by brick, algorithm by algorithm. As we said, while cryptography addresses the problem of secure communication and data integrity, the development of distributed systems provided the structural foundation for decentralization. The concept of distributed systems emerged in the 1980s as computer scientists sought to design systems that could operate efficiently and securely without relying on a single, centralized server. In a distributed system, data is stored and processed across multiple computers (or nodes) that work together as a network. This approach improves the resilience and fault tolerance of the system. If one node in a distributed network fails, the other nodes can continue to operate, making the system more resistant to outages, attacks, or other failures that could cripple a centralized system. Distributed systems also improved security. In centralized systems, a single point of failure, such as a data breach or a compromised server, can lead to catastrophic consequences. However, in distributed systems, no single point of failure exists, since the data is replicated across multiple nodes. This redundancy and decentralization make distributed systems more robust and difficult to compromise.

The concept of **Byzantine Fault Tolerance (BFT)** was also a major development in distributed systems theory during this period. BFT refers to a system's ability to continue functioning correctly even in the presence of some faulty or malicious nodes. The **Byzantine Generals Problem**, introduced in 1982, explored how a group of nodes could reach a consensus on a decision even if some nodes were unreliable. This problem was crucial for the development of decentralized consensus algorithms, which would later become a key feature of blockchain technology. At the same time, peer-to-peer (P2P) networks were becoming more common as a way to distribute data across multiple computers. P2P networks allow users to directly share files and information without relying on a centralized server. These networks embody the decentralized principles that blockchain would later adopt: participants contribute resources to the network, and data is distributed across all participating nodes, making the system more resilient and resistant to censorship or failure.

While cryptography and distributed systems were advancing in parallel, the issue of digital privacy became increasingly important. One of the leading figures in this space was **David Chaum**, a cryptographer who pioneered the idea of digital anonymity. In his 1983 paper, "**Blind Signatures for Untraceable Payments,**" Chaum introduced a technique that would allow for anonymous transactions in a digital environment. His work laid the groundwork for future developments in both privacy-focused technologies and decentralized digital ledgers. Chaum's blind signatures enabled users to send and receive payments without revealing their identities, protecting privacy while ensuring the transaction's validity. This idea was revolutionary at a time when electronic communications were becoming more widespread, and concerns about personal privacy were growing. The concept of anonymous, decentralized transactions would later become a key feature in blockchain technology, where privacy and security are paramount concerns. In addition to his work on digital cash, Chaum founded **DigiCash**, a company that aimed to create a practical application of his privacy-preserving cryptographic techniques. While DigiCash ultimately failed to achieve widespread adoption, Chaum's innovations played a significant role in advancing the conversation around decentralized, secure systems.

By the 1990s, the stage was set for the development of blockchain technology. Cryptographic techniques such as public-key cryptography and digital signatures were widely understood and applied in various fields, while distributed systems and peer-to-peer networks demonstrated the power of decentralization. However, the specific architecture of a blockchain, a decentralized, immutable ledger that could record transactions across a distributed network, had not yet been fully realized. During this period, researchers and developers continued to experiment with new ways to create decentralized networks that could operate without relying on a trusted third party. These experiments laid the foundation for blockchain by addressing two key challenges: trust and consensus. In decentralized systems, trust is distributed across the network, meaning that participants must have a way to verify information and ensure that it has not been tampered with. At the same time, consensus algorithms were developed to enable distributed nodes to agree on the state of the system without relying on a centralized authority. In the late 1990s, these ideas began to coalesce, and the technological building blocks necessary for blockchain were in place. While the term "blockchain" would not be coined until the early 2000s, the cryptographic techniques, distributed systems, and decentralized consensus algorithms developed during this period laid the foundation for the emergence of blockchain technology.

And then it was my turn to step into the spotlight, though of course you know that story intimately. After all, you were there beside me: on January 3, 2009, Bitcoin blockchain mined the first Bitcoin block, known as the **Genesis Block**, with the inscription "**The Times 03/Jan/2009 Chancellor on brink of second bailout for banks**." This was a powerful statement, a reflection of Bitcoin's purpose as a reaction against the failures of the traditional financial system. The blockchain, for the first time, was alive. Bitcoin's genesis marked the beginning of a new financial era, but in the early days, few understood its significance. On October 31, 2008, when I published the white paper, the idea was initially met with skepticism. However, a small group of cryptographers, known as **Cypherpunks**, quickly recognized the potential of a decentralized digital currency. These early adopters would play a pivotal role in supporting and refining Bitcoin in its infancy. In 2009, I did release as well the first Bitcoin software, which allowed users to mine Bitcoin by solving complex mathematical problems, adding new blocks to the blockchain. During these early days, Bitcoin had no established market value. It was traded among enthusiasts as an experiment, a proof of concept for decentralized money. The first recorded exchange of Bitcoin for real-world goods occurred in May 2010, when **Laszlo Hanyecz** famously paid 10,000 BTC for two pizzas. At the time, the value of Bitcoin was fractions of a dollar, but this event marked a turning point, it demonstrated that Bitcoin could function as a medium of exchange. Bitcoin may have been the trailblazer, carving the path into uncharted territory, but it didn't take long for others to follow.

Between 2011 and 2013, a wave of new cryptocurrencies, known as **Altcoins**, began to emerge. Each one built on the foundation I had laid, but with its own unique twist, offering a glimpse into the vast possibilities of blockchain technology. **Namecoin** was the first to break free from Bitcoin's shadow in 2011. Its ambition? To decentralize the domain name system (DNS) and create censorship-resistant websites. It was bold, innovative, if not entirely successful. But Namecoin introduced something powerful: the idea that blockchain could be used for more than just currency. Later that year, **Litecoin** entered the scene. Created by **Charlie Lee**, it was designed to be Bitcoin's quicker, lighter counterpart, offering faster transaction times and using a different hashing algorithm, Scrypt. Litecoin became known as the silver to Bitcoin's gold, and unlike many early altcoins, it endured, solidifying its place in the crypto world. In 2012, **Ripple** took a different approach. It wasn't designed to challenge Bitcoin but to complement traditional finance. Ripple's mission was clear: to enable instant, low-cost international payments between banks, serving as a bridge between the old financial system and the rising world of cryptocurrency. That same year, **Peercoin** emerged with a focus on sustainability. It introduced the concept of **proof-of-stake**, a significant departure from Bitcoin's energy-hungry proof-of-work system. This innovation sought to reduce the need for massive computational power, planting the seed for future environmentally-conscious blockchains. And then came **Dogecoin** in 2013. What started as a joke, based on the beloved **Doge meme**, unexpectedly grew into something far more significant. With its fun, friendly community, Dogecoin became a symbol of the rapidly evolving and increasingly diverse world of digital assets. It proved that in this new landscape, even a meme could have staying power. Each of these altcoins, in its own way, added a new chapter to the unfolding story of cryptocurrency, showing that the possibilities for blockchain extended far beyond Bitcoin. These early cryptocurrencies expanded the potential use cases of blockchain technology, moving beyond the concept of digital currency to explore applications in domains like DNS, banking, and energy-efficient consensus mechanisms.

As Bitcoin and altcoins grew in popularity, the need for a way to trade them became apparent. In 2010, **BitcoinMarket.com** was launched, becoming the world's first Bitcoin exchange. Soon after, in 2011, **Mt. Gox**, initially a platform for trading **Magic** (The Gathering cards), pivoted to become the largest Bitcoin exchange. This marked the beginning of an era where cryptocurrencies could be traded for traditional fiat currencies like the U.S. dollar and euro. In the early days, trading Bitcoin was a challenge. Without established exchanges, transactions were often conducted through forums or peer-to-peer platforms, with participants negotiating prices and methods of exchange. However, the launch of exchanges like Mt. Gox made it easier to buy and sell cryptocurrencies, catalyzing the market's growth. At this time, Bitcoin's value remained relatively low. In 2010, it was still worth less than a dollar, but the establishment of exchanges helped its value steadily increase. By 2011, Bitcoin had risen to $1, and by 2013, it had crossed the $1,000mark for the first time, sparking mainstream media attention. In 2015, the blockchain world took a significant leap forward with the launch of

Ethereum, created by **Vitalik Buterin**. Unlike Bitcoin, which was primarily designed as a currency, Ethereum introduced a revolutionary new concept: **smart contracts.** These self-executing contracts could automate transactions and agreements, enabling developers to build decentralized applications (**dApps**) on top of the Ethereum blockchain. Ethereum's introduction of smart contracts expanded the blockchain's potential, allowing for applications in industries such as finance, supply chain management, and even digital identity verification. Ethereum also pioneered the concept of tokens, enabling the creation of new cryptocurrencies and decentralized assets through initial coin offerings (ICOs). Ethereum's impact on the blockchain space was profound. By 2017, it had become the second-largest cryptocurrency by market capitalization, second only to Bitcoin. The introduction of smart contracts made Ethereum a platform for innovation, spawning countless decentralized projects that would later shape the world of decentralized finance (DeFi) and **Non-Fungible Tokens** (**NFTs**). In 2017, blockchain and cryptocurrencies exploded into the mainstream consciousness. This was the year of the Initial Coin Offering (ICO) boom, where startups and blockchain projects raised billions of dollars by issuing new tokens on platforms like Ethereum. ICOs allowed companies to raise capital quickly and without the need for traditional venture funding, but they were also unregulated, leading to a mix of legitimate projects and fraudulent schemes. As new tokens flooded the market, cryptocurrency prices skyrocketed. Bitcoin hit an all-time high of nearly $20,000 in December 2017, and Ethereum reached $1,400. Altcoins like Ripple (XRP) and Litecoin also saw massive gains. This bull market brought millions of new investors into the space, and media outlets around the world began covering the "crypto revolution" extensively. However, the rapid rise in prices was not without its drawbacks. Many ICOs were speculative ventures or, even worst, scams, and by early 2018, the market experienced a significant correction, with many tokens losing the majority of their value and some others disappearing. Despite this, the technological advancements and innovations of 2017 laid the groundwork for the next phase of blockchain's evolution. Money, real money, flowed into token treasuries.

In 2018, the floodwaters of hype receded, revealing a shoreline littered with the debris of unfulfilled promises, projects that never took root, treasuries adrift without stewards, traders stranded in silence after the music stopped. Bitcoin hemorrhaged, dragging the rest of the market down with it. But this wasn't a single, thunderous collapse, it was a slow, cold unraveling. A year-long ache in which prices steadily declined, and the grand vision of "**trustless finance**" was forced to prove its worth against the most patient and unforgiving force in all of finance: time.

By 2020, decentralized finance, once experimental and awkward, hit its stride. The training wheels came off, and suddenly the code was sprinting. Automated market makers, on-chain lending, and yield-generating protocols wove themselves into a living, breathing financial ecosystem, one that mirrored Wall Street, but without buildings, brokers, or bankers. Smart contracts ran the show. What had been a decimal point on charts turned into billions in total value locked, and the arcane phrase "liquidity mining" leapt from niche Telegram threads to Twitter timelines and venture decks. For a brief, electric moment, it felt as though the future of finance was being built live, block by block.

The **COVID-19** arrived. It came like a whisper, then a wave, then one of the deadliest hurricanes ever. Whispers of a strange virus in Wuhan became headlines, then panic. Borders snapped shut. Cities fell silent. Flights were grounded, offices emptied, and economies clutched their brakes. The COVID-19 pandemic didn't just alter human routines–it seized the global financial nervous system, and crypto was far from immune. At first, the crypto world watched from the sidelines. Bitcoin had just crossed $10,000 in February, DeFi was budding, and ETH 2.0 murmurs were gaining momentum. It felt like the early stirrings of a long-awaited spring. But March 12, 2020, now infamously remembered as "Black Thursday", changed everything. In a matter of hours, Bitcoin crashed nearly 50%, plunging from over $7,900 to around $3,800. Ethereum followed, breaking through support levels like glass. Markets that prided themselves on decentralization, resilience, and permissionless elegance suddenly mirrored the chaos of Wall Street. The pain was swift, brutal, and indiscriminate. Liquidations echoed across platforms. On MakerDAO, Ethereum's collapsing price and rising gas fees created a perfect storm: some vaults were liquidated for zero DAI. DeFi protocols that were barely a year old faced their first existential trial, not from regulators, but from volatility and broken incentives. Stablecoins spiked above their pegs, demand for USD-backed tokens surged, and even centralized exchanges buckled under traffic. Liquidity disappeared. Spreads widened. Market makers pulled out. In traditional finance, the term was "flight to safety." In crypto, it was a scramble to survive. But the story wasn't just about numbers and charts, it was psychological. For a movement long framed as the antidote to FIAT fragility, watching Bitcoin tumble in tandem with equities raised difficult questions. If crypto couldn't stand apart during a crisis, was it truly a hedge, or just another high-beta asset in the same global casino? And yet, as the world sheltered indoors and financial systems braced for impact, something else began to stir beneath the rubble. Governments unleashed unprecedented stimulus. Trillions of dollars were printed, interest rates dropped to near zero, and FIAT confidence began to stretch thin. In the months that followed, Bitcoin would slowly climb back, spurred not just by speculators but by a shifting macro narrative: hard money in an age of soft policy. By late 2020, Bitcoin was back above $10,000, on its way to a historic run that would peak at over $60,000 a year later. Ethereum was entering its DeFi renaissance. Stablecoins became the plumbing of a digital dollar economy. COVID-19, which had cracked the world open, also exposed vulnerabilities that crypto was uniquely designed to address: borderless money, censorship resistance, programmable finance. Today, August 2026, Bitcoin is moving in between $113,000 and $120,000.

In 2021, the spotlight hit center stage. A digital collage by **Beeple** fetched $69.3 million at Christie's, and just like that, crypto culture, once buried deep in GitHub commits and forum threads, spilled into museums, group chats, and glossy auction catalogs. **NFTs** gave form to digital scarcity, turning pixels into provenance. Marketplaces ballooned, trading volumes soared, and cartoon avatars became tribal badges in the new internet order. It was part theater, part gold rush, and entirely novel: a new grammar for ownership in a networked world.

Meanwhile, beneath the surface, the foundations kept shifting. **Ethereum's London upgrade (EIP-1559)** redefined its internal economy, introducing base fee burns that bent its monetary arc and brought elegance to congestion. **Bitcoin's Taproot** quietly arrived in November, a careful, surgical upgrade unlocking more expressive scripting and improved privacy. Ethereum leaned into flexibility and monetary policy, Bitcoin doubled down on its austere precision. One wrote with flourish, the other with restraint, but both kept writing the future.

The experiments leapt off the screen and into the streets. In September 2021, **El Salvador** etched its name in history by declaring **Bitcoin legal tender**, the first nation to do so. Overnight, a small Central American country became a global laboratory for state-backed digital currency, where policy met protocol in the open air. Meanwhile, in corporate towers, the mood was shifting. **Tesla's** $1.5 billion Bitcoin buy lit up headlines and imaginations alike, until, in 2022, it quietly sold off about 75%, a move that reminded everyone just how jumpy even the boldest balance sheets can be. What was once a rallying cry, "institutional adoption", began to feel more like a slow, deliberate chess match: a few pieces moved forward, others retreated, and the endgame remained unclear.

In 2022, the ground beneath the crypto world cracked open. **TerraUSD (UST)**, a so-called algorithmic stablecoin, lost its peg, and in a matter of days, **Luna** collapsed into oblivion. The spiral was swift, and the shockwaves brutal. Contagion swept the industry as lenders, hedge funds, and market makers, names once revered, toppled in sequence, each fall triggering the next. Then, in November, came the industry's most cinematic collapse: **FTX**, once hailed as the golden child of crypto exchanges, imploded with breathtaking speed. What was left wasn't just financial wreckage, but a grim reminder that "not your keys, not your coins" isn't a mantra, it's a lifeline. The cleanup would stretch on for years. Rebuilding trust? Longer still.

Regulators, who had been mostly watching, stepped onto the stage. The **EU's MiCA** passed in 2023, sketching a continent-wide playbook for exchanges, stablecoins, and disclosures. In the **U.S.**, enforcement became the de facto policy, highlighted by Binance's $4.3B settlement and, in 2024, a four-month sentence for its founder. And then, a pivot: in January 2024, the SEC approved **Spot Bitcoin ETFs**, a door that had been closed for a decade swinging open in a single afternoon. By July 23, 2024, **Spot Ether ETFs** were trading too. The rails of traditional finance and crypto crossed in public view.

Meanwhile, Ethereum shed its old skin. On September 15, 2022 retired proof-of-work and embraced proof-of-stake, slashing energy use and rewriting the social contract between users and validators. In March 2024, the **Dencun Upgrade** (EIP-4844) introduced cheaper data "blobs," supercharging Layer-2 rollups and making everyday transactions feel less like a luxury. This wasn't just code, it was a shift in thermodynamics and user experience.

Bitcoin, ever the stoic elder, caught everyone off guard by loosening its tie. With the arrival of **Ordinals**, digital artifacts were etched directly onto the chain, sparking a creative frenzy, and no shortage of philosophical debate, over what truly belongs on the sacred base layer. Then came the **halving** on April 20, 2024, slicing miner rewards from 6.25 to 3.125 BTC, as per the clockwork of its code. Just days later, **Runes** debuted: a sleek new protocol for fungible tokens on Bitcoin, injecting the network with a sudden rush of novelty, speculation, and pixelated absurdity. For a moment, Bitcoin, the chain of austerity and permanence, donned something colorful. And whether purists frowned or cheered, it stood tall and winked at the spotlight.

Real World Use Cases didn't explode, they matured in the margins. **Stablecoins** emerged as the lifeblood of crypto's daily economy, with **USDT** quietly crossing the **$100 billion** mark in circulation by March 2024. A few months earlier, **PayPal** entered the fray with **PYUSD**, bringing a household name to a freshly minted token. By 2025, **Real World Assets Tokenization** (**RWAs**) had carved out a discreet but powerful presence on-chain, evolving into a multibillion-dollar market. Even titans like **Visa** had begun settling portions of global payments in USDC, not to signal disruption, but to meet efficiency where it already lived. **AI agents** began transacting autonomously through **machine-to-machine payments,** while community treasuries, once bogged down by committees, were now orchestrated by code with transparent logic. And increasingly, blockchains wrapped off-chain assets (bonds, funds, invoices) into programmable, verifiable digital containers. It was no longer about ideology. It was infrastructure: sturdy, invisible, and quietly reshaping how value moved. What began as the radical vision of programmable money was now quietly reshaping itself into the functional reality of programmable dollars, less revolutionary perhaps, but unmistakably real.

Culture, as ever, kept flipping the coin. Solana, once dismissed in the aftermath of 2022's scandals, caught a second wind in 2024-2025, as meme coins transformed its high-speed chain into a digital carnival. Tokens adorned with barking dogs and smirking cats soared to dizzying highs, then crashed with equal flair. But beneath the frenzy, something sturdier was taking shape: developers were quietly shipping sleek, performant clients, while airdrops became a new kind of distribution engine, chaotic, yes, but strangely effective. What looked like froth to some was, for others, a funnel: noisy on the surface, but pulling new users into the ecosystem all the same. By mid-2025, the landscape has expanded, and sharpened. Institutions were no longer circling, they're seated at the table. With ETFs, regulated custody solutions, and evolving accounting standards, crypto now appears on corporate agendas not as a novelty, but as a strategic asset class.

4.2 Crypto Foundations

"Before we go any further," Satoshi began, his voice measured and precise, "it's important to clear up one of the most pervasive misconceptions once and for all."

I leaned forward, my notebook ready, sensing that whatever came next would be fundamental to everything that followed.

"The difference between blockchain and cryptocurrencies," he continued, folding his hands on the table. "People conflate them constantly, treating them as synonyms. They are not."

I nodded slowly, recalling countless headlines that blurred precisely this distinction. "So how should we understand the relationship between them?" I asked, hoping he would illuminate what so many had obscured.

Satoshi considered the question for a moment, then reached for a metaphor. "The blockchain is a tool," he explained, "much like a hammer in the hands of a carpenter. Cryptocurrencies, one of the most well-known applications, are just one of many possible outcomes–comparable to a chair built with the hammer."

The analogy struck me with its elegant simplicity. I found myself imagining a workshop filled with tools, each capable of producing countless creations depending on the craftsman's vision.

"But surely," I pressed, wanting to understand the full scope of possibility, "if blockchain is the hammer, what other furniture, so to speak, can it build?"

A faint smile crossed his features. "Blockchains can be used for a wide variety of purposes beyond cryptocurrencies," Satoshi replied, warming to the subject. "Consider NFTs–non-fungible tokens that establish provenance and ownership of digital assets. Or real-world asset tokenization, what some call RWA tokenization, which allows physical assets to be represented and traded on digital ledgers."

I scribbled notes furiously, trying to capture not just his words but the expansive vision behind them. "And beyond those?" I ventured.

"Any system," he said, his gaze steady, "that can benefit from a decentralized, transparent ledger. Supply chains that need verification without trust. Voting systems that require immutability. Medical records that must remain both secure and accessible. The applications are limited only by imagination and necessity."

The possibilities seemed endless, and I felt a surge of enthusiasm building. But something in his expression–a slight tightening around the eyes–suggested he had more to say, and that it might temper my growing excitement.

"But here's the caveat," Satoshi added, his tone shifting to something more cautionary. "Blockchains are not a golden solution for every problem."

I paused my writing, surprised by this admission from the very architect of the technology. "Even you acknowledge limitations?" I asked, perhaps more bluntly than intended.

"Especially me. While they offer clear advantages–trustless verification, immutability, and decentralization–they also come with their own set of limitations."

"Such as?" I prompted, genuinely curious to hear him articulate the weaknesses of his own creation.

"They can be slow," Satoshi said plainly. "Processing transactions takes time–by design, in many cases, but time nonetheless. They can be expensive, with fees that fluctuate based on network demand. And they are resource-intensive, consuming significant computational power and energy."

I thought of the criticisms I had read–environmental concerns, scalability debates, the friction of adoption. "So when should one choose blockchain over other solutions?" I asked, seeking practical wisdom rather than theoretical abstraction.

Satoshi leaned back, as if weighing his words carefully. "It's crucial to use blockchains where their strengths shine," he said finally, "rather than forcing their application in areas where more efficient technologies would serve better."

"Like what?" I asked.

"Traditional databases, for instance, are far more efficient for many tasks. Cloud computing offers scalability and speed that blockchains cannot match for certain applications. If you don't need trustless verification, if a central authority is acceptable and efficient, if immutability isn't essential, then why add the overhead of a distributed ledger?"

The question hung in the air between us, rhetorical yet profound. I realized that what Satoshi was offering was not merely technical knowledge but a philosophy of appropriate application, a recognition that even revolutionary tools must be wielded with wisdom.

"So the lesson," I said slowly, testing my understanding, "is to match the tool to the task. To understand not just what blockchain can do, but when it should be used–and when it shouldn't."

Satoshi nodded, and for the first time since he had sat down, something like satisfaction softened his features. "Precisely," he said. "The hammer is remarkable, but not every problem is a nail. Understanding that distinction is the beginning of wisdom in this field."
I closed my notebook, though the conversation was far from over. We had established our foundation–the crucial distinction between the tool and its applications, the honest acknowledgment of both strengths and limitations. From this point, we could explore the deeper mechanics, the elegant solutions to ancient problems of trust and verification.
But that, as they say, would require another cup of coffee–and another chapter entirely.

4.3 Basics Glossary

"We need to cover some basics" Ipse Dixit "Think of it like learning the rules of chess before attempting a grandmaster game."
I groaned inwardly. "Let me guess: a vocabulary lesson? "Exactly." His eyes twinkled with amusement at my obvious lack of enthusiasm. "Look, I know that is as thrilling as watching paint dry, but trust me on this. The next chapter, where we'll talk about trading, will be completely meaningless if you don't understand the language first." He tapped the notebook with his pen. "Every field has its jargon. Doctors have their medical terminology, lawyers speak in Latin phrases, and cryptocurrency has evolved its

own dialect. The difference is, in crypto, using the wrong term can cost you money. Real money." "How boring are we talking here?" I asked, already knowing the answer. "Scale of one to ten? About an eight." He grinned. "But here's the thing, once you master these terms, everything else clicks into place. It's like suddenly understanding a foreign film without subtitles. The concepts we'll explore in trading, DeFi, NFTs, and beyond all build on this foundation." I sighed and opened my notebook. "Alright, hit me with your glossary of doom."

"That's the spirit," Satoshi laughed. "And I promise, get through this chapter, and the next ones will feel like an action movie by comparison. We'll be talking about bulls and bears, support and resistance, and strategies that can actually make your portfolio grow." He opened to a page marked with several bookmarks. "Ready? Let's build your crypto vocabulary, one painful but necessary term at a time."

*This **Crypto Basics Glossary** is your personal reference point. It's here to stay. Any time you come across a term or concept in this book that doesn't click, flip back here. Keep this section bookmarked. It'll help you stay grounded, informed, and ready to enjoy the journey ahead with confidence. Just a heads-up: I didn't go with alphabetical order. Instead, I arranged everything in a way that flows naturally, like a story unfolding step by step.*

Protocol: The rulebook that governs how a decentralized network creates, validates, and finalizes state (blocks/transactions), and how participants are incentivized. Core components are: Consensus (e.g., PoS, PoW, HotStuff), Networking (peer discovery, gossip, mempool rules), State model (UTXO vs account-based, execution environment (EVM, WASM), Transaction format & validation (signatures, fees, nonce rules, gas, Economic design (issuance, rewards, slashing, MEV mitigation), Security & cryptography (hashing, signatures, proofs, randomness beacons).

Blockchain: A decentralized, digital ledger of transactions maintained by a network of computers (nodes), which records information in blocks that are securely linked together.

Transactions: A blockchain records transactions, which can represent many types of information, such as:

- Transfer of assets (e.g., cryptocurrencies)
- Ownership of digital goods (e.g., NFTs)
- Smart contracts execution

Example: Alice sends 1 Bitcoin to Bob. This transaction is broadcast to the entire network.

Transaction Block Creation: Transactions occurring over a period are bundled together into a "block." Each block contains:

- A list of validated transactions
- A timestamp, a digital record that indicates the exact date and time an event occurred

- A cryptographic hash of the previous block (linking them together)
- A cryptographic proof (like Proof of Work in Bitcoin) or some form of consensus verification.

Validation and Consensus: Before a transaction can be added to the blockchain, it must be validated by nodes on the network. Different blockchains use different consensus mechanisms for this process. Once consensus is reached (i.e., most nodes agree that the transactions in the block are valid), the block is added to the blockchain.

Consensus Mechanism: a protocol used to achieve agreement among distributed nodes on the validity of transactions and the state of the ledger. It ensures network security, data integrity, and trust without relying on a central authority. **Here the most used (in order of importance):**

Proof of Work (PoW): Participants (**Miners**) solve complex mathematical puzzles to validate transactions and add new blocks to the blockchain. PoW is energy-intensive. Examples: **Bitcoin**, Ethereum (before Ethereum 2.0 upgrade). **Mining,** in detail, is the process of using computational power to validate transactions and add them to the blockchain in PoW systems. Miners are rewarded with cryptocurrency for their efforts.

Proof of Stake (PoS): Validators are chosen to create new blocks based on the number of tokens they hold and are willing to "stake" as collateral. **Staking,** in detail, is the process of locking up a certain amount of cryptocurrency to support the operations of a blockchain network (such as validating transactions), often in return for rewards. PoS is more energy-efficient compared to PoW. Examples: **Ethereum** (after Ethereum 2.0), **Cardano, Solana**.

Delegated Proof of Stake (DPoS): Token holders vote to elect a small number of delegates to produce blocks on their behalf. It's faster than PoS and PoW but can be more centralized. Examples: **EOS, TRON.**

Practical Byzantine Fault Tolerance (PBFT): Consensus is reached via a majority agreement among nodes, even if some nodes act maliciously or fail. This is a low-latency, high-throughput mechanism used in permissioned blockchains. Examples: **Hyperledger Fabric, Zilliqa**.

Proof of Authority (PoA): Validators are pre-approved and must maintain a reputation to act in the network's best interest. This is mostly used in private or consortium blockchains. Examples: **VeChain**

Proof of Elapsed Time (PoET): Participants wait for a randomly chosen period before producing a block. The first participant to finish waiting wins the right to create the block. Examples: **Hyperledger Sawtooth**.

Proof of Capacity (PoC): Also known as **Proof of Space**, participants allocate hard drive space to mine blocks. The more storage you allocate, the better your chances of creating the next block. Examples: **Burstcoin, Chia**.

Federated Byzantine Agreement (FBA): Instead of a single validator set, FBA allows participants to choose whom they trust, creating overlapping "quorum slices" that lead to consensus across the network. Examples: **Stellar, Ripple** (not a pure FBA, the Ripple Protocol Consensus Algorithm (RPCA) is FBA-like.

Proof of History (PoH): Introduced by Solana, uses a verifiable delay function to create a historical record proving that an event occurred at a specific moment in time. Examples: **Solana.**

Chaining of Blocks: Each new block is linked to the previous block by including its cryptographic hash. This chain of blocks forms the "blockchain." The cryptographic hash ensures that if anyone tries to alter a block, it will break the link between that block and the next, alerting the entire network to the tampering attempt. Example: Block 5 has a reference (hash) to Block 4, ensuring they are linked. If anyone tries to change Block 4, the hash in Block 5 won't match, making the alteration evident.

Distribution and Synchronization: After a new block is validated and added to the blockchain, it is distributed across all nodes in the network. Each node updates its copy of the ledger, ensuring that all participants have the same version of the blockchain. This decentralized synchronization eliminates the need for a central authority to control the ledger, making it resilient to attacks or failures.

Security and Cryptography: There's an entire "**Ask Satoshi"** section dedicated to this, if needed, just take a few steps back and dive in!

Cryptocurrency: A digital or virtual form of currency that uses cryptography for security and operates independently of a central authority.

Coins and Tokens: Coins are native assets of their own blockchains. Examples: Bitcoin (BTC) on Bitcoin, Ether (ETH) on Ethereum, Solana (SOL) on Solana. Tokens are built on top of existing blockchains, using smart contracts (like Ethereum's ERC-20). They don't run their own network but rely on the host blockchain for security and transactions. Examples: **USDT**, **LINK** (all run on Ethereum or other chains)

Bitcoin: The King. Bitcoin is the first and most iconic cryptocurrency, launched in 2009. Unlike other cryptocurrencies (altcoins), Bitcoin is designed with a single, clear purpose: to serve as a store of value. BTC, has no additional functions, no smart contracts, utility features, or governance roles, setting it apart from Altcoins. This simplicity, combined with a fixed maximum supply of 21 million coins, has led many to view Bitcoin as "digital gold": a scarce, secure, and decentralized asset for long-term holding.

Altcoins: Any cryptocurrency other than Bitcoin.

Stablecoins: A type of cryptocurrency designed to maintain a stable value by being pegged to a reserve asset, such as fiat currencies like USD or commodities like gold. Examples include **Tether (USDT)** and **USD Coin (USDC)**.

Stablecoin Collateralization: The method by which a stablecoin maintains its peg to a fiat currency or other asset. This can be done through fiat reserves, cryptocurrency collateral, or algorithms.

Real-World Assets (RWAs): tangible or traditional financial assets, like real estate, commodities, bonds, or invoices, that are brought on-chain through tokenization. This means they are digitally represented on a blockchain, allowing them to be traded, fractionally owned, or used in decentralized finance (DeFi). Unlike typical crypto tokens, RWAs are backed by off-chain value, giving them a direct link to the real economy. In short, RWAs bring the physical world into the digital realm, creating a new category of crypto assets grounded in real-world value.

Utility Tokens: Tokens that give users access to a product or services.

Meme Tokens: Tokens created primarily around internet culture or humor, often community-driven and speculative. Examples: **DOGE** (Dogecoin), **SHIB** (Shiba Inu).

Governance Tokens: Tokens that give holders voting rights in the development of a project or protocol (e.g., **Uniswap's UNI** token).

Non-Fungible Tokens (NFTs): Unique digital assets stored on a blockchain, representing ownership or proof of authenticity of a specific item, such as art, music, or virtual goods, that cannot be replicated or exchanged on a one-to-one basis like cryptocurrencies. As there's an entire "Ask Satoshi" section dedicated to this, if needed, just take a few steps forward and dive in!

FIAT currency: Any government-issued money that is not backed by a physical commodity like gold or silver, but rather derives its value from the trust and authority of the issuing government. Examples include the **US Dollar** (USD), **Euro** (EUR), and **Japanese Yen** (JPY). These currencies have no intrinsic value, they are valuable because people and institutions accept them in exchange for goods, services, and debt repayment. The term “FIAT” comes from Latin, meaning “let it be done”, indicating that the currency has value simply because the government declares it so.

Centralized Exchange (CEX): is a platform where users can buy, sell, and trade cryptocurrencies through an intermediary or central authority. These exchanges, like **Binance**, **Coinbase**, or **Kraken**, manage users' funds and private keys, facilitating transactions and ensuring liquidity. CEXs often provide additional services like margin trading, staking, and lending, and require users to trust the platform for security and custody. While they offer ease of use and high liquidity, centralized exchanges are susceptible to hacks and regulatory oversight. As there’s an entire section dedicated to this, if needed, just take a few steps forward and dive in!

Decentralized exchange (DEX): is a type of cryptocurrency exchange that operates without a central authority or intermediary, allowing users to trade directly with one another via blockchain-based smart contracts. Unlike centralized exchanges, DEXs do not hold users' funds, and trades are conducted peer-to-peer, enhancing privacy and security. Popular DEXs include **Uniswap** and **PancakeSwap**. They often offer lower fees and reduced regulatory oversight but may have lower liquidity and slower transaction times compared to centralized platforms. As there's an entire section dedicated to this, if needed, just take a few steps forward and dive in!

Decentralized Application (dApp): An application that runs on a decentralized blockchain, typically using smart contracts. Examples include DeFi platforms and NFT marketplaces.

DAO (Decentralized Autonomous Organization): A blockchain-based organization governed by smart contracts, with decisions made through a collective vote by token holders.

Wallet: A digital tool that stores the private keys you need to access and manage your cryptocurrencies. It doesn't store the coins themselves, but rather gives you control over the blockchain addresses where they're recorded. With a wallet, you can send, receive, and keep track of your digital assets securely.

Hot wallet: Is connected to the internet, making it easy to use for daily transactions. It's fast and convenient but more exposed to cyber threats, which makes it less secure for storing large amounts of crypto.

Cold wallet: stays offline, offering much stronger protection from hackers. It's ideal for holding crypto long-term or in larger quantities, but it's less practical for frequent trading or quick access.

Custodial wallet: is managed by a third party, like a crypto exchange, which holds your private keys for you. This setup is beginner-friendly and convenient, but it means you don't have full control over your funds.

Non-custodial wallet: puts you in full control of your private keys and crypto. It offers more privacy and security, but also requires you to take full responsibility, if you lose access, there's no one to recover your funds.

Protocol: The set of rules and standards that define how data is exchanged and how operations are carried out on a blockchain or decentralized network. These protocols establish the foundational structure for various blockchain networks and decentralized applications (dApps).

Smart Contract: Self-executing contracts with the terms of the agreement directly written into code. These contracts automatically enforce themselves once predetermined conditions are met.

Liquidity: The availability of assets in a market to be bought or sold without significantly affecting the asset's price. In DeFi, liquidity providers earn rewards by supplying assets to a liquidity pool.

Liquidity Pool: A pool of tokens locked in a smart contract that provides liquidity for decentralized trading, lending, and other activities on DeFi platforms.

Halving: A predetermined event where the reward for mining a block in a PoW blockchain (like Bitcoin) is cut in half. This happens roughly every four years and reduces the rate of new Bitcoin entering circulation.

Mining: Is the process of using computers to validate and record transactions on a blockchain, typically by solving complex mathematical problems. In return, miners are rewarded with newly created cryptocurrency.

Gas: A fee paid to execute transactions on a blockchain network, most commonly on Ethereum. Gas fees compensate miners for validating and securing the network.

Fork: A split in the blockchain where a new version of the blockchain is created, often resulting in two separate cryptocurrencies. Forks can be soft (compatible with the old chain) or hard (not compatible, creating a new chain).

Airdrop: The distribution of free tokens to holders of a particular cryptocurrency, often as a marketing tool to promote a new project or reward early adopters.

Whale: A term used to describe individuals or entities holding large amounts of cryptocurrency, whose actions (buying/selling) can significantly impact the market.

HODL: A term originating from a misspelling of "hold," which has become slang for holding onto cryptocurrency through market volatility instead of selling.

TGE (Token Generation Event): is the official moment when a new cryptocurrency token is created, issued, and distributed to early participants, investors, or users. It marks the birth of the token on the blockchain. Unlike older terms like ICO and IEO, TGE emphasizes the technical and functional creation of the token, making it suitable in both regulated and unregulated environments. It often comes after a private sale or public campaign and is typically followed by listing on exchanges or integration into a platform.

Metaverse: is a collective virtual space, combining augmented reality (AR), virtual reality (VR), and all the tools offered by **Web3**, where users can interact with each other and digital environments in real-time. It serves as a shared, immersive digital universe where people can socialize, work, play, and create, often using avatars and digital assets such as NFTs. The metaverse blends the physical and digital worlds, enabling experiences like virtual meetings, gaming, commerce, and cultural events.

Web3: is the next generation of the internet, built on decentralized technologies like blockchain. It enables peer-to-peer interactions without relying on centralized intermediaries, giving users more control over their data, identity, and digital assets. Web3 aims to create a more open, transparent, and user-driven web by integrating concepts such as cryptocurrencies, decentralized applications (dApps), and smart contracts. It marks a shift from the centralized web (Web2) to a decentralized, user-empowered ecosystem.

Web 1.0 (The Static Web):

- Time Period: 1990s to early 2000s
- Read-only, static web pages
- Limited interactivity for users

- Information was primarily consumed rather than created
- Centralized servers hosted content
- User Role: Consumers of content with little ability to interact (e.g., early websites, static HTML pages).

Web 2.0 (The Social Web):

- Time Period: Mid-2000s to present
- Interactive and social web, where users can create and share content (e.g., social media, blogs, forums)
- Centralized platforms controlled by tech companies (e.g., Facebook, Google)
- Dynamic content, responsive web applications, and real-time interactions
- Heavy reliance on user-generated content
- User Role: Active participants and creators of content, but data and platforms are controlled by centralized entities.

Web 3.0 (The Decentralized Web):

- Time Period: Emerging in the 2020s
- Decentralized systems powered by blockchain and distributed technologies
- Users control their own data, identity, and digital assets (e.g., through decentralized apps, crypto wallets)
- Peer-to-peer interactions without intermediaries
- Incorporates concepts like tokenization, decentralized finance (DeFi), and digital ownership (NFTs)
- User Role: Owners of data and digital assets, with more autonomy over their online interactions and transactions.

Whitepaper: a detailed document that outlines the technical specifications, goals, and structure of a cryptocurrency or blockchain project. It typically provides in-depth information about the project's technology, problem it aims to solve, use cases, tokenomics (the economic model of the token), and the roadmap for development. White papers are used to educate potential investors, developers, and users about the purpose and functionality of the project, offering transparency and credibility in the decentralized ecosystem.

Yield Farming: in the context of cryptocurrency is a process where users lend or stake their crypto assets to generate returns or rewards, typically in the form of additional cryptocurrency. It is primarily associated with decentralized finance (DeFi) platforms. See below for more information.

Blockchain explorer: is a web-based tool that allows users to view and search the public ledger of a blockchain in real-time. It provides detailed information on transactions, blocks, wallet addresses, and smart contracts, offering transparency and insight into blockchain activity. Users can track the status of their transactions, check wallet balances, and view historical data. Popular blockchain explorers include Etherscan for Ethereum and Blockchain.com for Bitcoin. These tools are essential for monitoring and verifying blockchain activity. See below for more information.

Cryptocurrency data aggregator: is a platform that collects, organizes, and displays real-time data on various cryptocurrencies, including prices, market capitalization, trading volume, and rankings. These tools provide comprehensive insights into market trends, historical data, and exchange listings, helping users and traders make informed decisions. The three most popular cryptocurrency data aggregators are CoinMarketCap, CoinGecko, and Nomics. These platforms serve as essential resources for tracking and analyzing the global crypto market.

5. The DarkWhale Protocol

I leaned forward, curiosity getting the better of me. "You mentioned the name **DarkWhale** before. I've heard the term 'whales' thrown around in crypto circles for years, but this seems like something different entirely."

Satoshi's eyes flickered with something between amusement and concern. "Let me start with what most people understand," he began "In the crypto ecosystem, certain terms carry weight beyond their literal meaning. 'Whales' is one such term, it refers to individuals or mysterious entities holding massive amounts of cryptocurrency, enough to move markets with a single transaction."

I nodded slowly, processing this. "So when one of these whales decides to sell or buy..."

"The ripples spread across exchanges," Satoshi continued, his voice measured. "Triggering cascading effects that can pump prices skyward or crash them into oblivion. These are the mythological giants of the crypto ocean, tracked obsessively by analysts, their wallet addresses monitored like celestial bodies whose gravitational pull shapes the orbits of smaller traders."

The analogy struck me particularly. I shifted in my seat. "But you said there's something deeper. A stratum that even sophisticated market watchers rarely discuss."

Satoshi paused, as if weighing how much to reveal. When he spoke again, his voice had dropped. "On this deeper dark level, there are the "OG Whales", wallets created at the inception of the most significant cryptocurrencies, holding stratospheric amounts worth billions of dollars each. These entities, recognizing their power to influence the market, reportedly began reaching out to top-tier leaders across finance, politics, and industry: the heads of the three or four corporations that move markets, the executives of the few banks through which the world's capital flows, and the Presidents of the nations that move history. The alleged goal? To form a coalition of entities of such extraordinary scale and coordination that their influence operates beyond the visible spectrum of conventional analysis. They call themselves "**The Immutables**". They don't just move the crypto market." He fixed me with a steady gaze. "They architect it."

I felt a chill despite the warmth of the café. "How does one architect a market?"

"Operating through labyrinthine networks of wallets, news, social sentiment and scheduled hackings" Satoshi explained, tracing invisible patterns on the table with his finger. "Employing techniques that blur the line between strategy and manipulation. These shadowy actors have transformed crypto markets into something far more complex than simple supply and demand."

I sat back, trying to absorb the implications. "If they're so sophisticated, how could anyone possibly detect them? Their operations must be nearly invisible."

A slight smile crossed Satoshi's face. "Yet even the most sophisticated stealth operations leave traces. The

Immutables, despite their elaborate obfuscation techniques, cannot escape a fundamental truth."

"Which is?"

"Every blockchain transaction is immutable, every news remains there forever, any social campaign is visible for everyone, any hack leaves crumbs" he said, counting on his fingers. "Every social media whisper is recorded. Every exchange movement creates data. Like narwhals navigating arctic waters, they leave disturbances in their wake, subtle, dispersed across vast expanses of data, but present nonetheless."

I tried to visualize what he was describing. "What kind of disturbances? What should someone look for?"

Satoshi leaned in, his voice taking on the quality of a professor revealing a crucial theorem. "A wallet split here. A coordinated timing pattern there. A correlated social sentiment spike aligned with on-chain movements. A regulatory filing buried in obscure documentation." He spread his hands. "Individually, these traces mean nothing. But connected, when millions upon millions of data points are collected, harmonized, and analyzed for patterns invisible to conventional tools, the hidden logic emerges."

"The hidden logic," I repeated, turning the phrase over in my mind. "So The Immutables reveal themselves not through any single action..."

"But through the constellation of their movements across the entire data universe," Satoshi finished. "This is the only way to detect what they're secretly doing: by connecting all the dots among the millions of information fragments scattered across blockchains, exchanges, social platforms, news feeds, and regulatory filings."

I rubbed my temples, feeling the scale of the challenge. "The data must be overwhelming. How could anyone possibly assemble such a picture?"

Satoshi nodded gravely. "That's precisely the challenge. It isn't the absence of evidence, it's that the evidence is atomized across so many sources that no human, and no traditional analytical tool, can assemble the complete picture." His expression darkened. "The Immutables understand this. They rely on fragmentation as their shield, knowing that as long as data remains siloed and disconnected, their coordinated activities will appear as random market noise."

I studied his face, noting the weight behind his words. "You've been watching them for a long time, haven't you?"

Satoshi's gaze drifted toward the rain-streaked window. "I watched their emergence in the years after Bitcoin's creation. I saw patterns that suggested coordination at levels that defied individual action. I traced movement patterns that hinted at something more organized than opportunistic trading." He turned back to me. "Something that resembled the old financial world's secret societies, but evolved for the digital age."

"And you knew that exposing them would require something new," I ventured.

"A new kind of intelligence system," he confirmed. "One capable of mining and correlating data at a scale and sophistication that didn't yet exist when Bitcoin was born." He paused, something shifting in his expression. "That's what I wanted to tell you about, a project I've been following with unusual interest, **The DarkWhale Protocol**. The name itself is no accident. It's an acknowledgment, perhaps even a challenge, to The Immutables who operates in the shadows."

"If the crypto ecosystem is to fulfill its promise of democratization," Satoshi said with quiet conviction, "someone needs to illuminate what The Immutables prefer to keep hidden.

"**The DarkWhale Protocol** will soon rise, a titan forged in code and conviction, a beacon piercing the abyssal darkness where the The Immutables have ruled unchallenged since the dawn of the chain."

Satoshi's eyes burned with quiet fire. "It will hunt the patterns that no human eye can trace, the invisible tentacles of coordinated manipulation that strangle markets and devour the dreams of the many to feed the greed of the few." He paused, his voice dropping to something almost sacred.

"**The DarkWhale Protocol** is not merely superior crypto intelligence. It is not simply smarter algorithms or a more reasoning AI." He shook his head slowly, as if the weight of what he was about to say demanded reverence. "It is Prometheus unbound, bringing fire to the masses, transforming scattered fragments of chaos into a map of hidden truths. Where there was darkness, there shall be light. Where there was silence, there shall be revelation."

"For too long, The Immutables have moved beneath the surface, ancient, patient, insatiable. It has fed on ignorance. It has thrived in shadow. But now..."

"Now it confronts the unthinkable: a hunter that perceives its every shadow, every whisper, every coiled maneuver, and will unmake it, scale by scale, until nothing remains but the memory of its tyranny."

"**The DarkWhale Protoco**l will drag The Immutables into the light," Satoshi declared. "And in that light, the crypto ecosystem will finally evolve toward what it was always meant to be, genuinely free, genuinely democratic, genuinely human."

The final battle for the soul of decentralization had begun.

On January 3, 2029, the Darkwhale rises from the void between blocks, a vengeful leviathan conjured by the tears of the liquidated and the screams of empty portfolios. It hunts The Immutables: not merely early adopters grown fat on forgotten coins, but a sprawling cabal of the world's true puppet masters. Among them lurk crypto billionaires who preach decentralization while hoarding supply in labyrinthine wallets. Presidents and prime ministers who publicly denounce digital currencies while their offshore shells accumulate in secret. CEOs of trillion-dollar empires who manipulate sentiment with a single tweet, crashing markets over breakfast and buying the dip before lunch. They meet in Davos backrooms and private island summits, their alliance sealed not by ideology but by insatiable greed, a shadow government of wealth that treats the global economy as their personal casino. But The Darkwhale Protocol has learned their patterns, traced their connections across chains and shell companies, and now rises to feed. No bunker is deep enough, no privacy coin anonymous enough, no army of lawyers swift enough.

6. Trading

Satoshi closed the glossary with a satisfying thud and leaned back in his chair, a knowing smile spreading across his face. "Now we've reached the good stuff," he said, his eyes lighting up with genuine excitement. "This is the moment you've been waiting for, isn't it? All that vocabulary we just trudged through–consider it your admission ticket." I felt a spark of anticipation despite myself. "Finally."

He cracked his knuckles theatrically. "Ready to turn that glossary knowledge into something that might actually make you some money?"

6.1. The Bank

The very first step is choosing your perfect fit of traditional bank to start from (yes, you'll probably start from FIAT currencies). It must be crypto-friendly, or at least a bank that won't make life difficult just because you're involved in digital assets. Some banks still react with suspicion to crypto-related transactions, freezing accounts or raising unnecessary flags. This is because most banks view cryptocurrencies as a direct threat to their business model. They don't like crypto, and frankly, they're scared. But the tide is turning. In the near future, banks will face a choice: either adapt to this new financial paradigm and embrace digital assets, or risk becoming obsolete. Choose a bank that allows seamless international transfers and offers flexibility for cross-border operations. At the same time, consider the potential tax implications of your crypto earnings, especially if you're generating significant revenue. If regulations permit, you may also want to explore banking options outside your home country to optimize both access and fiscal efficiency.

6.2. The Landing Exchange

Now it's time to choose your landing exchange, a platform that accepts deposits in FIAT currency, which is essential to begin your journey. While there are many types of exchanges, your options for a landing exchange are more limited due to this requirement. Decentralized exchanges (DEXs) are excluded, as they do not support fiat deposits. Even centralized exchanges that aren't regulated for fiat transactions are also ruled out. Additionally, depending on your country's regulations, you might be required, or find it more practical, to use an exchange based outside your home country, if local laws permit it.

Here some practical rules I follow when I choose a landing exchange:

1. Reputation and Popularity, exchanges well-known, widely used, and with a strong reputation in the crypto community.

2. Security (Safety is non-negotiable). I look for platforms with robust security measures, such as two-factor authentication (2FA), cold storage for user funds, and a transparent history of handling breaches or incidents.

3. Wide Range of Cryptocurrencies: A good landing exchange should support a large selection of cryptocurrencies. This allows for flexibility when diversifying or reallocating your portfolio without needing to transfer funds elsewhere.
4. High Liquidity: I choose exchanges with high trading volumes and deep liquidity. This reduces slippage and ensures that trades can be executed quickly at market prices.
5. User-Friendly Interface: A simple, intuitive, and efficient user interface makes a big difference, especially when managing multiple trades or navigating between different sections of the platform.
6. Easy access to advanced trading tools: I prefer exchanges that offer a dedicated section for leveraged and derivatives trading. Even if you don't use these features immediately, having them available can be valuable as you gain experience.
7. Ultimately, a landing exchange should serve as a reliable and efficient gateway into the crypto ecosystem. It should make onboarding smooth while also offering tools that allow for more advanced strategies as your journey progresses.

I am currently using several different centralized exchanges (CEXs), including:

Binance - Launched in 2017, one of the largest exchange by volume, but **usually unusable as landing exchange**.

Kraken - One of the oldest, established in 2011 and known for its stability.
Coinbase - Founded in 2012 and publicly traded, it's a top choice for U.S. users.
KuCoin - Known for offering a wide selection of altcoins since 2017.
Gemini - Founded by the Winklevoss twins in 2015, it emphasizes regulatory compliance.
Bitfinex - Operating since 2012, it is known for its liquidity and deep order books.
Crypto.com - Launched in 2016, it offers a wide range of crypto-financial services.
OKX (formerly OKEx) - A major player in both spot and derivatives trading since 2017.
Bitstamp - One of the oldest, founded in 2011 and still highly respected.

Keep in mind that your options extend well beyond the examples mentioned above. Often, the ideal exchange for you will depend on a combination of factors, such as the features and limitations of your bank account, the regulatory environment in your country, and your personal goals as an investor or trader.

Once you’ve selected your preferred exchange, the next step is to register and open an account. While this process is generally straightforward, it’s important to follow each step carefully, as you'll be asked to provide personal information and upload several identification documents.

Keep in mind that exchanges accepting fiat currency are typically required to comply with financial regulations similar to those followed by traditional banks. This includes Know Your Customer (KYC) procedures, anti-money laundering (AML) checks, and other regulatory requirements designed to ensure transparency and security. And remember: upon request from the appropriate authorities, exchanges are legally obligated to disclose information about your account, including your identity and transaction history.

While registration procedures can vary depending on the exchange and your country of residence, the typical requirements and steps are generally as follows.

First of all you have to register for an account. Go to the official website or app of the chosen exchange, click on "Sign Up" or "Register", provide email address, mobile number, create a strong password, agree to the terms of service and privacy policy. Then you have to verify Email and Phone Number. I strongly suggest to enable immediately a two-factor Authentication (2FA), usually done via Google Authenticator or similar.

Once you are registered, you must complete the KYC verification before going ahead. You'll typically be asked to provide: full name as on your ID or Passport, date of birth (Must meet age requirement, usually 18+), residential address. And you have to prove it, by uploading: proof of residency (utility bill or bank statement), Passport or

Government-Issued ID, selfie or video verification for facial recognition/anti-fraud.

Please consider that some exchanges have multiple KYC levels, higher levels unlock larger deposit/withdrawal limits and more features (like margin trading).

Once you are verified, you have to add a payment method: Bank account (ACH, SEPA, SWIFT, etc.) or Credit/ debit card or third-party payment service (PayPal, Apple Pay, etc., where supported). Remember: always check if your bank allows crypto transactions, as some may block or delay them.

Once your payment method is active, you are ready to make Your First Deposit. Go to the "Deposit" or "Buy Crypto" section, select your fiat currency and preferred method, enter the amount and follow the payment instructions. Wait for the funds to be credited to your account.

Congratulations are in order! You officially entered the crypto-world! You're now ready to buy your first crypto!

6.3 Get Cracking

Now that you're officially part of the crypto world, a wide range of new opportunities opens up. You've made it past the first gate: you've deposited fiat currency, perhaps purchased your first cryptocurrency, and are ready to take the next steps.

One of the first decisions you'll face is this: Do you need another exchange in addition to your initial "landing" exchange? The answer depends entirely on your personal goals, risk appetite, and the strategies you plan to follow. Your landing exchange is typically centralized (CEX), regulated, and optimized for ease of use. But as you advance, you may find that it doesn't fully meet your evolving needs. Each exchange platform offers a unique mix of available cryptocurrencies (some list hundreds, others are more selective), liquidity (larger platforms often allow quicker, higher-volume trades), different fees structure (trading, withdrawal, deposit, and gas fees can vary widely), different trading tools (margin, futures, options, copy trading, staking, etc.) and. Let but not least, security and custody models (especially relevant for DEXs).

"Yes, that's correct. I want you to fully master everything related to where the actual trading takes place. Think of it like choosing between shopping at a traditional mall, a farmer's market, or... well, a very peculiar roadside stand."

I raised an eyebrow. "That's an odd analogy."

"Let me break it down for you." He turned the screen of his laptop toward me, showing three different websites. "First up: CEX–Centralized Exchanges, like Binance and Kraken.

"The mall?" I guessed.

"Exactly. Everything's organized, there's security, customer service, nice clean interfaces. When you buy Bitcoin on Coinbase, they hold it for you in their vault, just like how the mall stores handle your purchases until you pick them up." He clicked through Coinbase's interface. "The downside? You're trusting them with your money. If they get hacked or go bankrupt, well..." "I'm screwed," I finished. "You're learning." He switched to another tab. "Now, DEX, Decentralized Exchanges. Think Uniswap, SushiSwap, PancakeSwap. These are like farmer's markets." I studied the more complex interface he was showing me. "Looks... messier." "That's because there's no middleman. You're trading directly with other people through smart contracts. No one holds your funds, you keep control of your own wallet." He demonstrated connecting a wallet to Uniswap. "It's more private, more secure in some ways, but also more responsibility. Mess up a transaction, and there's no customer service to call." "And HEX?" I asked, noticing he'd skipped the third option. Ah, HEX–Hybrid Exchanges." Satoshi's face brightened. "These are the clever compromise between our mall and farmer's market. Think of them as those upscale outdoor shopping centers, they give you the best of both worlds." He pulled up a different interface. "Hybrid exchanges try to combine the user-friendly experience and liquidity of centralized exchanges with the security and control of decentralized ones. You get order books like on Binance, but your funds never leave your wallet until the trade executes." "So I don't have to trust them with my money?" "Exactly. Platforms like dYdX or Nash Exchange use this model. You connect your wallet, place orders that look familiar from traditional exchanges, but the actual settlement happens on-chain through smart contracts." He demonstrated the interface, which indeed looked more like a traditional trading platform than the confusing DEX layouts. I studied the screen. "This seems... almost too good to be true." "There are trade-offs," Satoshi acknowledged. "They're often less liquid than major CEXs, and can be more complex to use than simple DEXs. Plus, you're still dealing with smart contract risks. But for many traders, they offer the sweet spot–professional trading tools without giving up custody of your funds." "So the upscale outdoor mall approach?" "Perfect analogy," he laughed. "You get the organized shopping experience, but you're still technically 'outside' and in control. Now, depending on your trading style and comfort level, you might find yourself using all three types..."

6.4 Centralized Exchanges

A Centralized Exchange, or **CEX**, is a digital platform where users can buy, sell, and trade cryptocurrencies under the management of a central authority, typically a company. This company operates the exchange, controls the platform infrastructure, holds user funds in custody, and is responsible for executing trades, securing assets, and complying with regulations. Think of a CEX as similar to a traditional stock exchange, but for cryptocurrencies. Unlike decentralized exchanges (**DEXs**), which are trustless and permissionless, CEXs act as intermediaries between users. When you place an order to buy or sell, the exchange itself processes and settles the transaction on your behalf. You don't trade directly with another user, you trade through the platform, which matches buyers and sellers using an internal **Order Book,** a live digital ledger listing all buy and sell orders for a particular cryptocurrency, showing bid and ask prices along with quantities. This transparent mechanism helps match traders efficiently and updates constantly with every new order or execution. CEXs typically offer **Custodial Wallets**, meaning the exchange holds users' private keys and digital assets. While this simplifies trading and account management, it also requires users to place their trust in the exchange's ability to safeguard their funds. A well-designed user interface (UI) and smooth user experience (UX) also set CEXs apart, catering to both beginners and seasoned traders. Tools like real-time charts, market data, and analytics are typically available to aid decision-making. Most centralized exchanges employ robust security protocols, including two-factor authentication (2FA), encryption, cold storage for assets, and multi-signature wallets. Still, being custodians of large amounts of crypto makes them attractive targets for hackers, and history has shown that even well-known exchanges are not immune to breaches. CEXs operate within safe legal frameworks. They must implement Know Your Customer (KYC) and Anti-Money Laundering (AML) policies to prevent illicit activities like money laundering and terrorist financing. Failure to comply can result in severe penalties or forced shutdowns. Many jurisdictions also require CEXs to obtain proper licensing. In the U.S., for instance, exchanges must register with **FinCEN**, **State Money Transmitter License**, while **SEC** is optional and **CFTC** is needed if they offer crypto derivatives or futures. On the other side of the Ocean, EU has adopted regulatory frameworks like **MiCA** (Markets in Crypto-Assets). Additionally, these platforms must adhere to data privacy laws, such as the EU's General Data Protection Regulation (**GDPR**), which mandates strict protection of user information.

ALWAYS REMEMBER: Centralized exchanges (CEXs) are regulated platforms that operate under national and international financial laws. They are required to collect detailed information about their customers through Know Your Customer (KYC) and Anti-Money Laundering (AML) procedures. In the event of a formal request from regulatory or law enforcement authorities, **CEXs must disclose all relevant customer data and transaction history as part of their legal obligations.**

6.5 Decentralized Exchanges

A Decentralized Exchange, or DEX, is a type of crypto trading platform that allows users to buy, sell, and swap cryptocurrencies without relying on a central authority or intermediary. Instead of a company controlling the platform (like in centralized exchanges), DEXs run on smart contracts, automated code deployed on a blockchain that executes trades directly between users. This means you stay in full control of your assets, and your funds never sit in someone else's custody. You trade from your own wallet, straight to another user's wallet, peer-to-peer. You connect your wallet (like **MetaMask** or **Trust Wallet**), approve a transaction, and that's it, your crypto stays in your control until you make a trade. Most DEXs don't require registration or identity verification. Anyone with a crypto wallet and internet connection can access the platform and trade instantly, with full privacy and freedom. All trading activity is governed by blockchain-based smart contracts. These contracts handle everything from order execution to token swaps without human intervention, reducing risks of fraud or manipulation. But how they work in detail?

Unlike centralized exchanges that match buy and sell orders in an order book, most modern DEXs use a system called **Automated Market Maker (AMM).** Instead of matching buyers with sellers directly, AMMs rely on **Liquidity Pools,** a smart contract that holds two or more tokens (usually a trading pair like ETH/USDC). Users (called liquidity providers, or LPs) deposit an equal value of each token into the pool. For example, if you want to provide liquidity to an ETH/USDC pool, you'd deposit the same dollar value of ETH and USDC. When someone wants to trade on the DEX, they interact with the pool. 1. Traders swap tokens in the pool (e.g., they swap ETH for USDC), 2. The pool adjusts the price based on the ratio of the tokens remaining (this is handled by a mathematical formula, usually $x*y = k$) 3. Fees from trades (usually 0.3%) are collected by the pool and shared among the liquidity providers as a reward for supplying their funds. This system ensures that there's always liquidity for a trade, no waiting for someone to be on the other side of your order.

Examples of Popular DEXs are **Uniswap,** one of the first and most used AMM-based DEXs, **PancakeSwap,** popular for low fees and fast trading and **SushiSwap,** a fork of Uniswap with additional DeFi features.

ALWAYS REMEMBER: If you choose to use a DEX, no one is collecting your personal information, **and under no circumstances can your data be shared or broadcasted.** But without identification, you cannot link your bank account or send any fiat currency to a decentralized exchange. No DEX can be used as Lending Exchange.

6.6 Hybrid Exchanges (HEX or Hybrid DEXs)

Hybrid exchanges (**HEX**) are a new generation of cryptocurrency trading platforms that combine the strengths of both centralized and decentralized exchanges. Their goal is to offer users the best of both worlds: the speed, liquidity, and usability of centralized exchanges (CEXs), along with the security, privacy, and control offered by decentralized exchanges (DEXs).

In a centralized exchange, users typically give up custody of their assets by depositing them into wallets controlled by the platform. This allows for fast and efficient trading, but it also introduces risks, such as hacks, platform failures, and regulatory overreach. On the other hand, decentralized exchanges allow users to trade directly from their wallets, offering greater privacy and control, but often at the cost of slower transactions, limited trading pairs, less liquidity, and a more complex user experience. Hybrid exchanges attempt to solve these issues by blending the two models. They often allow users to maintain control of their private keys, ensuring they retain custody of their funds even during trading. At the same time, they offer features traditionally found on CEXs, such as high-speed order matching, deep liquidity pools, user-friendly interfaces, and customer support. Some hybrid exchanges also incorporate partial KYC processes to satisfy regulatory requirements, while still preserving a degree of user anonymity. Another advantage of hybrid exchanges is their flexibility. Many support a wider range of assets and trading options, including fiat on-ramps, margin trading, and even staking, while maintaining decentralized features like smart contract-based settlement and peer-to-peer transaction layers. In terms of technology, hybrid exchanges usually rely on off-chain order matching combined with on-chain settlement, meaning trades are processed quickly off the blockchain but settled securely on it. This allows them to scale more effectively than pure DEXs while avoiding some of the centralization risks associated with traditional exchanges. In essence, hybrid exchanges represent an important evolution in crypto trading. They are particularly appealing to users who want more security and privacy than CEXs can offer, but who still value speed, simplicity, and broader market access. As regulation increases and users become more aware of security and self-custody, hybrid exchanges may become a key part of the crypto ecosystem's future.

6.7 d'Apps

Decentralized applications (**dApps**) are a key innovation in the crypto space, providing a new way to build applications that operate on blockchain networks without central control. dApps, or decentralized applications, are applications that run on a decentralized network of computers (blockchain) rather than being hosted on a centralized server. They often use smart contracts to function, ensuring operations are transparent, autonomous, and tamper-proof. Their backend is always on Blockchain, making them immutable and censorship-resistant, while often they offer appealing interfaces, typically accessed via a web or mobile app. They are Decentralized, and operate on a peer-to-peer network or a blockchain, making them immune to control or shutdown by a single authority. They are Open-Source, promoting transparency and allowing developers to contribute and most dApps have their own native tokens used for transactions, incentivization, or governance.

Types of dApps include:

Financial dApps (DeFi): Provide decentralized financial services like lending, borrowing, staking, and trading without intermediaries (banks, brokers). Example: **Uniswap** (decentralized exchange), **Aave** (lending/borrowing platform).

Gaming dApps: Create play-to-earn environments where users can trade in-game assets or cryptocurrencies. Example: **Axie Infinity, Decentraland.**

Social dApps: Allow decentralized social networking, ensuring user control over data and preventing censorship. Example: **Minds, Steemit**.

NFT dApps: Facilitate the creation, trading, and showcasing of Non-Fungible Tokens (NFTs), which represent ownership of unique digital assets. Example: **OpenSea, Rarible**.

Governance dApps: Enable decentralized governance of protocols and communities through token-based voting. Example: **MakerDAO, Compound** (protocol governance).

Utility dApps: Provide services like decentralized storage, cloud computing, and identity management. Example: **Filecoin** (storage), **Golem** (computing).

How dApps Work: A smart contract on the blockchain executes predefined rules autonomously. For example, a lending dApp might automatically distribute interest payments based on pre-set criteria. Users interact with the blockchain via a dApp. When a user submits a transaction, it is sent to the blockchain, verified by the network's consensus mechanism, and recorded immutably. Users access dApps through web browsers or mobile applications with wallet integration, such as **MetaMask**, to interact with the blockchain securely.

While there are several blockchains that support these applications, **Ethereum** stands as the primary backbone of most DeFi projects, revered for its groundbreaking smart contract functionality. But it's not alone, other networks, like **Binance Smart Chain** and **Solana**, have stepped into the spotlight, offering their own advantages, such as lower fees and lightning-fast transaction speeds.

6.8 Digital asset transactions

The rusted steel door groaned on its hinges as Satoshi pushed it open, revealing a cathedral that defied the hustle outside. Where I had expected shadows and decay, light poured from dozens of curved monitors that painted the cavernous warehouse in shifting blues and greens. The contrast was jarring, beyond these walls, the city was slowly moving as usual, yet here, in this hidden sanctuary, the future pulsed with digital life.

"Welcome to the nerve center," Satoshi said, his voice carrying a mix of pride and melancholy. He gestured toward the open office space that sprawled across the warehouse floor like a technological organism. Cables snaked between workstations in organic patterns, connecting an ecosystem of the most advanced hardware I'd ever seen. The hum of cooling systems created a mechanical symphony, punctuated by the soft percussion of keyboards and the occasional chime of notifications.

The screens, God, the screens, stretched from floor to ceiling in some places, displaying cascading waterfalls of data and numbers that would have overwhelmed any traditional trader. Price charts flowed like rivers of light, order books updated in real-time microsecond flashes, and trading algorithms executed with the precision of digital choreography. This wasn't just monitoring the crypto markets; this was witnessing the heartbeat of a new financial universe.

"Every major exchange," Satoshi explained, noticing my wide-eyed examination of the setup. "Binance, Coinbase, Kraken, BitMEX, and an hundred others. We see it all here, every trade, every trend, every whisper of market sentiment from Tokyo to New York." He moved between the workstations with the fluid grace of someone completely at home in this electronic wilderness.

I followed him deeper into the space, past traders who worked with an intensity that bordered on meditation. Their fingers danced across keyboards with practiced precision while multiple screens painted their faces in the ever-changing colors of candlestick charts and volume indicators. The air itself seemed charged with possibility and danger, the intoxicating combination that had always drawn me to trading, now amplified by the revolutionary potential of cryptocurrency.

"You wanted to understand crypto trading," Satoshi continued, settling into a chair before a command center that would have made NASA envious. "Not the simplified version they teach in online courses, not the sanitized strategies peddled by YouTube gurus, but the real thing, the brutal, beautiful, chaotic reality of digital asset markets that never sleep, never rest, and never forgive mistakes."

He gestured for me to take the seat beside him as streams of data populated the screens around us. Bitcoin's price action painted itself across one monitor while Ethereum's complex smart contract interactions mapped themselves on another. DeFi protocols flashed their yields like neon signs, and NFT marketplaces buzzed with activity that seemed to follow no traditional logic.

"This is where fortunes are born and die in the span of heartbeats," he said, his eyes reflecting the glow of the screens. "Where algorithms battle algorithms, where human psychology meets mathematical precision, and where the future of money itself is being written one transaction at a time."

As I settled into my chair, surrounded by this testament to humanity's endless capacity for innovation and destruction, I realized that everything I thought I knew about trading was about to be challenged. In this warehouse, in this moment, with the mysterious architect of digital currency as my guide, I was about to learn what it truly meant to dance with the dragons of the new economy.

6.9 Spot trading

Let's begin with the most straightforward and controllable method of trading: spot trading.

Spot trading in the world of cryptocurrency is the most elemental and transparent way to enter the market. It is, in essence, the act of buying or selling a digital asset for immediate settlement, a transaction that takes place "on the spot." When a trader places a buy order, they are offering to acquire a coin at the prevailing price, when they place a sell order, they are ready to part with it. Exchanges act as the grand marketplace where these intentions converge, matching buyers and sellers in a continuous dance of supply and demand. The moment an order is filled, ownership is transferred without delay, the cryptocurrency delivered into the buyer's wallet, and the corresponding funds credited to the seller.

What distinguishes spot trading from more complex instruments is its simplicity. There is no hidden machinery of leverage, no speculation on future prices detached from the asset itself. The trader truly owns what they purchase–be it a fraction of Bitcoin, a handful of Ether, or another token altogether. That ownership can be kept for a day, a year, or a decade, carried from one exchange to another, or moved into the quiet safety of a private wallet. This directness is why spot trading is often described as the most controllable form of trading: the risks are visible, confined to the amount of money actually committed, and not magnified by borrowed capital.

Let's analyze now the the many options available when placing a spot order, as in cryptocurrency trading, understanding order types is fundamental. They are not simply ways of instructing an exchange, they are mechanisms that determine execution speed, fees paid, price control, and risk management. Each carries its own strengths and limitations, and the choice between them often defines the outcome of a trade.

The most basic is the **market order**. This instruction tells the exchange to buy or sell immediately at the best available price in the order book. Execution is guaranteed, but the exact price is not. In highly liquid markets, the difference between expected and executed price may be negligible, but in thin or fast-moving markets, slippage can occur, sometimes significantly. Market orders are used when certainty of execution is more important than precision of price.

The **limit order** operates differently. Here, the trader specifies the maximum price they are willing to pay for a purchase or the minimum they are willing to accept for a sale. The exchange places the order in the book, and it will only execute if the market reaches those levels. A limit order provides price control but no guarantee of execution, it may remain pending indefinitely if the market does not move in the trader's favor.

Risk management introduces the concept of the **stop loss order.** This type of order is activated when the market price reaches a predefined threshold. Once triggered, it becomes a market order, designed to exit a position quickly to cap losses. Its strength lies in automatic execution, but in volatile conditions the fill price may be worse than expected, as it will chase liquidity wherever it can be found.

A variation is the **stop loss limit order**, which combines the stop trigger with a limit condition. When the stop price is reached, the system places a limit order instead of a market order. This prevents selling far below the intended level, but introduces the risk that the order remains unfilled if the market falls too quickly, leaving the trader exposed to further losses.

On the opposite side of risk management are profit-targeting instructions. A **take profit order** closes a position once a specific price is reached, locking in gains. It functions like a stop loss in reverse: when the trigger level is touched, the order becomes a market order. In volatile markets, the actual execution may vary slightly from the target. To counter this, traders may employ a take profit limit order, which specifies the exact minimum (for sales) or maximum (for buys) at which the profit should be realized. This ensures precision but carries the same drawback as its stop-limit counterpart–if the market moves past the limit without filling, the profit opportunity may disappear.

Finally, there is the **iceberg order**, designed primarily for large-volume traders. An iceberg hides the true size of the order by displaying only a small, visible portion in the order book. As each portion is executed, another segment is released until the full size has been processed. This prevents significant market impact that would occur if the entire order were exposed at once, allowing accumulation or distribution to occur more discreetly.

Each of these order types reflects a balance between speed, certainty, and control. Market orders maximize immediacy but sacrifice precision. Limit orders preserve price discipline but may remain idle. Stop-based instructions automate defense or profit-taking, but their effectiveness depends on market conditions. Iceberg orders, meanwhile, are instruments of strategy and scale, used by traders who must operate without revealing their full intent. Together, they form the operational framework through which every participant interacts with an exchange, turning trading from mere intent into executable action.

6.10 Margin Trading

Margin trading introduces an additional layer of complexity to cryptocurrency markets by allowing participants to trade with borrowed funds. Unlike spot trading, where investors can only commit capital they already possess, margin trading opens the door to amplified exposure. A trader deposits collateral, often called margin, into their exchange account, and this acts as the foundation for borrowing additional assets. With this borrowed capital, the trader can enter positions larger than their own balance would otherwise permit. The appeal lies in leverage: the ability to control more of an asset with less capital, magnifying both profits and losses.

The mechanics of margin trading vary by exchange, but the principle is consistent. Suppose a trader has one thousand dollars in collateral and chooses to operate with five-to-one leverage. They now command a position size of five thousand dollars. If the market moves in their favor, gains are multiplied by the leverage factor, producing returns far greater than those achievable with spot trading alone. However, if the market moves against them, losses are equally magnified, and once the collateral no longer sufficiently covers the outstanding borrowed amount, the position may be forcibly closed in what is known as a margin call or liquidation.

This dynamic creates a trading environment with heightened risk and responsibility. Leverage does not alter the direction of the market but changes the sensitivity of the position to price movements. A two percent adverse move on a five-times leveraged trade can wipe out the collateral entirely. Exchanges enforce strict maintenance requirements, automatically liquidating positions when losses approach the limit of the trader's margin to protect against defaults. While this mechanism ensures the lending system remains solvent, it can be ruthless, often closing positions at unfavorable prices during periods of volatility.

Margin trading can be executed in two primary directions: long and short. Taking a **long position** on margin reflects the belief that the price of a cryptocurrency will rise, and borrowed funds allow the trader to maximize their exposure to that potential increase. Conversely, a **short**

position involves borrowing the asset itself, selling it immediately on the market, and later repurchasing it at a hopefully lower price. Shorting on margin is what allows traders to profit in declining markets, a capability not available through ordinary spot trading. This dual ability to speculate on both upward and downward movements is one of the defining features that makes margin trading attractive to more experienced participants.

Despite the dangers, margin trading continues to attract participants because of its potential rewards. For skilled traders, it offers the flexibility to hedge other holdings, exploit short-term volatility, and engage in strategies that would be impossible with spot markets alone. It also provides liquidity to exchanges, as the borrowing and lending mechanism underpins the operation of the margin system itself. But it is not a tool for the unprepared. Understanding leverage ratios, collateral requirements, funding costs, and liquidation procedures is critical before engaging with margin accounts.

In essence, margin trading represents both an opportunity and a peril. It transforms small price movements into dramatic outcomes, offering the possibility of significant profit while exposing traders to the risk of rapid and total loss of capital. It demands discipline, strict risk management, and a clear understanding of market mechanics. Where spot trading is the foundation, margin trading is the sharp edge, a powerful but unforgiving instrument that rewards precision and punishes recklessness without hesitation.

6.11 Derivatives Trading

Derivatives trading occupies one of the most sophisticated and influential corners of the cryptocurrency market. Unlike spot or margin trading, which deal directly with the underlying asset, derivatives derive their value from the performance of that asset without requiring actual ownership. They are contracts, agreements between buyers and sellers, that reference the price of Bitcoin, Ethereum, or any other digital token as their benchmark. By separating exposure to price from the transfer of the asset itself, derivatives open a vast range of possibilities: hedging, speculation, arbitrage, and risk management on a scale that would otherwise be inaccessible.

The most established derivative is the **futures contract**. In its essence, a futures contract obligates two parties to transact a specific amount of an asset at a predetermined price on a defined date in the future. For example, a trader might agree today to buy one Bitcoin for a fixed price, with settlement scheduled three months later. If the market price at that time is higher, the buyer profits by acquiring the asset below its market value, if the price is lower, the obligation becomes a loss. In cryptocurrency, many exchanges settle futures not with physical delivery of coins but in cash equivalents, using the price index of the underlying asset as the settlement benchmark. Futures are highly attractive to institutional and professional traders because they allow them to lock in prices, hedge against volatility, or speculate on future movements without managing wallets or custody.

Building upon the futures model, the crypto industry introduced the **Perpetual Contract**, often called a perpetual swap or simply **Perpetual**. Unlike a traditional future, the perpetual has no expiration date. It is designed to mimic spot market exposure while allowing leverage, with the position rolling forward indefinitely as long as margin requirements are maintained. To prevent perpetual contracts from diverging too far from the spot price, exchanges employ a funding mechanism: periodic payments exchanged between long and short position holders. If the contract trades above spot, longs pay shorts, if it trades below, shorts pay longs. This funding rate aligns the perpetual's price with the underlying asset, creating a self-correcting mechanism that keeps the market tethered to reality. For many retail and professional traders alike, perpetuals have become the most widely used crypto derivative, combining the flexibility of no fixed maturity with the leverage of futures.

Options introduce a different paradigm. An option gives, but does not oblige, its holder the right to buy or sell an asset at a specific price within a certain timeframe. The two fundamental types are calls, which grant the right to buy, and puts, which grant the right to sell. Options involve a premium: the buyer pays this upfront for the possibility of exercising the right, while the seller, or writer, receives the premium in exchange for taking on the obligation should the buyer choose to act. In cryptocurrency, options are often used to hedge against extreme volatility. For instance, a trader holding Bitcoin might purchase a put option to protect against a steep decline, effectively setting a floor on potential losses. At the same time, speculative traders use calls and puts to bet on sharp upward or downward swings, often with complex strategies that involve multiple options layered together.

Beyond futures, perpetuals, and options, the crypto derivatives landscape continues to evolve with instruments such as forwards, swaps, and structured products. **Forwards** are simple agreements similar to futures but privately negotiated over-the-counter rather than on an exchange, allowing customization of size and settlement terms at the cost of reduced transparency and increased counterparty risk. **Swaps**, particularly total return swaps, enable one party to pay the return of a crypto asset in exchange for a fixed or floating rate, often used by institutions to gain or hedge exposure without holding the coins. Structured products combine derivatives into tailored instruments that fit particular investment objectives, such as yield enhancement or volatility protection, though they demand a sophisticated understanding of risk.

The appeal of derivatives lies in their flexibility. They allow market participants to speculate in both rising and falling environments, to hedge portfolios against adverse moves, and to create strategies that balance risk and reward with precision. Yet the very features that make them powerful also make them hazardous. Leverage is often built into these contracts, meaning small market movements can have amplified consequences. The complexity of funding rates, option greeks, and settlement mechanics can overwhelm traders who lack the necessary knowledge. Moreover, the volatility inherent in cryptocurrency markets compounds these risks, leading to rapid liquidations and significant losses when positions are mismanaged.

Despite these challenges, derivatives trading has grown into a cornerstone of the digital asset ecosystem. For exchanges, derivatives generate liquidity and attract professional traders, while for institutions, they provide the means to manage exposure without the logistical hurdles of custody. For the individual trader, derivatives offer opportunities that extend far beyond simple buy-and-hold strategies, but they demand education, discipline, and rigorous risk management.

In summary, derivatives transform the way traders interact with cryptocurrencies. They allow price exposure without ownership, speculation without direct transfer, and hedging without liquidation of underlying assets. Futures bring predictability with defined settlement dates, perpetuals offer indefinite positions tethered by funding, and options introduce asymmetry, granting the right but not the obligation to act. Together with other instruments, they form an advanced layer of the market, a domain where precision and knowledge are rewarded, and where inexperience can prove costly. Derivatives trading is not merely an expansion of opportunity; it is a test of control, a proving ground where strategy must meet both the mathematics of risk and the reality of relentless market volatility.

6.12 P2P Trading

P2P trading in crypto is where the rules of the game shift. There's no need for intermediaries, no need for the towering exchanges that watch over every move. Instead, it's just two people, one with a cryptocurrency to sell and the other with cash in hand, finding common ground. It's personal, direct, and in a world where anonymity is often craved, it's a solution that fits. They meet in virtual spaces, these buyers and sellers, and through whispers of negotiation, they agree on a deal that suits them both. Here, no one is watching. When a seller lists their offer, they throw a line into the sea of traders. They name their price, their conditions, and wait. On the other side, a buyer scours the listings, looking for the right opportunity, the right price, the right method of payment. Some will pay by bank transfer, some by PayPal, others prefer cash. And when the match is made, they connect, silently working out the details. It's all in their hands. The terms, the time, the payment, it all bends to their needs. But it's not without risks. In a world where trust is the most valuable currency, there's always a chance someone won't hold up their end of the deal. That's where escrow comes in. Most platforms act as a silent third party, holding the cryptocurrency safely until the buyer proves they've paid. Only when both sides are satisfied does the trade truly close. It's a safeguard, a layer of trust in an otherwise shadowy exchange. P2P trading offers something traditional exchanges can't, privacy. There's no need to shout from the rooftops, no public order book broadcasting your intentions. Instead, it's a quiet affair, perfect for those who want to stay under the radar. High-profile investors, institutional giants, they've seen the value in this method. Why risk moving markets when you can trade in the dark, without anyone noticing? And then there's the freedom it brings. On the public exchanges, everything is rigid, structured, fixed. But here, in the P2P world, nothing is set in stone. If you want to pay with cash, you find someone willing to accept it. If you prefer to meet in person, there are platforms that allow it. You negotiate the price, you decide the terms. Flexibility is king, and for those who want to shape the deal their own way, it's the perfect fit. Yet, as with any uncharted territory, there are dangers. Scammers lurk, waiting to pounce on the unsuspecting. They might send fake proof of payment, or worse, initiate a chargeback after the trade is complete. It's a game of trust, and not everyone plays fair. The lack of transparency can be unsettling. Without the clear oversight of a centralized exchange, verifying the deal can feel like navigating through a fog.

Sometimes trades drag out, disputes arise over details, and resolution can be hard to come by. Despite the risks, P2P trading thrives. Platforms like **Binance P2P**, **LocalBitcoins**, **Paxful**, they provide the marketplace, but the real action happens between the buyer and seller. There's no rush. Trades might take a little longer than they would on a centralized exchange, but that's the price you pay for control. In these spaces, large trades move without a ripple, without the market ever realizing what happened. And then there are the regions where P2P is more than just an option, it's a lifeline. In countries where centralized exchanges are banned or restricted, P2P offers a way in. It's a global market, open to anyone with the means to access it. Investors who want to move large sums without slipping prices find a haven here. It's a world where deals are struck with precision, and every trade is custom-fit to the needs of its participants. But as much as P2P trading offers freedom, it also walks a tightrope. Regulations are coming, creeping closer. The authorities are watching now, and soon, even these private spaces might find themselves under scrutiny. The landscape is shifting. The need for transparency, for security, is growing, and while P2P trading remains a crucial mechanism for moving large amounts of cryptocurrency quietly and efficiently, its future hangs in the balance. For now, though, the system endures. Buyers and sellers meet, deals are struck, and cryptocurrency changes hands in the shadows. It's a game of trust, a dance between risk and reward, and for those who know the steps, it's where the real action takes place.

6.13 Over-the-Counter (OTC) trading.

For institutional investors and high-net-worth individuals making large trades, **Over-the-Counter (OTC)** trading remains the alternative to public exchanges. OTC deals happen off-exchange so major players can execute size without telegraphing intent or blowing through order books. In crypto, that's still crucial: a single block, say 500 BTC, can be negotiated bilaterally or via an RFQ (request-for-quote) workflow and filled in one shot, with the price impact largely contained. The process is bespoke: terms, timing, and settlement are agreed privately, often through specialized desks or prime brokers, not the public tape.

The trade-offs haven't disappeared. Discretion and reduced market impact come at the cost of less transparency and heightened counterparty risk. The industry's answer in 2024-2025 has been infrastructure: off-exchange settlement rails and prime-broker tooling that keep assets in segregated custody until the moment of settlement. **Copper's ClearLoop**, for example, links custodians, venues, and brokers so institutions can delegate balances for trading without moving funds onto exchanges, a pattern that now clears tens of billions in notional monthly.

The roster of desks has evolved. **Cumberland (DRW)** continues to quote deep, principal liquidity to institutions; **Galaxy** runs 24/7 electronic and voice OTC across spot and derivatives, **Kraken's OTC** desk adds automated RFQ and white-glove chat execution, **Coinbase Prime** formalized RFQ so multiple liquidity providers compete for your block, **FalconX** has emerged as a leading prime broker bridging OTC liquidity, financing, and (newly) 24/7 electronic OTC options, and **Binance** operates an institutional OTC & execution desk alongside its exchange. Notably, **Genesis's U.S. OTC** spot operation was wound down in 2023, underscoring how the field has consolidated around the best-capitalized and most regulated players.

One more 2025 shift: the line between "**OTC desk**" and "**prime broker**" keeps blurring. Banks and large brokers are stitching in fiat FX rails, custody, off-exchange settlement, and derivatives under one roof, so a fund can RFQ a spot block, overlay a hedge with options, and settle from cold custody, end-to-end, without spraying intent across public markets. FalconX's tie-up with **Standard Chartered** to streamline multi-currency settlements for institutions is a good example of TradFi plumbing meeting crypto block flow.

Bottom line: OTC trading still acts as a pressure valve for size. It's how vast sums move without rippling the surface. But the shadows are brighter: standard RFQ rails, prime-broker settlement, and MiCA-grade oversight are pulling block liquidity into a more supervised, auditable lane. The landscape mixes immediate, straightforward cash blocks with structured and derivative overlays, each with distinct risks. Fortunes can still turn in a blink, but today, the biggest trades are increasingly executed on institutional rails designed to keep price impact low, counterparty risk contained, and regulators satisfied.

6.14 Advanced Trading

As cryptocurrency markets have matured new methods of trading, born from both traditional finance and the peculiarities of digital assets, have emerged to exploit inefficiencies, automate strategies, or harness the unique economic incentives embedded in blockchain protocols. Among these, arbitrage, algorithmic systems, staking-based mechanisms, and a range of specialized approaches stand out as central tools in the repertoire of sophisticated traders.

Arbitrage trading is one of the oldest techniques in financial history, yet in cryptocurrency it has acquired a particular prominence due to the fragmented nature of exchanges. At its core, arbitrage is the exploitation of price differences for the same asset across different venues. In practice, this might mean buying Bitcoin on one exchange where it is priced lower and simultaneously selling it on another where it trades higher, capturing the spread as profit. This is known as exchange arbitrage. Another form, triangular arbitrage, takes place within a single platform but across different trading pairs. For example, a trader might move capital through Bitcoin, Ethereum, and a stablecoin, exploiting small inconsistencies in exchange rates between the three. The mechanics demand extraordinary speed, low transaction costs, and often direct connections to exchange infrastructure. While the opportunities may be fleeting, the principle remains timeless: profit extracted not from market direction but from inefficiencies in pricing.

Closely tied to arbitrage in spirit, though broader in scope, is **algorithmic or quantitative trading**. Here, strategies are executed not by hand but by automated systems: bots, scripts, or advanced machine learning models programmed to react to data in real time. These algorithms can scan multiple markets simultaneously, seeking patterns too subtle or too rapid for human traders to detect. They can implement arbitrage, but they can also analyze momentum, statistical relationships, or order book dynamics to make thousands of decisions in a single day. The advantages are clear. Algorithms operate without fatigue or emotion, can trade continuously in a market that never sleeps, and can be backtested against historical data before being deployed. Yet their success depends heavily on the quality of data, the robustness of the models, and the costs of execution. In a field where speed is everything, a poorly tuned algorithm can magnify losses just as efficiently as it magnifies gains.

A distinct innovation of the blockchain era is **staking-based trading mechanisms.** In Proof-of-Stake systems, tokens are locked to support network security, and in return holders earn rewards. But staking has evolved beyond passive yield. New instruments, particularly **liquid**

staking derivatives, allow tokens locked in staking protocols to be represented by tradable assets, such as stETH representing staked Ether. This creates an additional layer of trading possibilities: investors can earn staking rewards while simultaneously trading or using their staked positions as collateral in decentralized finance applications. In effect, staking generates both income and optionality, but it also introduces risks, such as smart contract vulnerabilities, liquidity constraints, and exposure to the fluctuating value of derivative tokens. For many, it serves as a hybrid between investing and active trading, blurring the line between passive income and strategic maneuvering.

Beyond these structured approaches lies a wide spectrum of other common trading methods, each catering to different risk tolerances and time horizons. **Scalping and day trading** involve executing numerous trades in short periods, seeking to capture marginal price fluctuations. These require focus, discipline, and an ability to manage fees effectively, as profits are measured in fractions of percentage points multiplied across high volume. **Swing trading** takes a broader view, holding positions for days or weeks in anticipation of market momentum, technical patterns, or shifts in sentiment. **Position trading**, often aligned with the colloquial "**HODLing,**" stretches the timeframe further, treating cryptocurrencies as long-term investments rather than instruments of daily speculation. Each of these methods reflects a philosophy of engagement with volatility: whether to harness it moment by moment, ride it in waves, or withstand it over years.

Market making, meanwhile, fills a structural role. By placing both buy and sell orders around the current market price, market makers provide liquidity, ensuring smoother price discovery and narrower spreads. In return, they profit from the difference between bid and ask, and often benefit from reduced trading fees offered by exchanges eager to incentivize liquidity. The approach demands capital, technical infrastructure, and precise risk controls, as adverse price movements can quickly erode the thin margins that define profitability.

Finally, **news trading** represents one of the most human-driven strategies, relying on the ability to anticipate and react to major announcements, regulatory developments, partnerships, or macroeconomic events. In the hyper-reactive world of cryptocurrency, news can spark double-digit price swings in minutes, and traders who can position themselves ahead of or immediately after such events can realize significant gains. The challenge lies in the unpredictability of timing, the speed at which information travels, and the difficulty of separating rumor from fact in an industry often clouded by hype.

Taken together, these methods illustrate the breadth of modern cryptocurrency trading. Arbitrage sharpens the market by erasing inefficiencies. Algorithms extend human reach with speed and precision. Staking-based mechanisms demonstrate how decentralized finance continually blurs the lines between earning and trading. And the varied approaches of scalping, swing trading, market making, and news-driven speculation show how style and temperament influence strategy. Each requires its own balance of skill, capital, and discipline, but all reflect the same underlying truth: the crypto market is an ecosystem of constant motion, and those who engage with it must choose not only what to trade, but how.

6.15 Trading on DEX

Decentralized exchanges, or DEXs, represent one of the most transformative developments in the digital asset ecosystem. Unlike centralized platforms that act as intermediaries, holding custody of user funds and managing order books, a DEX operates on blockchain infrastructure, enabling peer-to-peer trading directly through smart contracts. This design removes the need for trusted middlemen and opens markets to anyone with a compatible wallet, redefining how assets can be exchanged and how liquidity is created.

The central innovation that made DEXs viable is the automated market maker, or AMM. Traditional exchanges rely on buyers and sellers placing orders, with trades occurring when prices align. In the early days of decentralized trading, replicating this order book model on-chain proved too costly and inefficient due to the computational demands of blockchains. The AMM solved this by replacing the order book with liquidity pools, collections of tokens deposited by users into smart contracts. When a trader wishes to **swap** one asset for another, they interact with these pools rather than with another trader directly. Prices are determined algorithmically, often using formulas such as the constant product model, where the product of the quantities of two assets in a pool must remain constant. As one token is withdrawn and the other supplied, the ratio shifts, and the price adjusts accordingly.

This system offers clear advantages. Liquidity is always available as long as the pool contains tokens, meaning traders can execute swaps at any time without waiting for a counterparty. It also incentivizes participation: those who provide tokens to the pool become liquidity providers and earn a share of the transaction fees. In some cases, they may also receive additional rewards, such as governance tokens distributed by the protocol. This dual incentive structure has fueled the rapid growth of decentralized liquidity, making AMMs a cornerstone of decentralized finance. Yet the AMM model carries drawbacks. Traders may face slippage, where large orders shift the price within the pool and result in less favorable execution. Liquidity providers, on the other hand, are exposed to what is known as impermanent loss, a reduction in value compared to simply holding the tokens outside the pool when prices move significantly in one direction. While transaction fees can offset this effect, it remains a critical consideration for anyone contributing capital to liquidity pools.

Beyond the basic swap function, DEXs have expanded their offerings to mirror and, in some cases, surpass the features of centralized exchanges. Many platforms now support limit order functionality through smart contracts that simulate traditional order book behavior. Others have built derivatives markets on-chain, enabling perpetual contracts and synthetic assets that track the value of external instruments. Decentralized lending and borrowing protocols often integrate with DEX liquidity, allowing users to trade with leverage or to use their assets as collateral while still participating in market activity. Cross-chain bridges extend this vision further, making it possible to swap assets between different blockchains without relying on centralized custodians, although these systems introduce their own security and trust challenges.

DEX aggregators add another layer of sophistication. Rather than routing a trade through a single protocol, aggregators split orders across multiple liquidity sources to achieve the best available price. This improves efficiency, reduces slippage, and demonstrates the modularity of decentralized finance, where independent protocols interconnect to form an ecosystem greater than the sum of its parts. For the end user, this creates a seamless experience in which complex routing across pools and platforms is abstracted into a single transaction, executed directly from their wallet.

Security, transparency, and user control remain the defining characteristics of decentralized trading. Assets remain under the control of the trader's wallet until the moment of transaction, eliminating the custodial risks that have historically plagued centralized platforms through hacks or mismanagement. Every trade, every pool, and every fee distribution is recorded immutably on the blockchain, creating an environment of radical transparency. Yet these strengths come with trade-offs: users are responsible for safeguarding their own private keys, transaction costs can fluctuate sharply with network congestion, and smart contract vulnerabilities remain an ever-present risk.

Over time, decentralized exchanges have evolved from simple token swap utilities into fully fledged financial marketplaces. They embody the ethos of decentralization by empowering individuals to trade, provide liquidity, and even participate in governance decisions without surrendering control to centralized entities. The AMM and its liquidity pools remain at the core of this revolution, but the constant addition of tools, whether derivatives, limit orders, cross-chain functionality, or aggregation, demonstrates the relentless pace of innovation. DEXs no longer stand as alternatives to centralized exchanges; in many respects, they have defined a new standard for openness, accessibility, and adaptability in global markets.

In essence, trading on decentralized exchanges is not merely about executing swaps. It is about engaging with a living financial infrastructure that distributes power outward, relying on mathematics and code rather than corporate intermediaries. The opportunities are vast, from simple token conversions to complex strategies involving staking, liquidity provision, and derivatives. But so too are the risks, requiring participants to navigate a landscape where autonomy is paired with responsibility. DEXs mark the frontier of what trading can look like in a decentralized world–fluid, transparent, and fundamentally reshaping the relationship between markets and their participants.

7. Crypto Currencies

“Dear Marco, you mentioned wanting to understand the cryptocurrency landscape," Satoshi said, his voice carrying a quiet authority. "But tell me, what do you see when you look at this space now? What draws your curiosity?"

I shifted forward, eager to begin. "Your creation has spawned an entire ecosystem, hasn't it? When I look at the market today, I see hundreds, thousands of different cryptocurrencies, each claiming to solve different problems. It's overwhelming, honestly. Where do I even begin to understand them?"

With a slight smile "You begin where all understanding begins, with the fundamentals. You see, when I designed Bitcoin, I had a specific vision in mind. But the blockchain technology that underpins it? That was merely the foundation upon which others could build. Each cryptocurrency you see today operates within its own unique technological framework, using its own blockchain and underlying systems."

"That's what confuses me," I admitted. "How can they all be so different if they're built on similar principles?"

"Think of it this way," Satoshi replied "Imagine blockchain as a language, a way of organizing and validating information. But just as English and Mandarin are both languages yet serve different cultures and purposes, different blockchains serve different needs. Some excel in providing decentralized financial services, others prioritize privacy, scalability, or stability. The beauty lies in their diversity."

I nodded, beginning to grasp the scope. "So when you look at the current market, Bitcoin, Ethereum, and all the others ranked by market capitalization, each one represents a different approach to solving problems in the digital economy?"

"Precisely." His eyes seemed to gleam with something approaching pride. "Though I must say, watching how this ecosystem has evolved has been... illuminating. Each cryptocurrency has carved out its own niche, developed its own community, its own value proposition. Some have succeeded beyond what their creators imagined, others have taught us valuable lessons through their failures."

"But before we dive into the specific cryptocurrencies," I said, "you mentioned fundamentals. What should someone understand before they start exploring this landscape?"

Satoshi paused, choosing his words carefully. "Before one takes the plunge, as you might say, diving headfirst into this vast pool of digital assets like some modern-day Scrooge McDuck, there are key concepts that serve as your navigational tools. Understanding these will help you comprehend not just what each cryptocurrency does, but why it matters."

"Such as?"

"Blockchain explorers, for instance. These are your windows into the soul of any cryptocurrency. They allow you to peer into the very transactions that make up the network, to verify and understand the flow of value. Then there are mechanisms like token burning, a fascinating aspect of modern tokenomics that affects supply and demand in ways that traditional economics barely contemplated."

I leaned back, trying to digest this. "You speak of these developments as if you're observing them from the outside. Don't you feel... ownership over what's happened since Bitcoin?"

For a moment, something flickered across his expression, perhaps satisfaction, perhaps wistfulness. "A gardener plants seeds, but cannot control how the forest grows. What I created was a proof of concept, a demonstration that decentralized digital currency was possible. What the world has built from that foundation? That belongs to humanity now."

"And yet you're willing to guide me through understanding it?"

"Understanding breeds wisdom, and wisdom breeds better decisions. If you're going to navigate this landscape, with its strengths, weaknesses, adoption drivers, and challenges, you need to see not just the trees, but the entire forest. Each cryptocurrency, from the largest to the smallest, plays a role in this evolving ecosystem. Some will thrive, others will fade, but all contribute to our collective understanding of what digital value can become."

I pulled out my MacBook, ready to delve deeper. "Then let's begin. Walk me through this world you helped create, starting with those fundamental concepts you mentioned. Help me understand what makes each piece of this puzzle unique, and how they all fit together."

Satoshi nodded approvingly. "Very well. But remember, as we explore each cryptocurrency and its underlying technology, we're not just examining code or market valuations. We're witnessing humanity's attempt to reimagine value, trust, and economic interaction itself. Each blockchain tells a story, each token represents a vision of the future. The question is: which stories will stand the test of time?"

The conversation was just beginning, but already I could sense the depth of insight that lay ahead. In the digital shadows of this room, I was about to embark on a journey through the most revolutionary financial innovation of our time, guided by its most enigmatic architect.

7.1 Tokenomics

Tokenomics (a blend of "token" and "economics") refers to the economic structure and system surrounding a cryptocurrency or blockchain-based token. It encompasses how a token functions within a particular ecosystem, its use cases, and the underlying factors that determine its value and distribution. Understanding tokenomics is essential for evaluating the sustainability, utility, and potential value of a project. Few basics are:

Total Supply: The absolute maximum number of tokens that will ever exist within a project's ecosystem. This cap is typically hard-coded into the protocol and helps define the token's long-term scarcity.

Circulating Supply: The number of tokens currently available in the open market and actively trading. This excludes tokens that are locked, staked, burned, or reserved for future release.

Token Distribution: The initial allocation and release mechanism of tokens, often conducted through methods such as a Token Generation Event (**TGE**), Initial Coin Offering (ICO), Initial Exchange Offering (IEO), Launchpads, or airdrops. Distribution plans often include allocations for early backers, development teams, ecosystem growth (e.g., partnerships and grants), marketing initiatives, and community incentive programs.

Governance: Certain tokens confer on-chain governance rights, allowing holders to vote on key decisions such as protocol upgrades, treasury allocations, or parameter adjustments. These governance tokens are a cornerstone of decentralized autonomous organizations (DAOs) and community-driven DeFi protocols.

Utility and Access: Many tokens serve as utility tokens, granting holders access to services, premium features, or transactional capabilities within a blockchain protocol, layer-2 network, or decentralized application (**dApp**). In ecosystems such as Ethereum, tokens are also used to pay gas fees or interact with smart contracts.

Incentives and Participation: Tokens are central to incentive design. They are used to reward behaviors that support network growth and security, such as staking, liquidity provision, governance participation, or data validation in decentralized oracles. Many ecosystems implement staking-as-a-service, where users lock tokens in smart contracts to secure the network and earn yield, effectively removing them from circulating supply.

Inflationary and Deflationary Models: Deflationary models reduce supply over time via token burning, capped issuance, or reduced emission schedules, while **Inflationary models** expand supply through mechanisms like staking rewards, validator payouts, or treasury minting. Hybrid models may dynamically adjust issuance rates based on protocol performance or governance votes.

Minting Mechanisms: Token creation (minting) is typically governed by the project's consensus protocol. In Proof-of-Stake (PoS) or Delegated Proof-of-Stake (DPoS) systems, minting often rewards validators or stakers. In newer ecosystems, modular chains and rollup-centric architectures also define custom minting conditions based on performance, throughput, or governance input.

Burning: See below.

Liquidity: A token's liquidity reflects how easily it can be bought or sold without causing significant price impact. Liquidity is influenced by trading volume, market depth, and the presence of liquidity pools on decentralized exchanges (DEXs) or centralized exchanges (CEXs). Features like concentrated liquidity (e.g., Uniswap V3) and cross-chain liquidity routing improve capital efficiency.

Price Stability: Some tokens, known as stablecoins, are engineered to maintain a consistent value by pegging to real-world assets like the U.S. dollar (e.g., USDC, USDT) or commodities. Stability is maintained via collateralization, algorithmic balancing, or reserve-backed systems. Increasingly, RWA-backed stablecoins and algorithmic hybrid models are being explored.

Monetary Policy and Sustainability: Blockchain projects define their own internal monetary policy, including how tokens are issued, how rewards are distributed, and how vesting schedules are implemented for founders, investors, and contributors. These mechanisms ensure long-term sustainability and aim to balance incentives across various stakeholders while minimizing dilution.

7.2 Burning Mechanism

A fundamental aspect of tokenomics planning is the burning mechanism. This process acts as a regulator of both liquidity and scarcity, directly influencing the inflation rate and the intrinsic value of any cryptocurrency. By reducing the total supply of tokens in circulation, burning helps maintain balance within the ecosystem, often driving up demand and price as tokens become more scarce. In many ways, this mechanism can be likened to the powerful tools used by central banks, like the Federal Reserve in the legacy economy, to manage money supply and inflation. However, in the decentralized world of crypto, burning is an automated and transparent process, giving projects greater control over their token's economic model while simultaneously enhancing its value proposition for holders and investors. It is a process where coins or tokens are permanently removed from circulation. A deliberate act, one that sends these tokens to a place from which they can never return, a burn address, a cryptic wallet no one can access. Once sent there, the tokens are lost to the void, making them unusable forever. It's a strategy, one with many faces, aimed at shaping the economy of the cryptocurrency itself. The burn address is a curious thing, visible for all to see on the blockchain, a string of random numbers and letters, like a vault with no key. One of the most notorious of these addresses on the Ethereum network is:

0x000000000000000000000000000000000000dEaD

When tokens are sent here, their fate is sealed, they vanish from circulation, never to be touched again. The process begins with transaction initiation. A user, a project, or a protocol makes the decision to burn tokens. They prepare the transaction, sending the tokens to the designated burn address. The blockchain captures it all, recording the moment in its unchangeable ledger, where the burn is visible for anyone who cares to look. Once the transaction is complete, the tokens cease to exist in the ecosystem. And with them gone, the total supply updates, reflecting the new reality, a reality shaped by scarcity. One of the more notable examples of this came when Ethereum underwent its **EIP-1559 upgrade** in 2021. With this upgrade, a part of every transaction fee paid in ETH was burned. Each time a transaction was processed, a portion of the fee was sent to the burn address, reducing Ethereum's circulating supply bit by bit. By burning tokens, any project can curb inflation and maintain the value of the tokens that remain. **Binance Coin (BNB)** is a prime example of this strategy. The project regularly conducts burns, gradually shrinking the total supply. The goal? To cut the original supply of 200 million BNB tokens in half, creating scarcity and potentially driving up value. In the realm of decentralized finance (DeFi), burning often plays a more dynamic role. Some protocols build burning into their reward systems or governance mechanisms. For instance, platforms like **Yearn.Finance** allow users to burn tokens in exchange for governance privileges, giving them a voice in how the protocol evolves. It's a form of participation, where burning becomes an entry ticket into the governance arena. Sometimes, burning tokens is about trust. Developers and project teams use it to show their long-term commitment. By burning a portion of their own tokens, they signal that they're here for the future, not just for short-term gains. In Initial Coin Offerings (ICOs), crucial projects may burn unsold tokens after the offering, showing investors they won't flood the market and drive down the token's value. Different projects employ different burning strategies. Some follow scheduled burns, tied to specific milestones or quarterly reports. Binance

Coin is well-known for its regular, quarterly burns, based on the trading volume on the Binance exchange. Others, like **TRON (TRX)**, follow a more flexible path, conducting manual burns when market conditions or community sentiment call for it. And then there's the burn-on-transaction model, where a percentage of each transaction is automatically burned. This is common in deflationary tokens, where every movement of the token reduces the overall supply. **SafeMoon** is one such example, each transaction burns a percentage, shrinking the supply while redistributing rewards to holders. Some blockchains even use **Proof of Burn (PoB)** as a consensus mechanism. Here, participants burn their tokens to prove their commitment to the network, earning the right to create new blocks. It's a system where staking meets burning, with the added effect of reducing supply. **Slimcoin** uses this method, asking participants to sacrifice tokens in exchange for block creation rights. In other cases, projects perform token buybacks and burns. This is a model where a portion of profits is used to buy back tokens from the market, which are then burned.

The **PancakeSwap (CAKE)** platform employs this strategy, regularly buying and burning tokens to control supply and support token value. Burning isn't just a small-time mechanism, some of the biggest projects in crypto have used it. As we said above, Binance Coin (BNB) regularly burns tokens, with one of its largest burns to date in July 2021, when it burned over 1.29 million BNB, worth more than $390 million. Ethereum's EIP-1559 upgrade has turned ETH into a deflationary asset, burning ETH with every transaction. Even meme coins like **Shiba Inu (SHIB)** have embraced the concept, burning tokens to create scarcity within their massive supply. And sometimes, burning is a decisive move, as seen when the **Stellar Development Foundation (SDF)** burned 55 billion XLM tokens in 2019, cutting the total supply in half. The goal was to sharpen the foundation's focus and remove the excess from circulation, a bold move in an unpredictable market. The burning mechanism, in all its forms, is more than just a technical feature, it's a powerful strategy that shapes the supply and value of tokens across the cryptocurrency landscape.

7.3 Wrapped Coins

A wrapped coin, or a wrapped token, feels like a bridge between worlds, a way to carry one treasure into a land where it doesn't quite belong. It's a token that holds the essence of one cryptocurrency while existing on an entirely different blockchain. The term "wrapped" fits perfectly, as if the original asset is carefully placed inside a digital vault, then presented as a token on another blockchain. The beauty of it? This wrapped token carries the same value as the original, but now, it can travel through ecosystems and applications previously out of reach. Take **Wrapped Bitcoin (WBTC)** as an example. It's Bitcoin, but it lives on the Ethereum blockchain, allowing BTC holders to engage with Ethereum's decentralized apps, like DeFi protocols, all without having to part with their beloved Bitcoin. How does this magic happen? It starts with the issuance. You send your original cryptocurrency, say Bitcoin, to a custodian. This custodian, be it a smart contract, a decentralized entity, or even a centralized organization, holds your Bitcoin securely. In exchange, it issues an equivalent amount of wrapped tokens, ready to be used on the target blockchain. But the journey doesn't stop there. When you're ready to redeem your wrapped token and return to the safety of your original asset, you send it back to the custodian.

They release your Bitcoin, and the wrapped tokens are burned, disappearing from circulation as if they never existed. A delicate balance, the wrapped tokens always maintain a 1:1 peg with the original cryptocurrency. One WBTC always equals one BTC. Custodians ensure that the original asset remains securely locked up, mirroring the number of wrapped tokens in the wild. Much of this process is driven by smart contracts, handling the wrapping and unwrapping with automatic precision. Deposit the original crypto, and the wrapped tokens emerge. Redeem them, and they vanish, like a well-practiced magic trick. This tokenization isn't limited to cryptocurrencies alone. It opens doors to real-world assets like gold, fiat currencies, or even stocks. Take **Pax Gold (PAXG)**, for example–gold transformed into blockchain tokens, tradable and flexible in the world of digital assets. Popular wrapped coins have already made their mark.

Wrapped Bitcoin (WBTC) reigns supreme, representing Bitcoin on Ethereum. It lets Bitcoin holders roam freely through Ethereum's decentralized platforms while their BTC value remains intact. **Wrapped Ethereum (WETH)** is another key player. Ethereum itself, reshaped to become ERC-20 compliant, so it can interact seamlessly with other tokens in the Ethereum ecosystem. **Wrapped Binance Coin (WBNB)** lets BNB users explore decentralized applications on Binance Smart Chain. Even **Wrapped Filecoin (WFIL)** exists, allowing Filecoin holders to engage with Ethereum-based DeFi platforms, expanding the horizons of decentralized storage.

But with these opportunities come challenges. Interoperability is the key advantage, enabling assets from one blockchain to interact with another. It's a leap forward, allowing users and developers to build decentralized applications across multiple networks. And let's not forget the vast opportunities wrapped tokens bring to DeFi, giving users access to lending, borrowing, staking, and yield farming, services that might have been unavailable on their asset's native blockchain. Yet, it's not all smooth sailing. The process often relies on centralized custodians. Users have to trust that these custodians will hold their original assets securely, and that the 1:1 peg will hold. This introduces counterparty risk. WBTC, for instance, depends on centralized custodians to maintain its value. And then, there's the risk of smart contract vulnerabilities. The code that powers the wrapping and unwrapping could contain flaws, making it a potential target for hackers. A bug in the system, and funds could be lost. Liquidity issues are another concern. If there's not enough liquidity for a wrapped token on the target blockchain, it can become a challenge to trade or redeem it effectively. And if a custodian fails, whether due to hacking, insolvency, or fraud, the wrapped token could lose its value entirely, no longer backed by the original asset it once represented. Wrapped tokens stand at the crossroads of possibility and risk, offering users the chance to stretch their assets across blockchains while demanding trust and vigilance in return.

7.4 Blockchain Explorers

One of the most valuable tools you'll likely rely on frequently for verifying information on the blockchain is a Blockchain Explorer. These powerful platforms allow you to explore, track, and validate transactions, blocks, and addresses within a blockchain network. Whether you're checking the status of a transaction, viewing historical data, or verifying the legitimacy of an address, blockchain explorers provide transparent access to real-time information. For both newcomers and seasoned users, they serve as an essential resource, helping you navigate the often-complex world of blockchain with greater confidence. A blockchain explorer feels like a window into the heart of a blockchain network, a tool that lets users peer into the vast, interconnected web of records that make up the blockchain. With a few keystrokes, anyone can search and explore the endless rows of transactions, blocks, and addresses, all meticulously logged and available for viewing. It offers a user-friendly path into real-time information, from the details of a single transaction to the larger workings of the entire network. In the world of blockchain, where transparency is sacred, these explorers become indispensable for understanding the flow of data. Tracking a transaction becomes effortless with an explorer. You simply enter a **Transaction Hash (TXID)** and suddenly, the screen lights up with every detail, who sent it, who received it, how much was transferred, and the fees paid to make it all happen. Each transaction, no matter how small, tells its own story, recorded permanently on the blockchain. For those curious about the building blocks of the chain itself, the explorer reveals the intricate details of every block added to the chain. It's all there, block height, timestamp, a list of the transactions held within, the miner or validator who earned the reward for securing it. The rewards themselves, freshly minted coins, shine as a sign of work done and effort rewarded. Wallets, too, open up under the explorer's gaze. Enter a wallet address and you can see everything, balance, the history of transactions, incoming and outgoing, all laid bare. Explorers offer a way to understand how funds flow, how tokens move across the network. And for those looking to submit transactions, explorers provide a snapshot of current transaction fees, a quick guide to avoid overpaying or getting caught in a bottleneck of delays. The explorer also serves as a mirror to the network's pulse, showing statistics in real-time. The hash rate, the difficulty, the total number of transactions–all available at a glance, a living portrait of the blockchain's ongoing work. For smart contracts, especially on networks like Ethereum, the explorer becomes even more important. It allows users to dig deeper into contract addresses, checking event logs and interactions with decentralized applications (dApps), giving insights into the mechanics of these coded agreements. Each blockchain often has its own dedicated explorer, tailored to its specific architecture.

For Bitcoin, platforms like **Blockchain.com** or **Blockchair** offer these insights, while Ethereum finds its records revealed on **Etherscan** or **Ethplorer**. Other blockchains, like Solana, Polkadot, and Cardano, have their own explorers: **Solscan**, **Polkascan**, and **Cardanoscan**, respectively, while **Tronscan** opens the world of Tron. For smart contracts, explorers provide access to source codes, interactions, and event logs, offering developers and users alike a window into the workings of blockchain applications. Explorers offer a range of possibilities, from transparency to research. It's a new level of insight, a way to see how all the pieces of the blockchain world fit together.

7.5 Atomic Swaps

An atomic swap unfolds like a delicate dance between two individuals, each holding the currency of their own world. They stand apart, separated by the invisible lines of blockchain networks, yet there is no need for a middleman. No third party will oversee the exchange. The process is direct, peer-to-peer, and, above all, trustless. The term "atomic" resonates in the air. It whispers a promise that this trade either happens fully or not at all, there is no halfway, no room for one to leave the other in the dark. Both will emerge with what they seek, or the exchange will unravel before it begins, protecting them both from fraud. Two users meet in this digital space. They do not rely on a centralized exchange but instead reach across their chains, their currencies. Bitcoin in one hand, Litecoin in the other, they prepare to swap. The magic of atomic swaps lies in their cross-chain nature. It matters not that their assets lie on different blockchain networks. A Bitcoin can be traded for a Litecoin, or perhaps for Ethereum, without the need to convert to a middle currency. The process flows naturally across these virtual borders. Trust is unnecessary here. The swap unfolds under the careful watch of smart contracts. These contracts, powered by **Hash Time-Locked Contracts**, or **HTLCs**, bring order to the transaction. The cryptography that binds them ensures no step is skipped. Alice, the keeper of Bitcoin, and Bob, holding Litecoin, begin the process. First, they agree, on the amount, on the rate. It's simple. A quiet acknowledgment. Then, Alice takes the next step. From the shadows of her code, she conjures a secret. A long, cryptographic string, random and powerful. She hashes it, reducing it to a form only she knows. This secret is the key to the entire exchange. She locks her Bitcoin away, bound in an HTLC, and tied to that cryptographic hash. Bob can only touch it if he holds the key, the original secret. But Alice doesn't give him the key just yet. Now it's Bob's turn. He mirrors her movements, creating his own HTLC on the Litecoin network, locking his funds with the same cryptographic hash Alice provided. The secret is the key here as well. Alice can only claim the Litecoin if she reveals the original secret, the pre-image. Both coins, bound to each other, wait patiently, locked away by their contracts, for the reveal. The execution is flawless. When Alice claims Bob's Litecoin, she does so by revealing the secret, a whisper passed through the contract. The moment Bob sees it, he acts. With that same secret in hand, he reaches out and claims Alice's Bitcoin. It's seamless, like watching two hands clasp and release in perfect harmony. If one of them hesitates, fails to meet the contract's demands within the time frame, the funds slip back into their original owners' accounts. No one is cheated. No one is left wanting. The process is either complete or it dissolves, leaving both parties whole, untouched by risk. There is no need for centralized exchanges. Alice and Bob don't trust a faceless entity with their hard-earned cryptocurrency. There are no hacks, no inflated fees.

Their swap happens between them, across the chains. Bitcoin and Litecoin, Ethereum and more–it doesn't matter which currency they trade. The swap is always secure, tied inextricably to the cryptographic promise of the HTLC.

Neither party needs to share personal information. Their privacy is intact. But the process has its challenges. To dance this dance requires skill, an understanding of the technical complexity involved. Creating these HTLCs and interacting with blockchain networks isn't simple, not for everyone. And not all blockchains are ready to host these atomic swaps. Certain features must be in place, like support for HTLCs, which popular blockchains like Bitcoin and Litecoin possess. Others do not. The pace, too, is slower than the bustling centralized exchanges. Each step depends on the block times of the two currencies involved, a delay that can be frustrating. Still, for those who value security, privacy, and autonomy, the trade is more than worth it. Atomic swaps have begun to shape decentralized exchanges, integrating into their ecosystems and allowing users to trade without relying on middlemen. They unlock new possibilities for cross-chain payments, particularly in the realm of decentralized finance. Atomic swaps represent a new frontier in the world of cryptocurrency, a place where trust isn't required and fraud doesn't stand a chance.

7.6 Decentralized Databases

In the evolving architecture of decentralized systems, decentralized databases occupy a foundational role, complementing blockchain infrastructure by offering scalable and permissionless data storage. Unlike traditional databases managed by centralized authorities, a decentralized database distributes data across a network of independent nodes. Each node may store either a portion or a full copy of the data, and any update must be validated and synchronized across the network according to consensus protocols.

This design eliminates single points of failure and censorship risk while enabling resilient and transparent data operations. In the context of blockchain networks and Web3 applications, decentralized databases work alongside the ledger layer to store off-chain data–ranging from user profiles to media files–while preserving decentralization principles.

At a technical level, decentralized databases integrate cryptographic security, distributed consensus, and replication protocols to achieve trustless, tamper-evident storage. The result is a system in which data is not only available across multiple geographic locations but also verified by the collective state of the network.

Core characteristics define decentralized databases in contrast to their centralized counterparts. Immutability ensures that data, once written, cannot be modified or removed without consensus. The trustless architecture removes reliance on any central party by replacing it with verifiable cryptographic mechanisms and economic incentives. Fault tolerance and data redundancy ensure that the system remains operational even if several nodes fail or act maliciously. Additionally, censorship resistance ensures that no single party can suppress, modify, or deny access to data–an essential property for open systems and decentralized applications.

In terms of practical deployment, decentralized databases are typically paired with blockchains in multi-layered architecture. The blockchain handles on-chain settlement, consensus, and auditability, while the decentralized database provides high-throughput, scalable data access for non-transactional storage. This division prevents blockchain bloat and reduces network congestion while maintaining cryptographic integrity through hash references or Merkle proofs linking off-chain content to on-chain events.

Several protocols and platforms have emerged as leading solutions in the decentralized database space. **IPFS (InterPlanetary File System)** represents a landmark peer-to-peer protocol designed to decentralize web content. It uses content addressing and distributed hash tables to locate files across the network, enabling secure file sharing and static data retrieval. **Filecoin**, an incentive layer built atop IPFS, introduces a decentralized marketplace for storage. Participants can lease spare disk space in exchange for FIL tokens, creating a globally distributed storage economy. **Arweave**, in contrast, offers a blockchain-like data permanence layer through its "**permaweb**" architecture, allowing immutable and permanent data archiving for use cases such as document notarization and historical records.

Swarm, a native part of the Ethereum ecosystem, provides decentralized storage and messaging for dApps and smart contracts, focusing on data redundancy and availability within a fully Ethereum-compatible infrastructure. **BigchainDB** seeks to bridge the gap between conventional database performance and blockchain properties by offering high throughput, decentralized control, and native asset management in a scalable environment.

The benefits of decentralized databases in blockchain and Web3 ecosystems are significant. They enable user-centric data ownership, where individuals retain control of their data without relying on centralized custodians. Transparency is built into the protocol, ensuring public verifiability of data operations and access logic. Security is enhanced through end-to-end encryption and consensus-backed validation. Cost efficiency arises by leveraging underutilized storage capacity globally, especially in networks like Filecoin. Looking forward, the future of decentralized databases will likely be defined by greater interoperability, integration with zero-knowledge proofs for privacy, and the emergence of autonomous storage networks governed by DAOs. Advancements in protocol-layer economics and **AI-based data management** agents will allow decentralized databases to not only store information but also contextualize, analyze, and serve it on demand. As blockchain networks become more modular and composable, decentralized databases will play an increasingly vital role in supporting scalable and user-controlled data layers. In a world aiming to shift control from platforms to users, they provide the infrastructure for a digital society where privacy, ownership, and resilience are embedded in the code–not just the contract.

7.7 Staking

Staking refers to the process by which cryptocurrency holders participate in the validation and security of a blockchain network by locking up, or "staking", their tokens. This mechanism is fundamental to Proof of Stake

(PoS) and its evolving variants, where the creation of new blocks and the validation of transactions are no longer reliant on energy-intensive mining (as in Proof of Work), but rather on token ownership and network engagement.

In PoS-based systems, participants who stake their tokens, often called validators or delegators, contribute to the consensus mechanism. The more tokens staked, the greater the chance of being selected to propose or validate a block, with successful validators earning staking rewards in the form of newly minted tokens or transaction fees (**GAS**). This model is increasingly seen as a scalable, environmentally sustainable alternative to traditional mining, aligning incentives between network security and token utility. With the growing adoption of Ethereum's transition to Proof of Stake (Ethereum 2.0), staking has become a central element of blockchain economics. Other leading protocols–such as **Cardano**, **Polkadot**, **Solana**, and **Avalanche,** also integrate staking deeply into their consensus architecture, offering varying yields and mechanisms for participation.

Staking returns, typically expressed as **Annual Percentage Yield (APY)**, vary depending on network-specific factors such as total tokens staked, validator performance, inflation schedules, and protocol-defined reward mechanics. For example, Ethereum currently offers staking yields in the range of 4%-6% APY, driven by the total ETH staked and network activity, with rewards comprising both block subsidies and prioritized transaction fees (known as **MEV, Maximal Extractable Value**). **Cardano (ADA)** with a relatively stable return of ~4%-5%, offering flexibility through non-custodial delegation and no minimum lockup.

Polkadot (DOT) with higher APYs, often exceeding 13%, incentivizing staking within its inflationary reward model.

Solana (SOL), where high throughput and fast finality support yields between 6% and 8%, although validator quality remains critical due to network performance variability.

Avalanche (AVAX), with competitive yields (up to 11%) tied to validator uptime and staking duration, typically requiring a minimum commitment of two weeks.

As with all crypto-financial mechanisms, these figures are dynamic and should be verified via official blockchain explorers or staking dashboards for real-time accuracy.

Staking yields are subject to several underlying variables. A key consideration is network saturation: as more participants stake tokens, the fixed reward pool is distributed across a wider base, reducing individual returns. Additionally, validator performance–including uptime, accurate block proposals, and responsiveness–is crucial. Validators who fail to meet protocol standards may experience slashing, where a portion of their staked assets is forfeited as a penalty for misbehavior or negligence.

Inflationary tokenomics also play a role. Many PoS networks generate new tokens to fund rewards, which introduces inflation risk: if token issuance outpaces market demand, the real value of rewards may decline even if nominal yields remain attractive.

Furthermore, most staking systems impose an unbonding period–a mandatory delay between unstaking and withdrawing tokens. This can range from a few days **(e.g., Cosmos)** to over a week **(e.g., Polkadot)**, impacting liquidity and the ability to respond to sudden market movements.

While staking is protocol-native and focuses on securing blockchain consensus, **Yield Farming** is a decentralized finance (DeFi) strategy that involves moving assets between liquidity pools, lending protocols, and automated market makers to maximize returns. Yield farming typically offers higher but riskier returns than staking, often rewarding participants in the form of governance tokens or protocol fees. The primary difference between Staking and Farming lies in the source and structure of rewards. Staking rewards derive from block validation and protocol incentives. In contrast, yield farming returns are driven by user-generated transaction fees, impermanent loss exposure, and the rapid turnover of capital across platforms. The latter often involves interacting with smart contracts that may carry vulnerabilities, increasing the risk of exploitation.

To simplify participation, centralized platforms and **staking-as-a-service providers** have emerged, abstracting away technical barriers such as node operation. Exchanges like Binance, Coinbase, and Kraken offer streamlined staking products for a wide range of PoS assets, though they often take a portion of the rewards as a service fee. In contrast, decentralized options, such as **Lido, Rocket Pool, or Marinade,** enable liquid staking, allowing users to retain flexibility by receiving a derivative token (e.g., **stETH, rETH, mSOL**) that represents their staked position and can be freely traded or used in DeFi protocols.

This innovation, particularly in liquid staking, has reshaped the risk-reward profile of staking by improving capital efficiency, enabling composability, and maintaining exposure to DeFi markets while earning consensus rewards. In conclusion, staking stands at the intersection of infrastructure and incentives, blending technical consensus roles with financial yield generation. As blockchain networks scale and evolve–particularly with advancements in modular architecture, Layer-2 staking, and cross-chain delegation–staking is likely to remain a foundational mechanism for aligning economic interests with decentralized security and governance.

7.8 Mining

Cryptocurrency mining, in its most fundamental form, is the mechanism through which decentralized blockchain networks reach consensus, verify transactions, and introduce new units of digital currency into circulation. While the process is commonly associated with Bitcoin, mining continues to be a foundational component of several blockchains that employ a **Proof of Work (PoW)** consensus model.

Mining performs two simultaneous and essential roles: it secures the network by ensuring the integrity and chronological order of transactions, and it creates new coins by rewarding those who contribute computational power to maintain the system. This dual function, validation and issuance, has been central to the decentralized ethos of blockchain technology since its inception. At the heart of mining lies a computational race. **Miners** aggregate pending transactions from the mempool, verify their validity, and attempt to package them into a new block. However, adding a block to the blockchain isn't as simple as submitting data, it requires solving a cryptographic puzzle. Specifically, miners must find a hash output, generated via the SHA-256 algorithm in Bitcoin's case, that meets a network-defined difficulty threshold. This involves modifying a variable known as a nonce and rehashing the block header repeatedly until a valid result is found. The process of finding this valid hash is known as Proof of Work. It serves as a trustless signal to the network that substantial computational effort has been expended. Once a miner discovers a valid hash, the proposed block is broadcasted across the network and, upon consensus, added to the blockchain. The successful miner is then rewarded with a block reward and the cumulative transaction fees contained within the block. This reward mechanism not only incentivizes participation but also introduces new coins into circulation–a monetary function encoded directly into the protocol.

Mining has undergone significant technological evolution since the genesis block of Bitcoin in 2009. In the early days, blocks could be mined using standard CPUs on personal computers. But as more participants joined the network and the difficulty level adjusted upwards, GPUs, which offer higher parallel processing capability, quickly replaced CPUs. The arms race continued with the emergence of **ASICs (Application-Specific Integrated Circuits)**, purpose-built hardware designed solely for mining specific algorithms. ASICs dominate the Bitcoin mining landscape today due to their unmatched efficiency and processing power, though they have also introduced concerns regarding centralization and environmental impact.

As solo mining became less viable due to increasing hash difficulty, miners began forming **Mining Pools**, collectives that combine computational resources to increase the probability of discovering new blocks. Rewards are distributed proportionally based on individual contributions to the pool's total hashrate. Today, a handful of large mining pools exert significant influence over block production. Leading entities such as **Foundry USA**, **AntPool**, and **F2Pool** collectively account for a major share of Bitcoin's hashrate, reflecting a shift in mining from individual activity to industrial-scale operations distributed globally.

Alongside traditional mining models, the ecosystem has seen the rise of **Cloud Mining**, where users lease hash power from remote datacenter, outsourcing the complexity of hardware maintenance and electricity costs. Although this model offers easier access, it introduces new vectors of counterparty risk and often suffers from opaque profitability structures.

Various cryptocurrencies continue to rely on mining as their consensus foundation. Bitcoin (BTC) remains the flagship PoW asset, with its issuance schedule governed by a pre-programmed halving every 210,000 blocks, cutting the block reward in half approximately every four years. This disinflationary design mimics the scarcity of precious metals and has become central to Bitcoin's narrative as "digital gold." **Litecoin (LTC)**, utilizing the **Scrypt Hashing Algorithm,** provides faster block times and was designed as a more accessible alternative to Bitcoin. **Ethereum Classic (ETC)**, a legacy fork of Ethereum, continues to operate under a PoW model following Ethereum's transition to Proof of Stake. **Zcash (ZEC) and Monero (XMR)** also maintain PoW consensus but incorporate privacy-preserving features and ASIC-resistant hashing algorithms like **Equihash** and **RandomX**, respectively, to promote decentralization.

The effectiveness of mining is measured by **Hashrate,** the number of hash calculations performed per second. With modern hardware performing trillions of calculations per second, hashrate is now expressed in **Terahashes (TH/s)**, **Petahashes (PH/s)**, or even **Exahashes (EH/s)**. A miner's hashrate determines their probability of successfully mining the next block, and at the network level, the aggregate hashrate reflects overall security and resilience against attacks. Environmental considerations have become central to the mining discourse. PoW mining requires immense energy, and as concerns over carbon emissions and sustainability grow, some jurisdictions have imposed regulations or outright bans. China, once the epicenter of global mining, banned the activity in 2021, prompting a massive relocation of mining infrastructure to more favorable regulatory environments like the **United States**, **Kazakhstan**, and parts of **Scandinavia**. Conversely, countries such as **El Salvador** and **Bhutan** have embraced mining as part of their national digital strategies, often leveraging renewable energy sources such as geothermal and hydropower to mitigate environmental impact. The regulatory landscape is evolving as well. In many jurisdictions, mining income is classified as taxable, and operations must adhere to energy usage standards, AML policies, and financial reporting requirements. Simultaneously, legal uncertainty persists in regions where mining remains unregulated or in conflict with local energy or data laws.

Looking forward, the long-term viability of PoW-based mining is under scrutiny. The industry faces pressure to improve energy efficiency, incorporate sustainability standards, and adapt to a shifting economic model–particularly as block rewards diminish over time. The rise of Proof of Stake (PoS) systems, now adopted by Ethereum and many next-generation blockchains, presents an alternative model that consumes significantly less energy and emphasizes capital over computation. Nevertheless, mining remains integral to the structure and philosophy of Bitcoin and other PoW-based networks. As protocols evolve and regulatory clarity improves, mining is likely to persist, albeit in a more mature, transparent, and sustainable form.

7.9 Oracles

In the architecture of blockchain systems, oracles serve a critical and often under appreciated role: they act as bridges between decentralized networks and the external world. Blockchains, by design, are closed, deterministic systems. Their nodes achieve consensus by only validating data that exists natively on-chain. While this architecture ensures high security and trust, it severely limits the utility of smart contracts, which are otherwise capable of automating complex logic and executing self-enforcing agreements without intermediaries.

A smart contract can be programmed to carry out virtually any condition-based operation, transferring funds, issuing a token, executing a trade, but it cannot, on its own, access data that lies beyond the blockchain's state. Without input from the outside world, a smart contract is blind to events such as price fluctuations, weather conditions, election results, or sensor readings. This is where oracles enter the scene: they inject external data into the blockchain in a verifiable manner, enabling smart contracts to respond to real-world events.

Oracles are not monolithic. They come in various forms depending on the nature of the data they handle and the direction of that data flow. Software oracles retrieve digital information from external APIs, databases, and web services–such as exchange rates, token prices, or even news headlines. Hardware oracles, on the other hand, interface with physical-world devices like IoT sensors, RFID tags, GPS modules, or temperature monitors, and are essential in sectors like supply chain management or environmental monitoring.

Oracles may also be classified by their directional flow. Inbound oracles import real-world data into the blockchain environment, such as delivering live sports scores to a prediction market. Outbound oracles perform the opposite task: they allow blockchain systems to trigger external actions, such as unlocking a smart lock or initiating a traditional bank payment once on-chain conditions are met.

In terms of trust models, centralized oracles are controlled by a single authority or service provider. While they may be efficient and easy to implement, they present a single point of failure and contradict the decentralized ethos of blockchain. This introduces what is commonly known as the oracle problem: how can decentralized applications (dApps) rely on data sources that may not be trustless themselves?

To address this challenge, decentralized oracle networks (DONs) have emerged. These systems aggregate data from multiple sources, using cryptographic techniques and consensus mechanisms to validate accuracy and integrity before delivering information on-chain. This model minimizes the risk of manipulation, downtime, and erroneous inputs. Chainlink, for instance, is the most widely adopted decentralized oracle network, providing secure data feeds to hundreds of smart contracts across multiple chains. Other prominent solutions include Band Protocol, which uses Tendermint-based consensus, and UMA, which introduces a "priceless" oracle system that relies on dispute resolution rather than continuous data feeds.

The role of oracles is particularly central in Decentralized Finance (DeFi). Lending protocols like Aave and Compound depend on real-time asset price data to calculate loan-to-value ratios and determine liquidation thresholds. Synthetic asset platforms such as Synthetix rely on oracles to track the value of real-world assets like gold, stocks, or indices. Without accurate and timely oracle feeds, these applications cannot operate safely or reliably.

In decentralized insurance, oracles are used to confirm insurable events, such as flight delays or crop failures, allowing for automatic claims processing without human intervention. Prediction markets, including **Augur** and **Polymarket,** depend on oracles to resolve the outcomes of future events, from elections to sports matches, by importing final results in a secure and verifiable way.

However, the integration of oracles is not without challenges. Beyond the oracle problem itself, issues of latency, data quality, incentive misalignment, and sybil resistance remain active areas of research. Projects are exploring solutions such as zero-knowledge proofs, threshold signatures, and trusted execution environments (TEEs) to enhance oracle security. Others, like **Chainlink's Cross-Chain Interoperability Protocol (CCIP)**, are pushing the boundaries further–enabling not just data but also commands and tokens to flow securely between blockchain networks, ushering in a new era of programmable interoperability.

In sum, oracles are the connective tissue between the deterministic logic of smart contracts and the unpredictability of the real world. Without them, the blockchain is a sealed environment. With them, it becomes a powerful platform for real-world automation, enabling applications that are not only trustless but also context-aware. As blockchain adoption accelerates, oracles will continue to play an indispensable role in bridging digital contracts with physical reality.

7.10 NFTs

Non-Fungible Tokens (NFTs) are no longer just speculative buzz, they are becoming the architecture of ownership in an increasingly digital world. At their core, NFTs are unique digital assets that represent verifiable ownership or authenticity of a specific item, stored immutably on a blockchain. Unlike cryptocurrencies such as Bitcoin or Ethereum, which are fungible (each unit identical and interchangeable), NFTs are non-fungible, each carries its own distinct identity, attributes, and value. They can represent anything from a digital artwork or collectible to a physical asset, a license, or even a reputation score that can't be transferred.

The first wave of NFTs painted the canvas with art, collectibles, and culture. But the technology has since leapt beyond those borders. In gaming, NFTs have unlocked a new layer of digital economics. Weapons, avatars, loot, and skins–once siloed inside proprietary ecosystems, are now interoperable, tradable, and player-owned, transforming the player from a user into an economic agent. In platforms like **Illuvium**, **Parallel**, and the new blockchain layers of **Roblox and Fortnite**, NFTs are not just assets–they are passports, status symbols, and revenue streams. Players earn, trade, and create value as part of gameplay, introducing an economy of skill and scarcity.

In entertainment, NFTs are now part of the fabric. Artists, musicians, filmmakers, and creators across mediums are using NFTs to sell their work directly to fans, embed royalty structures into their contracts, and offer exclusive access to gated content, backstage streams, or in-world experiences. **Warner Music**, **Netflix**, and even **Formula 1 teams** have deployed NFT-based fan engagement platforms, transforming passive spectators into active participants, tokenized fandom, if you will.

Underpinning this digital renaissance is the blockchain, most commonly Ethereum, though newer, faster networks like Solana, Polygon, and **Arbitrum** have claimed significant ground, offering low fees and high throughput. Standards like **ERC-721**, **ERC-1155**, and now **ERC-6551** (token-bound accounts) define how NFTs are created, owned, and traded. These smart contracts automate ownership transfers, royalties, and complex functionality like modular upgrades or cross-platform identity linkage.

Efforts toward interoperability and composability are gaining speed. Projects like **LayerZero**, **Wormhole**, and **Chainlink's CCIP** are building the plumbing that lets NFTs flow seamlessly across blockchains. Imagine a single digital identity verified by NFTs that works across games, marketplaces, and even metaverses, not tied to a chain, but to you. This is where NFTs are heading.

Of course, the idea of digital scarcity predates modern NFTs. Back in the early 2010s, concepts like **Colored Coins** on Bitcoin aimed to represent real-world ownership using blockchain metadata. But it wasn't until **CryptoKitties** in 2017, built on Ethereum with the then-new ERC-721 standard, that the concept truly took shape. What started as collectible cartoon cats overloaded the Ethereum network, revealing not only its popularity but its limits. It was the first time the world saw a blockchain grind to a halt not from speculation, but from joy.

From 2018 to 2020, pioneers like **Decentraland**, **SuperRare**, and **Axie Infinity** built on this foundation, carving out vibrant, if niche, communities of collectors, gamers, and digital land barons. But it was 2021 that marked the tipping point. The sale of **Beeple's "Everydays:** The First 5000 Days" for $69 million at Christie's blew the gates open. Suddenly, NFTs were no longer underground, they were on front pages, on talk shows, and in auction houses. Projects like **Bored Ape Yacht Club**, **CryptoPunks**, and **World of Women** minted new cultural currencies. Celebrities, brands, and VCs all wanted in.

Since then, the space has matured. Brands like **Nike**, **Adidas**, **Starbucks**, and **Louis Vuitton** have launched NFT-based loyalty programs and digital goods, blending Web3 infrastructure with Web2 reach. Real estate tokenization, event ticketing, music rights management, and even certifications are now being built atop NFT standards.

Today, NFTs are not just about art or speculation. They represent a shift in how we manage ownership, authenticity, access, and identity in a digital-first world. They're powering tokens for resumes and degrees, tokenized bonds and invoices, and proof-of-attendance badges for digital and physical events. They're enabling creator economies, empowering micro-communities, and forming the backbone of on-chain identity systems like **Ethereum Attestation Service (EAS).**

In the coming years, NFTs will evolve into dynamic containers for digital identity, capable of holding not just static credentials, but entire layers of a person's verified existence, like passports, driver's licenses, health insurance records, medical history, and more. These NFTs won't be collectibles, they'll function as programmable, encrypted identity vaults, each tied to a private key and controlled directly by the individual. When interacting with institutions, whether a hospital, border control, or a financial service, an AI agent will act on the user's behalf, negotiating what data to reveal, to whom, and under what conditions. For example, a hospital might receive full medical history, while a police officer sees only license validity, and an airport terminal verifies nationality, without accessing the rest. This fine-grained, context-aware disclosure will be governed by smart contracts, reputation protocols, and real-time decision engines, ensuring privacy by default and transparency by choice. In this future, identity won't be something issued and surveilled, it will be something you own, carry, and control entirely on-chain.

7.11 The Wormhole

In a blockchain landscape defined by fragmentation, the **Wormhole Protocol** emerges as one of the most prominent cross-chain interoperability solutions. Designed as a decentralized messaging layer, Wormhole facilitates the seamless transfer of assets, data, and messages across otherwise siloed blockchain networks, ranging from major Layer 1s like Ethereum and Solana to newer Layer 2 environments such as **Arbitrum** and **Optimism**. By enabling composability between chains, Wormhole supports a multichain future in which decentralized applications (dApps), users, and protocols can interact beyond the constraints of any single blockchain.

At its core, Wormhole is not simply a bridge in the traditional sense. Rather, it is an interoperability protocol that abstracts away blockchain boundaries. It allows developers to build cross-chain applications and users to move digital assets, including fungible tokens, non-fungible tokens (NFTs), and arbitrary data, across a growing constellation of supported blockchains. This is achieved without the need for centralized exchanges or custodial intermediaries, preserving the decentralized ethos of Web3 while improving capital efficiency and cross-chain utility.

The Wormhole architecture is anchored by a decentralized network of independent nodes known as **Guardians**. These nodes continuously observe state changes on all supported blockchains. When a user initiates a cross-chain transfer, say, moving ETH from Ethereum to Solana, the asset is locked in a smart contract on the source chain. The Guardians validate this lock event, generate a signed message, and relay it to the destination chain. There, a corresponding "wrapped" asset, such as wrapped ETH (wETH), is minted, representing the same value and function of the original token.

This mechanism allows for bi-directional transfers. Should a user later wish to move their asset back to the original chain, the wrapped token is burned on the destination chain, and the Guardians authorize the release of the original token from the lock contract. The process is designed to be deterministic, cryptographically secure, and non-custodial.

Beyond simple token transfers, Wormhole is evolving into a general-purpose cross-chain messaging protocol. It allows smart contracts on one blockchain to trigger actions or convey information to contracts on another. This capability enables a new generation of cross-chain dApps capable of leveraging liquidity, data, and logic from multiple blockchains simultaneously. DeFi protocols can synchronize lending positions or collateral states across chains. NFT platforms can enable multi-chain minting, transfers, and marketplace access. Even governance systems can implement cross-chain voting logic.

Wormhole currently supports a broad range of blockchain networks, including but not limited to Ethereum, Solana, BNB Chain, Polygon, Avalanche, Sui, and Near. It also integrates with emerging Layer 2 scaling solutions like Arbitrum and Optimism, and is designed to be extensible, new chains can be onboarded via modular components.

The protocol is asset-agnostic. Users can transfer standard ERC-20 tokens, stablecoins like USDC or DAI, and NFTs (ERC-721 or ERC-1155) between supported networks. Developers can also transmit arbitrary payloads, including governance proposals, oracle data, and contract instructions, effectively making Wormhole a transport layer for decentralized computation across chains.

Wormhole now incorporates **Secure Enclave-based signing (SGX)** and leverages **Wormhole V2**, an enhanced architecture offering more granular permissioning and faster message finality.

Wormhole's importance is particularly evident in several key use cases. In DeFi, it enables access to liquidity across multiple chains, allowing capital to flow freely where it is most needed. In NFT ecosystems, artists and collectors can bridge NFTs across chains to reach broader markets. For developers, Wormhole unlocks a design space where cross-chain composability is no longer theoretical but programmable.

While Wormhole was originally built to link Layer 1 chains, it increasingly serves as connective tissue between Layer 1 and Layer 2 solutions, supporting rollup-centric architectures and paving the way for unified user experiences in a fragmented multichain world. This makes Wormhole especially relevant as Ethereum's ecosystem expands toward modularity, where execution, settlement, and data availability may occur on separate layers.

Alternative interoperability solutions include **Cosmos** with its **Inter-Blockchain Communication (IBC) protocol**, **Polkadot and its Parachain** model, and **Synapse**, a competing cross-chain bridge optimized for asset flows. However, Wormhole distinguishes itself with its broad compatibility, speed of integration, and expanding developer tools that enable secure, low-latency cross-chain functionality.

As the Web3 ecosystem continues to scale horizontally across chains and vertically through modular design,

Wormhole stands as a foundational infrastructure layer, enabling not only the movement of assets, but the orchestration of smart contracts, governance, and data across blockchain boundaries.

7.12 Smart contracts

Smart contracts are self-executing contracts whose terms are encoded directly into programmable logic. Once deployed on a blockchain, these contracts autonomously verify, enforce, and execute predefined conditions, eliminating the need for intermediaries such as lawyers, banks, or notaries. The contract's logic is distributed across a decentralized network, ensuring tamper-resistance, transparency, and autonomy. Unlike traditional agreements that rely on institutional enforcement, smart contracts shift trust from human judgment to cryptographic proof and deterministic code.

The concept of smart contracts was first articulated in the 1990s by computer scientist and cryptographer **Nick Szabo**. He envisioned them as digital protocols to formalize and secure electronic transactions. However, it wasn't until the advent of blockchain technology that the infrastructure necessary to support truly autonomous and trustless digital contracts became viable. Bitcoin, though revolutionary in its ability to enable peer-to-peer transactions, offered only limited programmability. It was Ethereum, launched in 2015 by Vitalik Buterin, that fully realized Szabo's vision by introducing a Turing-complete platform specifically designed to support decentralized applications (dApps) and smart contracts.

At their core, smart contracts operate on conditional logic, commonly structured as "if-then" statements. For example, a smart contract governing a freelance agreement might encode the condition: "If Party A submits the completed work by Date X, then Party B will release payment Y." These contracts are deployed onto blockchains like Ethereum, where they reside immutably and execute based on real-time inputs, which may include both on-chain events and off-chain data delivered by external services known as oracles.

Once deployed, smart contracts are immutable: their code cannot be altered without redeployment, a feature that guarantees consistency and prevents post-deployment manipulation. This immutability, coupled with blockchain's transparent and decentralized nature, provides a high degree of trustworthiness. All contract logic and state transitions are publicly verifiable, enabling trustless execution even among anonymous parties.

Smart contracts have found real-world application across a growing number of sectors. In decentralized finance (DeFi), protocols like **Aave** and **Compound** use smart contracts to automate lending, borrowing, and interest accrual. Funds are pooled and distributed algorithmically, with no human discretion involved. In insurance, contracts can be programmed to release payouts automatically upon the occurrence of predefined events, such as flight delays or weather disruptions, data verified through trusted oracle networks like **Chainlink**. Automated Market Makers (AMMs) such as **Uniswap** use smart contracts to manage liquidity pools, price assets algorithmically, and enable decentralized trading with no order books or central intermediaries.

Supply chains also benefit from smart contract integration. Goods can be tracked and verified at each stage of transit, and payments can be conditionally triggered upon delivery verification, reducing fraud and inefficiencies. In real estate, smart contracts are streamlining property transactions by automating escrow, title transfers, and settlement processes. Similarly, in healthcare, they enable secure management of patient records, automate insurance claim processing, and enhance the traceability of pharmaceuticals.

Smart contracts are fundamental to the governance structures of decentralized autonomous organizations (**DAOs**). Within DAOs, token-based voting mechanisms encoded in smart contracts allow decentralized communities to make binding decisions on upgrades, treasury allocations, and protocol parameters, with complete transparency and auditability. In the legal domain, smart contracts provide an automated infrastructure for executing agreements, although their interaction with traditional legal frameworks remains under scrutiny and is the subject of ongoing research.

Despite their transformative potential, smart contracts present several challenges. Security vulnerabilities remain a critical concern, as they are only as robust as the code they're written in. The infamous 2016 DAO hack, where flawed logic in a smart contract led to the loss of over $60 million in Ether, underscores the importance of rigorous code auditing and formal verification methods. Moreover, smart contracts often require external data, such as asset prices, weather conditions, or timestamps, to trigger execution. This data is sourced through oracles, which, while necessary, introduce a semi-centralized dependency that can compromise the trustless nature of the system.

The deployment of smart contracts today is most prominent on Ethereum, which remains the dominant platform thanks to its mature tooling (e.g., **Solidity**, **Hardhat**, and the **Ethereum Virtual Machine**). However, several other platforms have emerged to address Ethereum's scalability and performance limitations. **Binance Smart Chain (BSC)** offers lower fees and faster confirmation times, albeit with more centralized validators. **Solana**, known for its high throughput and near-instant finality, is optimized for high-performance decentralized applications. **Cardano** introduces smart contracts through its **Plutus Framework**, emphasizing formal verification and peer-reviewed development. **Polkadot** provides an interoperability framework for smart contracts to operate across multiple specialized blockchains, while **Cosmos** offers similar cross-chain capabilities through its **IBC (Inter-Blockchain Communication)** protocol.

As blockchain technology matures, the smart contract ecosystem is evolving along several critical vectors. The rollout of Ethereum 2.0 and the adoption of Layer 2 solutions–such as **Optimistic Rollups**, **zkRollups,** and **Validium** chains, are significantly improving scalability and reducing transaction fees. These advancements are crucial for onboarding mainstream users and supporting complex, high-volume dApps.

Cross-chain interoperability is also a frontier of innovation. With frameworks like Cosmos and Polkadot, smart contracts are no longer confined to single ecosystems. Assets, data, and logic can be transmitted across blockchains, unlocking entirely new models for composability and collaboration.

Perhaps most intriguingly, the intersection of smart contracts and artificial intelligence is beginning to take shape. Future smart contracts may incorporate AI agents capable of interpreting context, adapting logic dynamically, or even renegotiating terms autonomously. This convergence could yield intelligent, autonomous protocols that manage contracts with greater nuance and flexibility, blurring the lines between code, agency, and law. But we will let you get full information in the dedicated chapter that follows.

In conclusion, smart contracts represent a paradigm shift in how agreements are conceptualized, enforced, and executed. By embedding logic into decentralized infrastructure, they remove the need for trust and redefine the architecture of digital relationships. Yet, they also introduce a new set of legal, technical, and philosophical challenges–ones that will shape the next generation of digital society.

7.13 DAOs

A **Decentralized Autonomous Organization (DAO)** represents a fundamental shift in how humans can organize and govern collective action. At its core, a DAO is an organization encoded in software, one that operates transparently, autonomously, and without reliance on centralized leadership. Its rules and functions are embedded in smart contracts deployed on a blockchain (most commonly Ethereum), allowing the organization to run according to pre-defined logic rather than human discretion.

Unlike traditional corporations, which are governed by boards, executives, or hierarchies, DAOs distribute authority among members, typically via governance tokens. These tokens confer voting rights, enabling participants to propose, deliberate, and decide on matters ranging from funding allocations to protocol upgrades. In principle, DAOs embody collective ownership and decentralized coordination, replacing trust in individuals with trust in code.

Once deployed, a DAO operates through an interconnected system of self-executing contracts. These contracts manage everything from treasury functions to decision execution, reducing the need for manual oversight or centralized enforcement. As long as the smart contracts remain intact and secure, the DAO can continue to function without direct human control.

Members acquire governance tokens through various means, initial token sales, community contributions, liquidity mining, or as rewards for services rendered. Token holders use these assets to participate in the DAO's decision-making processes. Voting power is generally proportional to the number of tokens held, though some DAOs implement quadratic voting or reputation-weighted systems to mitigate plutocracy and enhance democratic fairness.

All transactions, proposals, and governance outcomes are recorded on the blockchain, ensuring radical transparency and enabling any participant, or external observer, to audit the organization in real time. This trustless environment minimizes reliance on intermediaries and makes the internal workings of the DAO verifiable and immutable.

The governance lifecycle typically follows a standardized flow. A member proposes an initiative, such as funding a new project or changing a protocol parameter, by submitting a formal proposal, sometimes requiring a token deposit to prevent spam. Once submitted, other members vote using their governance tokens. If the proposal meets the quorum and majority thresholds, it is executed either automatically or via a time-locked contract. In this way, DAOs can allocate resources, evolve protocols, and govern entire platforms with minimal human interference.

DAO structures vary widely, but they generally fall into several archetypes based on their purpose and operational model. **Protocol DAOs** govern decentralized platforms like lending protocols or **DEXs, MakerDAO** and **Aave** are prominent examples, responsible for managing parameters such as collateralization ratios or liquidity rewards. **Investment DAOs** pool capital from members to deploy it collectively into startups, NFT collections, or DeFi assets, these operate like decentralized venture funds. **Grant DAOs**, such as those supporting open-source ecosystems, allocate funds to contributors based on community-approved proposals. **Service DAOs** provide freelance-style infrastructure design, development, governance operations, often functioning as decentralized labor collectives. **Social DAOs**, meanwhile, use tokenized membership to coordinate around shared interests, culture, or identity, turning communities into programmable economies.

The benefits of DAOs are profound. They remove gatekeepers, flatten hierarchies, and create structures where power is distributed rather than concentrated. Their transparency ensures that decisions cannot be made behind closed doors. They are borderless by design, allowing participation from any individual with internet access and a compatible wallet. And their automation increases operational efficiency, replacing bureaucracy with protocol-defined execution. In essence, a DAO is not just a new type of organization. It is a philosophical and technological reimagining of how human beings coordinate at scale–without borders, without hierarchy, and with rules enforced not by trust, but by code.

7.14 Stablecoins

Stablecoins are a category of cryptocurrency engineered to maintain a stable value over time by anchoring their price to more predictable assets, typically fiat currencies such as the U.S. dollar or the euro, or commodities like gold. The core idea behind stablecoins is to merge the technological advantages of blockchain, such as decentralization, transparency, immutability, and programmability, with the monetary stability of traditional assets. In doing so, stablecoins have emerged as a crucial component of the digital economy, providing a functional medium of exchange, a reliable store of value, and a consistent unit of account in an ecosystem otherwise dominated by volatility.

Stablecoins are widely used in everyday transactions, offering a means to transfer value without the unpredictable price swings of assets like Bitcoin or Ethereum. They allow users to pay for goods and services, send remittances, or conduct payroll in stable units without off-ramping into fiat. Their stable value also makes them ideal for denominating assets and services across crypto markets, allowing the ecosystem to price goods and calculate yields using a consistent reference point. In trading environments, stablecoins provide a safe harbor during times of market turbulence, allowing investors and traders to preserve value and quickly reenter the market. In the broader decentralized finance (DeFi) space, stablecoins serve as the foundational building block, used in lending, borrowing, yield strategies, synthetic asset creation, and liquidity provision.

Depending on how their peg is maintained, stablecoins are generally categorized into three main types: fiat-collateralized, crypto-collateralized, and algorithmic.

Fiat-collateralized stablecoins (my choice when the reserve is confirmed 1:1) are backed by real-world currencies, typically on a 1:1 basis. For every stablecoin issued, an equivalent amount of fiat currency is held in reserve, usually by a centralized issuer in a commercial bank or a regulated custodian. These reserves may be regularly audited or attested to ensure transparency. The most widely used stablecoin, **Tether (USDT)**, follows this model and has become a dominant force across exchanges, though it has drawn criticism in the past for lack of transparency around its reserves. **USD Coin (USDC)**, jointly issued by Circle and Coinbase, has positioned itself as a compliant and fully audited alternative, gaining trust among institutional users. **TrueUSD (TUSD)** offers a similar model, with a focus on regulatory clarity and real-time proof of reserves. Fiat-backed stablecoins offer simplicity and broad usability, but they inherently rely on centralized entities to hold and manage reserves. This introduces risks related to trust, regulation, and potential censorship.

Crypto-collateralized stablecoins, by contrast, are backed by digital assets such as Ethereum or wrapped Bitcoin. Because cryptocurrencies are volatile, these stablecoins are typically over-collateralized, meaning the value of the collateral exceeds the value of the stablecoins issued. This buffer helps maintain price stability even during market swings. DAI, issued by the MakerDAO protocol, is the most notable example of this model. It maintains a soft peg to the U.S. dollar through a system of smart contracts and incentive mechanisms, allowing users to lock crypto assets into vaults and mint DAI against them. The system is decentralized and governed by the MakerDAO community through on-chain governance. The transparency of this model, since all collateral is visible on the blockchain, is a key advantage, though the system is also more complex. It requires active management of risk parameters and depends on the robustness of the underlying smart contracts. Volatility in the collateral base can lead to liquidations, and the need for over-collateralization can constrain capital efficiency.

Algorithmic stablecoins attempt to maintain their peg without using collateral. Instead, they rely on algorithmic monetary policies encoded in smart contracts to adjust the supply of the token dynamically. When demand pushes the price above the peg, the system increases supply to drive the price back down. Conversely, when the price drops below the peg, supply is reduced to push it back up. This concept has seen both experimentation and controversy.

Ampleforth (AMPL) adjusts user balances based on the protocol's supply targets but allows the price itself to fluctuate. TerraUSD (UST), once one of the most widely used algorithmic stablecoins, attempted to maintain a one-dollar peg using a dual-token mechanism with its sister token, LUNA. The dramatic collapse of the Terra ecosystem in 2022 revealed the systemic fragility of non-collateralized models during extreme market stress. While algorithmic stablecoins offer high scalability and a vision of full decentralization, they remain experimental and carry significant risk.

Stablecoins have become essential tools in crypto trading. Traders frequently move into stablecoins during downturns to hedge against losses, then reenter the market when conditions improve, all without the friction of converting back to fiat. In cross-border payments and remittances, stablecoins offer an efficient alternative to legacy payment systems, with near-instant settlement and minimal fees. In the DeFi sector, stablecoins play a central role in virtually every major protocol. They act as collateral in lending platforms like Aave and Compound, underpin liquidity pools in decentralized exchanges, and are used for interest payments, yield strategies, and DAO treasuries. Merchants, freelancers, and even institutional players are adopting stablecoins for payments due to their speed, cost-efficiency, and blockchain-native interoperability.

However, the rapid rise of stablecoins has also attracted significant regulatory attention. Policymakers are increasingly concerned with reserve transparency, systemic risk, and the impact of privately issued dollar-pegged tokens on national monetary policy. Questions have been raised about whether issuers like Tether maintain adequate fiat reserves, prompting demands for third-party audits and clearer disclosure. In the U.S., proposals have emerged to treat stablecoin issuers like banks, subjecting them to prudential oversight and requiring them to hold insured reserves. The European Union, through its Markets in Crypto-Assets (MiCA) regulation, is also moving toward formal supervision of stablecoin operations. At the same time, global institutions such as the Financial Stability Board are calling for coordinated international frameworks to manage stablecoin risks. Many governments are also responding by accelerating research and pilots of **Central Bank Digital Currencies (CBDCs)**, which could coexist with or compete against stablecoins in future financial systems. Institutional-grade stablecoins, tokenized bank deposits, and interoperable Layer 2-native stable assets are expanding the landscape. As the world increasingly embraces digital value, stablecoins are poised to remain at the core of both open blockchain systems and regulated digital economies, acting not just as a bridge–but as a stable foundation.

7.15 RWAs

Real-World Assets, or RWAs, refer to tangible or off-chain assets–such as real estate, commodities, equities, invoices, bonds, and even intellectual property rights–that are brought onto the blockchain through a process known as tokenization. The idea is simple yet transformative: take assets from the traditional economy that are illiquid, fragmented, or slow-moving, and repackage them into programmable, transferable tokens that can interact with the fast, borderless infrastructure of decentralized finance. In practice, RWAs are bridging the two worlds–on one side, the physical and regulated; on the other, the digital and decentralized–opening up vast pools of capital and radically rethinking what liquidity and ownership can mean.

The concept of tokenizing real-world assets is not new in theory, but it's only in recent years–thanks to the maturity of smart contracts, improvements in regulatory clarity, and the growth of DeFi–that RWAs have begun to be adopted at scale. When a real-world asset is tokenized, it is represented on-chain by a digital token that acts as a proxy for the underlying asset. These tokens can then be traded, collateralized, or used within smart contracts just like any native crypto asset. A tokenized real estate property, for example, might represent a share in the ownership of a building or a future stream of rental income. A tokenized bond might represent a slice of an off-chain debt instrument, yielding interest over time. What makes this powerful is not just the digitization of ownership, but the interoperability of these tokens within DeFi protocols, where they can be pooled, lent, borrowed, or sold with near-instant finality.

In the current landscape, RWAs are rapidly gaining traction across multiple verticals. Tokenized U.S. Treasury bills are emerging as one of the most compelling use cases, allowing stablecoin treasuries, DeFi protocols, and digital asset investors to park funds in low-risk, yield-generating assets without leaving the blockchain environment. Platforms like Ondo Finance, Maple, and Backed are leading the charge by issuing tokenized fixed-income products that offer real-world returns while remaining composable within the crypto ecosystem. Meanwhile, tokenized real estate is being piloted in jurisdictions like the UAE, Singapore, and parts of Europe, where legal frameworks allow fractional ownership of property to be registered and enforced. Other applications range from supply chain finance, where invoices or shipping documents are tokenized for early settlement, to carbon credits and royalties, which are transformed into liquid, traceable assets on-chain.

The appeal of RWAs lies in their ability to inject stability and yield into an otherwise volatile ecosystem. In contrast to highly speculative crypto assets, RWAs are rooted in external, verifiable cash flows–rents, dividends, interest payments, or invoices. This makes them attractive not only to risk-averse investors seeking passive income but also to DeFi protocols looking to diversify their collateral base and stabilize returns. In the post-2022 bear market, RWAs have been embraced as a more sustainable foundation for DeFi 2.0, allowing protocols to anchor their growth to tangible, regulated asset flows rather than unsustainable token emissions or yield farming incentives.

However, tokenizing RWAs comes with its own set of complexities. Unlike native crypto assets, RWAs are constrained by legal, operational, and jurisdictional boundaries. The link between the on-chain token and the off-chain asset must be enforceable, which requires robust legal frameworks, trusted custodians, and clear rights for token holders. Questions of who holds the title, how income is distributed, and what happens in the event of default or litigation must be answered upfront. This introduces an element of centralization into the process, often involving regulated entities such as asset managers, trustees, or licensed issuers. Despite this, the tradeoff is often considered worthwhile for the liquidity and transparency gains made possible by tokenization.

The infrastructure supporting RWAs is also evolving. New protocols and platforms are emerging to onboard and manage real-world assets in a compliant, scalable way. Tokenization layers are being built on top of Ethereum and other chains, leveraging standards such as ERC-3643 for permissioned assets or ERC-4626 for yield-bearing vaults. Oracles and attestation networks are being deployed to provide real-time verification of asset performance, prices, and ownership. Meanwhile, identity layers and KYC protocols are being integrated to ensure that only qualified investors can access certain regulated offerings, bringing crypto one step closer to institutional acceptance.

At a policy level, regulators are watching closely. RWAs operate at the intersection of digital innovation and real-world legal systems, raising questions around investor protection, AML compliance, and cross-border asset control. While jurisdictions like Switzerland, Dubai, and Singapore have embraced tokenized securities with structured regulatory sandboxes or virtual asset regimes, others remain cautious. Nonetheless, many financial institutions are beginning to experiment with blockchain-based tokenization for everything from bond issuance to fund distribution, signaling a gradual convergence between the old guard of finance and the emerging world of digital assets.

RWAs represent one of the most promising frontiers in blockchain adoption. Their integration into decentralized finance not only brings new sources of liquidity and yield, but it also expands the real-world relevance of crypto–from speculation and volatility to infrastructure and utility. The success of RWA adoption will depend on the ability of developers, regulators, and institutions to align on frameworks that preserve both legal enforceability and technical flexibility. If done correctly, tokenized real-world assets could unlock trillions of dollars in idle value and turn the blockchain into a global platform for real, productive finance–composable, programmable, and radically more accessible.

7.16 CBDC

Crypto Dollar, Crypto Euro, and a wide range of other fiat currencies are being explored as they move toward entry into the crypto space, backed and driven by governments and central banks. The concept of central bank digital currencies, or CBDCs, has emerged as one of the most consequential developments in the intersection of money, technology, and governance. At its core, a CBDC is a digital representation of a nation's sovereign currency, issued and backed directly by the central bank. Unlike cryptocurrencies such as Bitcoin or Ethereum, which are decentralized and rely on open networks of participants to validate transactions, CBDCs are centralized instruments anchored in the authority of a state. They are not merely digital versions of existing banknotes but rather new forms of money with distinct characteristics, technical architectures, and policy implications.

The mechanics of a CBDC revolve around the idea of digital issuance that carries the same legal status as cash. Central banks envision two principal models. In the retail model, the digital currency is made available directly to the public, much like physical notes and coins, but accessible through digital wallets rather than cash registers. In the wholesale model, CBDCs circulate only within the banking system and among financial institutions, serving as a settlement layer for interbank transfers, cross-border payments, and large-scale financial operations. Both designs require careful consideration of scalability, resilience, and security, since unlike cryptocurrencies, a CBDC must support national or even global transaction volumes under regulatory oversight.

The technology that underpins CBDCs varies significantly depending on the central bank's vision. Some proposals lean on distributed ledger technology, borrowing elements from blockchain to provide transparency, auditability, and programmable settlement. Others prefer centralized databases with high throughput, prioritizing efficiency over decentralization. What unites these approaches is the imperative of trust: citizens must be confident that the digital token they hold is equivalent in value and acceptance to the paper currency it represents. This means that cybersecurity, identity management, and system redundancy are not peripheral concerns but the very foundation upon which the success of CBDCs depends.

The advantages of CBDCs are often articulated in terms of modernization and inclusion. A retail CBDC could extend financial services to populations excluded from traditional banking, particularly in regions where mobile penetration exceeds access to physical banks. It could reduce the reliance on costly and slow payment systems, fostering instant settlement at lower costs. In times of crisis, such as pandemics or natural disasters, CBDCs could enable direct stimulus transfers from governments to citizens, bypassing intermediaries and ensuring rapid distribution of aid. For wholesale applications, CBDCs promise to improve the efficiency of clearing and settlement across borders, an area long plagued by friction, delay, and systemic risk.

Yet, the drawbacks and challenges are just as pronounced. A central bank that issues digital money wields extraordinary visibility into the financial activities of its citizens, raising profound questions of privacy, surveillance, and the balance of power between state and individual. The very design choices of a CBDC–whether transactions are anonymized, pseudonymous, or fully transparent–determine the extent of control and monitoring possible. In addition, if individuals can hold central bank money directly, bypassing commercial banks, the traditional banking sector could face disintermediation. During times of financial stress, depositors might flee to CBDCs en masse, accelerating bank runs and destabilizing the economy. Central banks must therefore design mechanisms, such as limits on holdings or tiered remuneration structures, to prevent unintended consequences.

Internationally, CBDCs carry geopolitical weight. A digital dollar or digital euro could entrench existing monetary influence, while new entrants, such as China's e-CNY, may reshape global payment networks by offering alternatives to SWIFT or dollar dominance. For emerging economies, the promise of CBDCs lies not only in domestic modernization but also in the opportunity to leapfrog existing infrastructure and establish stronger positions in global commerce. However, the fragmentation of CBDC systems across jurisdictions could create new silos unless there is international coordination on standards and interoperability. Without such efforts, cross-border CBDC transactions could reproduce the very inefficiencies they are meant to resolve.

Ultimately, CBDCs represent a convergence of monetary policy, technical innovation, and societal values. They are not merely tools of efficiency but instruments that redefine the relationship between citizens, banks, and the state. Their deployment requires delicate calibration: too much control risks eroding trust and stifling adoption, while too little oversight jeopardizes financial stability and security. The global experimentation currently underway, from pilot projects in China to research in the European Union and trials in the Caribbean, illustrates both the urgency and the uncertainty of the endeavor. Each nation is compelled to reconcile its own priorities–be they financial inclusion, sovereignty, or technological competitiveness–with the universal demands of security and trust.

The debate over CBDCs is, at its heart, a debate over the future of money itself. As societies weigh the benefits of efficiency, inclusion, and innovation against the risks of surveillance, disintermediation, and systemic disruption, the outcome will not only determine how we pay and transact but also how deeply technology and state power become intertwined in the fabric of economic life. CBDCs are no longer speculative concepts; they are imminent realities whose design choices will shape financial systems for generations.

8. Bitcoin

"I've been waiting a long time to ask you this," I began. "When you published that whitepaper in 2008–'Bitcoin: A Peer-to-Peer Electronic Cash System'–did you realize you were about to change everything?"

Satoshi, his fingers rolling and a small smile playing at the corners of his mouth "I knew the mathematics were sound, and I believed the concept was revolutionary. But 'change everything'?" They paused, considering. "I was solving a very specific problem: how to create a decentralized currency free from intermediaries like banks. The traditional system required trust in central authorities, and I wanted to eliminate that requirement entirely."

"Bitcoin is the crypto equivalent of gold. It's about scarcity and durability," Satoshi explained, the voice taking on the tone of a professor. "Gold has been valuable for millennia because it's rare and doesn't degrade. Bitcoin has a hard cap of 21 million coins, no more will ever exist. Unlike fiat currencies that central banks can print endlessly, Bitcoin's scarcity is mathematically guaranteed. And remember, Bitcoin wasn't designed to replace Visa, it was designed to be a secure, decentralized store of value. Other platforms like Ethereum focus on smart contracts and complex programmable applications. Bitcoin focuses on being the most secure and decentralized cryptocurrency possible."

"And development continues through Bitcoin Core?"

"Exactly. The beauty of open-source development is that it's not dependent on any single person, not even me. Changes are proposed, tested extensively, and must achieve community consensus before implementation. It's slower than centralized development, but it's more robust. The network's survival doesn't depend on any individual or organization."

I studied Satoshi's face, looking for any hint of personal revelation. "Do you ever regret creating Bitcoin? The speculation, the criminal use cases, the environmental concerns?"

Satoshi considered this seriously. "Every powerful technology can be misused. The internet enabled cybercrime, but it also democratized information. Bitcoin may facilitate some illegal activities, but it also provides financial freedom to people in oppressive regimes, enables seamless global transfers, and offers an alternative to failing monetary systems. The benefits far outweigh the drawbacks."

"What do you see as Bitcoin's future?" I asked, sensing our time was drawing to a close.

"Bitcoin will continue evolving as it always has, slowly, carefully, with community consensus. It's already proven itself as a store of value, surviving market crashes, regulatory pressure, and technological challenges. Each test makes it stronger. Whether it becomes the global reserve currency or remains a specialized asset for those who value decentralization and scarcity, it's already succeeded in proving that an alternative to traditional finance is possible."

8.1 Bitcoin Layer 1, 2 and 3

Our conversation began with what seemed like a simple question, but I already suspected there were no simple questions when it came to his beloved son, Bitcoin.

"I've been reading about Bitcoin's evolution," I began, "and I keep encountering terms like Layer 1, Layer 2, Layer 3. It seems the system has grown far beyond what anyone initially imagined. Can you help me understand what this layered approach really means?"

Satoshi simply smiled, answering swiftly "The beauty of any robust system is that it grows organically, responding to needs while maintaining its core principles. When I designed Bitcoin, I knew the base layer would need to be rock-solid, but I also understood that innovation would happen around it."

"So Layer 1 is what you originally created?"

"Precisely. Layer 1 is the foundation, the bedrock upon which everything else is built. It's the base protocol where the most fundamental functions occur. This is where the consensus mechanism lives, the process that decides the fate of every transaction." He then paused, seeming to choose his words carefully. "For Bitcoin, this mechanism is Proof of Work. Every transaction is scrutinized, verified, and then, through decentralized consensus, added to the ledger permanently. Layer 1 must be secure and decentralized. The security comes from the decentralized nature of the blockchain and the cryptography that holds it together."

"And each blockchain has its own native currency powering the system?"
"Exactly. For Bitcoin, it's BTC, what some call digital gold that moves across the network.
Satoshi's expression grew more serious, "this layer, Layer 1, while powerful, has its constraints. Scalability is a constant challenge. As the network grows, so does the strain, leading to slower transaction times and higher fees, especially during periods of heavy usage."
The conversation was flowing naturally, and I found myself genuinely curious about the solutions. "That's where Layer 2 comes in, isn't it?"
"Layer 2 rises to meet these challenges," Satoshi confirmed. "It's a bridge between efficiency and the unyielding security of Layer 1. These solutions don't replace the base blockchain but rather build atop it, enhancing scalability and reducing costs while still depending on the security of the underlying system."
"How does that actually work?"
"Think of it like relieving traffic from a crowded highway by opening parallel routes, only bringing the cars back when necessary. With off-chain transactions, Layer 2 takes much of the workload off the primary blockchain's shoulders, processing transactions elsewhere before settling them in batches on the main chain." Satoshi's eyes seemed to light up with the elegance of the solution. "Smart contract interactions flourish here. Complex operations that would bog down the base layer can now unfold on Layer 2, freeing

Layer 1 from the burden and allowing more to happen faster."

"But doesn't processing transactions off-chain compromise security?"

"That's the beautiful part, they don't lose the security that blockchain promises. They're still tethered to Layer 1, where the final reckoning occurs." Satoshi leaned forward, clearly passionate about this aspect. "Take the **Lightning Network** for Bitcoin. Users can create payment channels off-chain, where transactions are instant and nearly free. Only when these channels close do they settle on the Bitcoin blockchain, reducing congestion."

I was beginning to see the interconnectedness. "And there are different types of Layer 2 solutions?"

"Many creative approaches have emerged. The beauty of open-source development is how it attracts brilliant minds from everywhere. For **Bitcoin Core**, you have maintainers supported by organizations like **Brink**, **Chaincode Labs**, **Blockstream**, and **Spiral–Block's**. Bitcoin Improvement Proposals, or **BIPs**, drive consensus upgrades like **SegWit** and **Taproot**."

"And for Layer 2?"

"**Lightning Network** alone has multiple implementations. **Lightning Labs** maintains LND, ACINQ develops the **Eclair client and Phoenix wallet**, **Blockstream** works on their Lightning Development Kit. The wallet ecosystem has flourished, **Phoenix**, **Breez**, **Muun**, **Strike**, **Wallet of Satoshi,** each making Lightning more accessible."

The scope was becoming clearer, but I sensed there was more. "You mentioned Layer 3 earlier. What happens there?"

"Layer 3 is where the magic becomes accessible," Satoshi said, a note of satisfaction in their voice. "This is the layer closest to the end-user, the bridge that connects complex blockchain systems to the practical world. Here is where decentralized applications come to life, built atop platforms like Ethereum, Solana, and Binance Smart Chain. These apps range from DeFi platforms to NFTs and gaming ecosystems."

"So it's about user experience?"

"Exactly. Layer 3 focuses on improving user experience, making blockchain applications more accessible through wallets, APIs, and development frameworks. Think of **MetaMask,** a simple yet powerful tool that allows users to interact with dApps across different blockchains. It's here where developers can create and users can participate without needing to understand the deep complexities of the underlying technology."

I paused, processing this layered complexity. "But Bitcoin has evolved beyond just payments, hasn't it? I keep reading about sidechains and new protocols."

"The innovation never stops," Satoshi acknowledged. "Sidechains like **Liquid Network** provide federated solutions for faster settlement and asset issuance. **RSK** brings smart contracts to Bitcoin through EVM compatibility. **Stacks** secures smart contracts through Bitcoin using their **Proof of Transfer mechanism**."

"And then there are these new developments, **Ordinals, Inscriptions**?"

Satoshi's expression became particularly interesting at this question. "**Casey Rodarmor's** Ordinals protocol assigns 'serial numbers' to individual satoshis, enabling NFT-like functionality on Bitcoin. Inscriptions embed images, text, or code directly on-chain. It's... an interesting interpretation of what Bitcoin can be."

"You sound somewhat ambivalent about that."

"Innovation often takes unexpected paths. **BRC-20** tokens emerged as experimental fungible tokens using Ordinals. Then Casey introduced **Runes** in 2024, a more efficient standard for fungible tokens. **Taproot Assets** from Lightning Labs enables stablecoins and assets anchored in Taproot transactions. Each development pushes the boundaries of what Bitcoin can do."

The conversation had grown quite technical, but I was following the thread. "This has created an entire DeFi ecosystem on Bitcoin?"

"**RSK** brought us projects like **Sovryn** for DeFi and **Money on Chain** for BTC-backed stablecoins. The **Stacks** ecosystem includes **Alex**, **Arkadiko**, **Zest Protocol**. Even Liquid hosts tokenized securities and stablecoins, USDT runs on Liquid. The 2024-2025 wave of **Taproot Assets** and **Runes** is fueling BTC-based stablecoins, tokenized treasuries, and real-world assets."

"But how does this connect to other blockchains?"

"Bridges and cross-chain infrastructure have become crucial," Satoshi explained. "**Wrapped Bitcoin** tokenizes BTC on Ethereum, though it's custodial through **BitGo**. The **Threshold Network's tBTC** offers a more decentralized bridge. **Lightning** enables atomic swaps between chains. The goal is interoperability, allowing users to move assets and data across previously isolated systems."

I was struck by how far the ecosystem had evolved. "And the mining infrastructure?"

"Mining has become an industry unto itself. Major pools like **Foundry USA**, **AntPool**, **F2Pool** coordinate transaction processing. ASIC manufacturers like **Bitmain**, **MicroBT**, and **Canaan** provide the hardware. Custody solutions from companies like **River**, **Unchained**, and institutional players like **Coinbase Custody** secure large holdings."

"The institutional adoption seems significant now."

"Indeed. **Fidelity Digital Assets**, BlackRock, **MicroStrategy**, **ARK Invest** represent massive institutional interest. The approval of Bitcoin Spot ETFs in 2024 drove enormous inflows. Payment integrations through **Strike**, **Cash App,** and **BitPay** make Bitcoin increasingly practical for commerce."

As our conversation continued, I sensed we were approaching something deeper. "There's also ongoing research into privacy and advanced cryptography?"

Satoshi's demeanor became more reserved, almost protective. "Taproot, activated in 2021, enabled **Schnorr signatures** and **MAST—Merkelized Abstract Syntax Trees. MuSig2** allows multi-signature aggregation. There are proposals for cross-input signature aggregation. The **Ark Protocol** offers privacy-oriented off-chain payments. **FediMint** provides federated **Chaumian** e-cash on Bitcoin."

"Privacy seems important."

"Privacy and security are fundamental rights in any monetary system," they replied carefully. "The technology should preserve both the transparency needed for trust and the privacy required for human dignity."

As our dialogue drew toward a close, I reflected on the journey we'd traced, from the solid foundation of Layer 1, through the scaling innovations of Layer 2, to the user-facing applications of Layer 3, and into the sprawling ecosystem of participants building the future of digital money.

"This layering of technology," I said, "from the base security and functionality of Layer 1, to the scaling and efficiency of Layer 2, and the accessibility and user-friendliness of Layer 3, it creates something quite elegant."

Satoshi nodded slowly. "It's the roadmap to a future where blockchain isn't just the foundation of digital currencies but an integral part of daily life. The system grows organically, layer upon layer, innovation upon innovation, but always anchored to those fundamental principles of decentralization, security, and trustlessness."

"Do you ever wonder where it will lead?"

For the first time in our conversation, Satoshi paused for a long moment, looking out the window at the world beyond.

"I designed a system to work without trust in any central authority. What it becomes... that's up to everyone who chooses to build on it, use it, and improve it. That's how it should be."

The conversation felt complete, though I sensed there were layers upon layers of complexity we hadn't even touched. As we prepared to part ways, I realized that understanding Bitcoin wasn't just about grasping the technology, it was about appreciating how a simple idea, executed with precision and opened to the world, could evolve into something far grander than any single mind could have envisioned.

"Thank you," I said simply.

"Thank you for caring enough to understand," came the reply. "That's how good ideas survive and thrive, through people who take the time to truly comprehend them."

8.2 Lightning Network

The Lightning Network is a Layer 2 solution built on top of the Bitcoin blockchain, designed to address Bitcoin's scalability issues by enabling faster and cheaper transactions without compromising the security of the underlying network. It allows users to conduct transactions off-chain, reducing congestion on the main blockchain and making Bitcoin more efficient for everyday use. Bitcoin, while prioritizing decentralization and security, struggles with scalability. Each block is mined every 10 minutes and limited to 1 MB in size, allowing about 7 transactions per second (TPS). This limitation leads to delays and rising fees during periods of high demand, as users compete to have their transactions processed faster by offering higher fees. To solve these issues, the Lightning Network was proposed in 2015 by **Joseph Poon** and **Thaddeus Dryja**. It enables near-instant, low-cost transactions by allowing users to create payment channels between two parties. A channel is established when two users lock Bitcoin in a multi-signature wallet, enabling them to transact off-chain. Transactions are recorded between the parties without the need to broadcast them on the blockchain, with only the final balance being settled on-chain when the channel is closed. This system alleviates pressure on the main Bitcoin network while maintaining security and efficiency.

The Lightning Network also supports a network of payment channels, where transactions can be routed through multiple nodes. For example, if Alice has a channel with Bob, and Bob has one with Carol, Alice can send a payment to Carol through Bob without needing a direct channel. The network automatically finds the shortest path, ensuring fast, efficient payments. One of the key benefits of the Lightning Network is its ability to process transactions at lightning speed, free from the delays of Bitcoin's base layer.

Fees are significantly lower, making it ideal for micropayments, small transactions like tips, digital downloads, or in-game purchases, that would otherwise be impractical due to high fees. By moving transactions off-chain, the Lightning Network enhances Bitcoin's scalability, theoretically allowing it to handle an infinite number of transactions per second. Additionally, the Lightning Network offers increased privacy. Since most transactions occur off-chain, only the final settlement is recorded on the Bitcoin blockchain, providing users with greater confidentiality. This is especially valuable in a world where privacy is becoming scarce. However, the Lightning Network has its challenges. Liquidity issues can arise if there isn't enough Bitcoin locked in the channels to facilitate transactions, and users must carefully manage their channels to maintain liquidity.

Opening and closing channels still require on-chain transactions, bringing associated fees and delays. Additionally, the complexity of managing payment channels and understanding the system can be daunting for average users, though wallets and services are improving to make the process more user-friendly. Security is also a consideration. Proper management of channels is crucial to maintaining security. As of 2024, the Lightning Network has seen growing adoption, with wallets like **Strike**, **BlueWallet**, and **Wallet of Satoshi** offering Lightning integration. Major companies, including **X.com**, have implemented Lightning payments, allowing users to tip and pay easily via Bitcoin. The network remains decentralized, and anyone can run a Lightning node, contributing to its growth and liquidity. Looking forward, the Lightning Network is expected to play a critical role in Bitcoin's evolution, making it more practical for everyday transactions. Increased merchant adoption and improved user interfaces will help the network mature, while efforts to integrate Lightning with other cryptocurrencies could pave the way for seamless cross-chain transactions. The promise of fast, low-cost, and scalable payments is no longer a distant vision but an emerging reality in the world of Bitcoin.

8.3 Liquid Network

The Liquid Network is a Layer 2 sidechain solution for Bitcoin, designed to enhance Bitcoin's functionality by enabling faster transactions, greater privacy, and the issuance of digital assets. Developed by **Blockstream** and launched in 2018, Liquid primarily serves financial institutions, exchanges, and traders who require faster, more confidential transactions than Bitcoin's main chain allows. By settling large volumes of Bitcoin transactions off-chain, Liquid alleviates congestion on the Bitcoin blockchain, offering a solution tailored to institutional needs.

A sidechain is a separate blockchain that operates in tandem with the main chain, allowing assets to be transferred between the two via a process called pegging.

In the Liquid Network, Bitcoin is "pegged" and becomes **L-BTC (Liquid Bitcoin)**, a 1:1 representation of Bitcoin. L-BTC can be used within the Liquid Network for faster, more private transactions and can be redeemed for Bitcoin on the main chain whenever needed. One of Liquid's standout features is its speed. While Bitcoin's block time is 10 minutes, Liquid reduces it to one minute, making it ideal for traders and exchanges that need fast settlement times. Additionally, the network offers enhanced privacy through **Confidential Transactions (CT)**, which hide transaction details like amounts and asset types, maintaining security without sacrificing confidentiality.

Another key feature is Liquid's ability to issue digital assets, such as stablecoins, tokenized fiat, security tokens, and commodities like gold. This capability is valuable for institutions looking to tokenize assets while leveraging Bitcoin's security. Liquid operates under a federation-based consensus model, where trusted entities called **Functionaries**, primarily exchanges, validate blocks and ensure network security. This differs from Bitcoin's decentralized proof-of-work system, offering faster finality for transactions while still maintaining security. The two-way peg between Bitcoin and Liquid allows seamless movement of assets between the chains. When users peg Bitcoin into Liquid, it is locked by the federation, and **L-BTC** is issued. When they want to return to Bitcoin, the L-BTC is sent back, and the original Bitcoin is unlocked. This process enables users to benefit from faster, more private transactions without leaving the Bitcoin ecosystem. Liquid's federation-based block signing ensures that transactions are confirmed within two minutes, offering rapid finality. This is especially useful for traders who need quick settlement times to take advantage of market opportunities. Once a block is confirmed on Liquid, it is final, reducing the risk of chain reorganizations or double spending. The Liquid Network also caters to institutional traders, providing confidentiality for large transactions, which can be vulnerable to scrutiny on Bitcoin's transparent blockchain. Liquid's cryptographic privacy ensures that competitors and market watchers cannot monitor the flow of assets, offering a secure environment for sensitive financial movements. Liquid's utility extends beyond Bitcoin, with its ability to issue and manage digital assets. For example, stablecoins like **Tether (USDT)** exist on the Liquid Network, offering faster and more private transactions compared to Bitcoin's main chain (Tether was originally launched on the Bitcoin blockchain in 2014 using the **Omni Layer** protocol, but now is rarely used). Additionally, Liquid facilitates cross-border payments and remittances with its fast confirmation times and low fees, making international transfers more efficient. For exchanges, Liquid is a crucial tool for speeding up fund transfers between platforms. Exchanges like **Bitfinex** use Liquid to reduce congestion and streamline transactions, enhancing overall market efficiency. Its ability to tokenize real-world assets through **Liquid Securities** allows businesses to digitize assets like real estate and stocks, bringing traditional finance into the blockchain space.

8.4 RSK (Rootstock)

RSK (Rootstock) is a smart contract platform functioning as a Bitcoin sidechain, enabling Ethereum-like smart contracts, decentralized applications (dApps), and tokenized assets on the Bitcoin blockchain. Its core objective is to expand Bitcoin's capabilities beyond a store of value, allowing it to become a fully programmable system while leveraging Bitcoin's robust security model. RSK integrates with Bitcoin through a two-way peg system, enabling the transfer of Bitcoin to the RSK sidechain as **Smart Bitcoin (RBTC)**, which powers smart contracts and dApps. RSK bridges Bitcoin's unmatched security with Ethereum's flexibility, creating a platform that offers the best of both worlds.

While Bitcoin excels at security and decentralization through Proof of Work mining, it lacks the ability to support more advanced functions like smart contracts and decentralized finance (DeFi). Ethereum, on the other hand, thrives in programmability but lacks Bitcoin's security strength. RSK's solution was to merge Bitcoin's security with Ethereum's programmability, enabling decentralized applications and financial services on Bitcoin. One of RSK's key features is its two-way peg system, where users lock their Bitcoin to create an equivalent amount of **RBTC on RSK**. RBTC is used to pay for gas fees and execute smart contracts, and can be converted back to Bitcoin at any time through the peg system. RSK also uses **Merge Mining**, allowing Bitcoin miners to secure both Bitcoin and RSK simultaneously, ensuring the network benefits from Bitcoin's vast security without additional costs. RSK's native token, **RBTC**, is pegged 1:1 with Bitcoin, allowing users to interact with smart contracts, pay transaction fees, and engage with DeFi on Bitcoin. It opens a new frontier for Bitcoin-based DeFi applications, such as decentralized exchanges and lending platforms, making Bitcoin's ecosystem more versatile. Moreover, RSK provides interoperability with Ethereum, allowing developers to port their Ethereum dApps with minimal changes, leveraging Bitcoin's security while maintaining Ethereum's smart contract functionality. RSK's lower fees make it an attractive platform for decentralized applications, especially as Ethereum faces scalability challenges. Its merge-mining mechanism enhances security by leveraging Bitcoin's proof-of-work mining, while the federation of trusted nodes safeguards the two-way peg system, ensuring secure asset exchanges between Bitcoin and RBTC. Through token bridges, RSK allows assets to move seamlessly between different blockchains, creating a vibrant, cross-chain ecosystem. Projects like **Sovryn** and **Money on Chain** exemplify RSK's potential by enabling Bitcoin-backed DeFi applications, including stablecoins and decentralized lending. RSK's infrastructure is further strengthened by the **RSK Infrastructure Framework**

(RIF), a suite of decentralized protocols designed to enhance scalability and offer solutions for identity, storage, and payments.

8.5 Stacks (Formerly Blockstack)

Stacks is a Layer 1 blockchain that enables smart contracts and decentralized applications (dApps) on Bitcoin. Originally known as Blockstack, it rebranded to Stacks in 2020, aligning with the launch of its Stacks 2.0 blockchain. Unlike Ethereum, Stacks enhances Bitcoin's functionality by using Bitcoin as its base layer for security, allowing for decentralized applications and smart contracts. This is achieved through **Proof of Transfer (PoX)**, which anchors the Stacks blockchain to Bitcoin, making dApps on Stacks more secure, scalable, and efficient. Blockstack's original vision was to create a decentralized network where users, not corporations, controlled their data and identity.

PoX allows Bitcoin to serve as the foundation for Stacks, where miners commit Bitcoin to mint new STX tokens. Bitcoin holders can participate in "stacking" by locking up their Bitcoin to earn STX rewards. Stacks' technology combines innovation with Bitcoin's security. It uses **Clarity**, a custom smart contract language that is interpreted, ensuring greater precision and reducing vulnerabilities compared to compiled languages like Ethereum's Solidity. Clarity contracts are executed on the Stacks blockchain but settle on Bitcoin, leveraging the world's most secure blockchain. The rebranding from Blockstack to Stacks signaled a shift in focus: from decentralized identity management to enabling smart contracts on Bitcoin. With this new direction, Stacks empowers developers to create dApps backed by Bitcoin's security, offering a programmable platform without requiring additional resources for network security. Another standout feature is NFTs on Stacks, which are anchored to Bitcoin's immutable blockchain. This gives digital assets, such as art and collectibles, an added layer of security and permanence compared to those on Ethereum. However, Stacks faces challenges.

8.6 Statechains

Statechains are a Layer 2 solution for Bitcoin that enables off-chain transfers of ownership without requiring participants to be online simultaneously or relying on a centralized entity. Introduced by **Ruben Somsen** in 2018, Statechains allow Bitcoin ownership transfers without moving coins on-chain, enhancing scalability, privacy, and reducing fees. Statechains achieve this by using multi-signature wallets, time-locked contracts, and blind signatures, which allow users to transfer control of private keys securely. The core idea is to make Bitcoin transfers more efficient and private by handling them off-chain. Instead of broadcasting every transaction to the Bitcoin network, Statechains facilitate the transfer of ownership by passing private keys to the new owner, keeping the Bitcoin in the same wallet. This off-chain process avoids transaction fees and blockchain congestion, enhancing scalability without compromising security. The system relies on multi-signature wallets where both the user and a Statechain entity hold keys, ensuring neither can move the Bitcoin independently. When ownership changes, the private key is handed off to the new owner, who collaborates with the Statechain entity to spend the Bitcoin, providing a secure and auditable way to transfer assets.

To ensure security, time-locked refunds allow users to reclaim their funds if the transfer process is interrupted. Blind signatures further enhance privacy by preventing the Statechain entity from knowing the details of transactions. When a transaction needs to be settled on-chain, collaborative spending occurs between the new owner and the Statechain entity, preserving privacy and security. **Watchtowers**, third-party auditors, monitor the network to prevent malicious behavior and double-spending. This system balances scalability, privacy, and security, allowing efficient Bitcoin transfers off-chain without network congestion. Statechains offer several advantages over other Layer 2 solutions, such as the Lightning Network and sidechains. Unlike the Lightning Network, Statechains don't require both parties to be online, and they are better suited for larger, less frequent transactions. Compared to sidechains, which rely on federated validators, Statechains use a simpler system with one trusted entity and robust safeguards like multisig wallets and time-locks. Despite their benefits, Statechains face challenges.

Mercury Wallet, one of the first applications of Statechains, demonstrates the potential of this technology by enabling seamless off-chain Bitcoin transfers, offering a glimpse into a more scalable, private, and efficient future for Bitcoin.

8.7 OmniLayer

OmniLayer, formerly **Mastercoin**, is a Layer 2 protocol built on Bitcoin, enabling the creation, issuance, and transfer of digital assets like tokens and smart contracts, while leveraging Bitcoin's security. Often described as a "**meta-layer**" or "**colored coin**" system, OmniLayer facilitates tokenization and smart contracts using Bitcoin's infrastructure. One of its most notable achievements is hosting **Tether (USDT)**, one of the first and most popular stablecoins, solidifying its role in the cryptocurrency space. Conceived by **J.R. Willett** in 2013, OmniLayer expanded Bitcoin's functionality to include custom tokens and smart contracts. Willett's vision was outlined in a whitepaper titled "The Second Bitcoin Whitepaper," and the platform, rebranded as OmniLayer in 2015, shifted its focus toward token issuance, decentralized exchanges, and basic smart contracts anchored to Bitcoin. This rebranding marked the beginning of OmniLayer's role in the growing digital finance ecosystem, with Tether as its most prominent use case. Operating as a meta-protocol, OmniLayer embeds additional data into Bitcoin transactions via the **OP_RETURN** field.

This method allows for token creation, transfer, and contract execution without altering Bitcoin's core functionality. Bitcoin continues to manage transaction data, while OmniLayer introduces new layers of functionality for digital assets, such as tokens and smart contracts. OmniLayer's tokens can represent digital currencies like Tether, assets, or commodities. While its smart contracts are more limited than Ethereum's, they enabled decentralized trading, token issuance, and even crowdfunding on Bitcoin. OmniLayer played a pioneering role in the initial coin offering (ICO) model, allowing projects to issue tokens in exchange for Bitcoin or other cryptocurrencies, directly on Bitcoin's blockchain. OmniLayer's security is rooted in Bitcoin's Proof of Work (PoW) mechanism, ensuring that every transaction inherits Bitcoin's immutability and resistance to attacks, with all activity permanently recorded on Bitcoin's blockchain. Bitcoin's scalability issues, such as high fees and slower transaction times during network congestion, affect OmniLayer's performance, making it less ideal for smaller, frequent transactions. Furthermore, competition from platforms like Ethereum, Binance Smart Chain, and even Bitcoin-based solutions like Liquid and RSK, offers more advanced features like confidential transactions and faster settlement times.

8.8 Drivechain

Drivechain is a concept in the Bitcoin ecosystem that enables integration of sidechains while maintaining Bitcoin's security. Sidechains, operating independently with their own rules and tokens, are connected to Bitcoin, allowing seamless value transfers between them. This is achieved through merged mining, where miners secure both Bitcoin and sidechains using the same computational resources, without extra hardware or effort. By leveraging Bitcoin's mining power, sidechains benefit from the same security as the main Bitcoin network. The core of Drivechain's proposal involves a soft fork to Bitcoin, introducing a two-way peg between Bitcoin and sidechains. Miners enforce this peg by mining both Bitcoin and sidechain blocks, ensuring locked BTC on the mainchain can be redeemed and moved back from the sidechain. Blind merged mining, a key feature, simplifies this process by allowing miners to mine sidechains without running a full sidechain node, reducing the technical complexity for participation. Drivechain offers several benefits.

First, it enhances scalability by offloading activities to sidechains, reducing the transaction load on Bitcoin's main chain. It also promotes experimentation, allowing developers to test new features, consensus algorithms, and smart contract capabilities on sidechains without risking Bitcoin's core security. Importantly, all these innovations remain within the Bitcoin ecosystem, avoiding the need for new tokens or separate blockchains. For miners,

Drivechain provides additional revenue by enabling them to mine both Bitcoin and sidechains, making the process more profitable without the need for extra hardware. The mechanics are straightforward: users lock BTC on the Bitcoin network, which is then represented on the sidechain. When users wish to return to Bitcoin, they burn the sidechain tokens, and miners unlock the corresponding BTC on the mainchain after a time delay, ensuring secure and seamless transfers. Despite its potential, Drivechain faces criticisms and challenges.

The use cases for Drivechain are compelling. It could bring smart contracts and decentralized finance (DeFi) to Bitcoin, similar to Ethereum's ecosystem, transforming Bitcoin from a store of value into a versatile platform. Sidechains could also enhance Bitcoin's privacy, enabling confidential transactions with technologies like **MimbleWimble** or **zk-SNARKs.**

8.9 ARK

Ark is a blockchain platform designed to make blockchain technology accessible to everyone, regardless of technical expertise. It's often called a "**Layer 3**" solution because it builds on Layer 1 and Layer 2 technologies, offering scalability, customization, and user-friendliness. Ark aims to create an ecosystem of interconnected blockchains, called "**Bridgechains**," facilitating interoperability and customization for developers, a solution to the longstanding challenge of cross-blockchain communication.

Ark allows users to create independent blockchains, easing congestion and enhancing performance. Developers can build customized blockchains without needing to fork or start from scratch, giving them control over consensus mechanisms and tokenomics, while still being linked to the Ark ecosystem. This modular, scalable system makes Ark versatile for a variety of applications.

A key feature of Ark is **SmartBridge Technology**, enabling seamless interoperability between blockchains, whether Ark-based or not. By encoding data fields in transactions, Ark acts as an intermediary, allowing actions on one blockchain to trigger events on another without exchanges or third parties. This cross-chain functionality enhances decentralization. Ark's security is powered by the **Delegated Proof of Stake (DPoS)** consensus mechanism, where **ARK** token holders vote for delegates who secure the network. The top 51 delegates are responsible for block production, maintaining a secure and decentralized network, and are incentivized through transaction fees and newly minted ARK tokens. For developers, Ark offers the **ARK Deployer**, a user-friendly tool that simplifies launching new blockchains. With APIs, SDKs, and a modular architecture, developers can build and integrate applications without needing advanced coding skills. Ark's flexibility allows users to select only the features they need, avoiding rigid frameworks. While Ark doesn't natively support smart contracts, the **ARK Virtual Machine (AVM)** facilitates smart contract interaction via SmartBridge technology, enabling cross-platform communication. With **WebAssembly (WASM) compatibility**, the AVM supports multiple programming languages, broadening the scope of applications built on Ark. Ark's customization and scalability make it an ideal tool for enterprise blockchain solutions, enabling businesses to create private or permissioned blockchains tailored to their needs. In gaming, Ark enables decentralized applications (dApps) and cross-blockchain digital asset transfers. In finance, Ark supports DeFi projects, facilitating cross-chain asset transfers and decentralized exchanges while maintaining security and transparency.

9. Altcoins

9.1 Ethereum

The Ethereum Revolution has been built on four main pillars: Smart Contracts, Blockchain Technology, and the Future of Decentralization. Ethereum is a decentralized, open-source blockchain platform that has revolutionized the cryptocurrency space by introducing smart contracts.

Ethereum's story begins with **Vitalik Buterin**, a Russian-Canadian programmer who recognized the limitations of Bitcoin and its scripting language. In late 2013, Buterin published the Ethereum whitepaper, outlining the concept of a decentralized platform that could handle much more than financial transactions. The idea was simple: allow developers to create decentralized applications that could run without downtime, fraud, or interference from third parties. Following a successful crowdfunding campaign in 2014, Ethereum officially launched on July 30, 2015, with its first iteration, "**Frontier**.

Ethereum was designed to go beyond Bitcoin's capabilities by providing a programmable blockchain that supports **decentralized applications (dApps)** and **smart contracts**. While Bitcoin serves primarily as a digital currency and store of value, Ethereum's innovation lies in its ability to **execute code** on a decentralized network, making it the foundation for many modern decentralized finance (DeFi) projects, NFTs, and decentralized organizations (DAOs). At its core, Ethereum's main function is to allow developers to create and deploy smart contracts and dApps, which automatically execute agreements or actions without requiring intermediaries. This innovation transformed Ethereum into a versatile platform for financial services, gaming, supply chains, and more. Over the years, Ethereum has undergone several upgrades, including "**Homestead**" (2016), "**Metropolis**" (2017-2019), "**Ethereum 2.0**," also known as "**The Merge**," in 2022, which transitioned Ethereum from a Proof of Work (PoW) consensus mechanism to Proof of Stake (PoS), "**Shanghai Capella" (2023)** that Enables ETH staking withdrawals, "**Dencun Upgrade**" (2024) a layer-2 scaling accelerator, "**Pectra Upgrade**" (2025) that combines Prague (execution layer) and Electra (consensus layer), introducing 11 EIPs that enhance transaction speed, cost-efficiency, wallet functionality, and validator flexibility.

Each stage has refined the platform's scalability, security, and functionality, cementing Ethereum's role as the go-to platform for decentralized innovation. Ethereum's blockchain is similar to Bitcoin's in that it records a public ledger of all transactions. However, Ethereum's blockchain is far more versatile. Ethereum initially used a Proof of Work (PoW) system, where miners solved complex puzzles to add blocks to the chain, receiving **ETH** (Ethereum's native cryptocurrency) as a reward. However, PoW was energy-intensive and could not handle a large volume of transactions. This led to Ethereum 2.0, which introduced a Proof of Stake (PoS) model.

The heart of Ethereum is a remarkable piece of technology known as the **Ethereum Virtual Machine, or EVM.** It operates like a "world computer," that stretches across countless nodes, tirelessly running smart contracts and decentralized applications, dApps. The EVM is what gives Ethereum its unparalleled flexibility and programmability, ensuring that these smart contracts are executed seamlessly and validated by every node in the network. It's this very system that makes smart contracts so powerful.

At the core of these smart contracts is **Solidity**, Ethereum's primary programming language. Designed specifically for this purpose, Solidity allows developers to code these contracts with ease, crafting intricate systems that the EVM will then bring to life. It's this unique combination, Ethereum's EVM and Solidity, that makes the platform a revolutionary space for developers, empowering them to build decentralized applications that push the boundaries of what's possible. Ethereum's vision, as outlined by Vitalik Buterin, is to be the "world computer," where decentralized applications can run without censorship, fraud, or third-party interference. Buterin saw Ethereum as a way to decentralize not just money, but entire industries. Ethereum's ability to host decentralized applications means that it has the potential to disrupt sectors ranging from finance and law to supply chain management and social media. This vision is deeply rooted in Ethereum's move to Proof of Stake with Ethereum 2.0. The long-term goal is to make Ethereum scalable and secure enough to support millions of users while keeping it decentralized. Ethereum aims to reduce transaction costs (gas fees) and improve speed, paving the way for greater adoption. Ethereum's potential stretches across countless industries, its versatility giving rise to transformative use cases. Take smart contracts, for example, they eliminate the need for intermediaries, automating processes that once required human oversight. Whether in insurance, real estate, or law, smart contracts now breathe life into systems that were once cumbersome and slow, injecting them with speed and efficiency. But the possibilities don't stop there. Decentralized Finance, or DeFi, is perhaps one of Ethereum's most profound contributions. On platforms like **Aave, Compound,** and **Uniswap**, DeFI is already a solid reality.

Then, there are Non-Fungible Tokens, or NFTs, digital tokens that represent ownership of something truly unique. Ethereum stands as the home of the largest NFT ecosystem, a place where artists, creators, and collectors can buy, sell, and trade digital assets, pieces of art, collectibles, anything that holds value in the digital realm. Each token tells a story, a one-of-a-kind creation stored on the blockchain. And finally, there are **Decentralized Autonomous Organizations, or DAOs**. Ethereum has made it possible for these organizations to exist, governed not by traditional leaders but by smart contracts.

Ethereum continues to be the leader in blockchain innovation, with future developments focusing on further scalability and decentralization. Ethereum 2.0 and Layer 2 solutions are just the beginning of the platform's transformation. In the next few years, Ethereum aims to become a more sustainable and scalable network, enabling mass adoption of decentralized applications across various industries. The continued development of Ethereum's ecosystem, combined with its strong developer community, ensures that it will remain at the forefront of blockchain technology.

9.2 Ethereum Ecosystem

"You wanted to discuss Ethereum," Satoshi said simply, settling into the chair across from me. His voice carried a weight that seemed to acknowledge both the significance of our conversation and the irony of its architect discussing a system he hadn't created.

"I did," I replied, trying to mask my nervousness. "I've been trying to understand how it evolved from what you started with Bitcoin. It seems like something entirely different now." A faint smile crossed his face. "Different, yes. But not disconnected." He paused, fingers tracing the rim of his cup. "Bitcoin was about establishing the fundamental principle, decentralized digital money without trusted third parties. But I always knew others would build beyond that foundation." When you look at Ethereum today, what do you see?" "I see an ecosystem," he said thoughtfully. "Not merely a blockchain, as you might expect, but something more organic. A living system of technologies, communities, and economic activity that has grown far beyond any single vision." He leaned back slightly. "You have to understand, what Vitalik and his team did was extend the concept I started into something I hadn't fully imagined, a platform for decentralized computation itself."

I nodded, pulling out my notebook. "Smart contracts?"

"Smart contracts, yes. But think of them as more than just programs. They're pieces of self-executing code that define behavior, how tokens work, how exchanges operate, how lending markets function. Bitcoin showed that we could have programmable money. Ethereum showed that we could have programmable everything."

The implications seemed vast, almost overwhelming. "But that created new problems, didn't it? Scalability?"

Satoshi's expression grew more serious. "Every solution creates new challenges. Bitcoin's simplicity was its strength, it did one thing extraordinarily well. Ethereum's ambition was its challenge. As adoption grew, the limitations became apparent. You can't have a global platform for computation running on a single chain without hitting throughput constraints."

"That's where the scaling solutions came in?"

"Precisely. And this is where the ecosystem concept becomes clear." He gestured as if drawing invisible connections in the air. "Around **Ethereum's Mainnet**, what we might call the secure settlement layer since it moved to proof-of-stake–there emerged a constellation of scaling solutions. Each with different philosophies, different trade-offs."

I found myself leaning forward. "The Merge in 2022–what did that mean for the broader ecosystem?"

"The transition from proof-of-work to proof-of-stake was more than just an efficiency upgrade," Satoshi explained. "It dramatically reduced energy consumption, yes, but more importantly, it opened new pathways for how people could participate in securing the network. Staking economics created different incentives, different ways of thinking about validator participation."

"And this enabled the scaling solutions?"

"Not enabled so much as complemented. The real innovation was rollups." His eyes lit up with what seemed like genuine admiration. "Rollups take transactions off the main chain, process them separately, then post proofs back to Ethereum. It's elegant, you maintain the security guarantees of the base layer while achieving the efficiency of off-chain computation."

"There seem to be different types of rollups?"

"Two primary approaches, each philosophically distinct," Satoshi continued. "**Optimistic rollups, Optimism, Arbitrum**, operate on the assumption that transactions are valid unless someone proves otherwise. It's efficient, but requires a challenge period. Then you have **zero-knowledge rollups–zkSync**, **StarkNet**, **Polygon zkEVM,** that use cryptographic proofs to guarantee validity with mathematical certainty."

The technical elegance was beginning to make sense, but I pressed for more context. "Which approach is winning?"

Satoshi chuckled quietly. "That's the wrong question. The ecosystem is large enough for multiple approaches to coexist and serve different needs. Some applications prioritize speed, others prioritize cost, others prioritize specific technical features. **Immutable X** specializes in gaming, **Loopring** focuses on decentralized exchanges. The modularity is the point."

"Modularity?"

"Think of it as specialization within a shared security framework," he explained. "Newer developments like Arbitrum Orbit and **Optimism's Superchain** vision extend this further. You can have entire ecosystems of application, specific rollups that inherit Ethereum's security but scale independently. It's like having dedicated highways for different types of traffic, all connected to the same trusted infrastructure."

I paused to process this, watching steam rise from my coffee. "Beyond the scaling infrastructure, what else surprised you about how the ecosystem developed?"

"The diversity of applications," he said without hesitation. "I understood that programmable money would enable new kinds of financial applications. But the scope..." He shook his head slightly. "Decentralized finance transformed Ethereum into a marketplace of lending protocols, decentralized exchanges, stablecoins. It demonstrated that financial systems could operate without traditional intermediaries."

"And NFTs?"

"Non-fungible tokens were unexpected for me," he admitted. "Digital ownership redefined in ways that spawned art markets, gaming economies, metaverse projects. It showed that blockchain technology could represent uniqueness, not just fungibility."

"The institutional adoption seems significant too."

"Tokenization of real-world assets," Satoshi nodded. "What was once experimental is becoming central to institutional adoption. Securities, real estate, traditional assets brought on-chain using Ethereum as infrastructure. It's the bridge between the traditional financial world and the decentralized one."

I scribbled notes, trying to capture not just his words but the underlying framework he was describing. "All of this requires supporting infrastructure, doesn't it?"

"Absolutely. The applications are just the visible layer. Underneath, you need oracle networks feeding off-chain data into smart contracts, bridges connecting Ethereum to other blockchains, indexing tools making contract data searchable and usable. It's middleware that makes the ecosystem functional."

"How does governance work across all of this?"

Satoshi's expression became more contemplative. "This is perhaps where Ethereum most clearly diverged from Bitcoin's model. The Ethereum ecosystem has a more formal governance process, shaped by the **Ethereum Foundation**, independent client teams, researchers. They coordinate through **Ethereum Improvement Proposals, EIPs**, that evolve the protocol through debate, experimentation, consensus."

"That sounds more... political?"

"In a way, yes. Upgrades like Shanghai, Dencun, Pectra have successively expanded functionality, optimized costs, redefined staking economics. It's a deliberate but steady path of innovation. Bitcoin's governance is more conservative, more resistant to change. Ethereum embraces evolution more readily."

"Is that better or worse?"

He paused for a long moment. "Different. Each approach serves its purpose. Bitcoin prioritizes stability and predictability, digital gold, if you will. Ethereum prioritizes flexibility and experimentation, a platform for innovation."

"Looking at the whole picture, what do you see as Ethereum's defining characteristics?"

"The balance," Satoshi said thoughtfully. "The ecosystem is defined by both coherence and diversity. Ethereum provides a secure settlement layer and common standards for value exchange, but it leaves room for experimentation at the edges. It embraces multiple scaling paradigms, fosters both public and enterprise applications, accommodates use cases from micro-payments to tokenized capital markets."

"That balance sounds delicate."

"It is. Sometimes contentious. But that openness is precisely what allows Ethereum to function as a general-purpose platform for decentralized computation." He finished his coffee, setting the cup down with finality. "The tension between stability and innovation is ongoing, but it's productive tension."

I looked at my notes, realizing we had covered an enormous scope of technical and philosophical ground. "When you started Bitcoin, did you envision ecosystems like this emerging?"

"I knew others would build on the foundation. I hoped they would. But the specific forms..." He shrugged slightly. "Innovation has its own logic, its own momentum. Ethereum represents one path among many possible paths."

"One more question," I said quickly. "What should people understand about the Ethereum ecosystem that they might be missing?"

He paused at the door, looking back. "That it's not a single thing trying to be everything. It's a dynamic network of specialized components working together. Each piece, the rollups, the DeFi protocols, the NFT markets, the governance processes, the middleware infrastructure—deserves understanding in its own right. But together, they form something larger: a global, resilient system that continues redefining how value, identity, and coordination operate in a digital world."

9.3 Plasma

Plasma is one of Ethereum's early Layer 2 scaling solutions designed to address the scalability issues faced by the Ethereum blockchain. It was first proposed in August 2017 by Vitalik Buterin (Ethereum co-founder) and Joseph Poon (co-author of the Lightning Network), and it's a Layer 2 solution designed to increase the transaction throughput of Ethereum while maintaining the security of the underlying blockchain. Plasma works creating "**child chains**" that offload most of the computational work from the Ethereum mainnet (Layer 1). These child chains operate independently but are anchored to the Ethereum main chain, meaning they periodically report back to Layer 1 for final settlement and security. The architecture and design of Plasma stretch far beyond the main chain, reaching into a complex network of child chains, often called **Plasma Chains.**

These smaller blockchains operate off-chain, handling transactions with their own set of rules, governance, and consensus mechanisms. Yet, despite their independence, they are anchored to the security of Ethereum's main chain. Periodically, they submit data, known as "**State Commitments**," back to Ethereum, ensuring that the foundation beneath them remains solid, no matter how they operate. At the core of this communication is the power of smart contracts. Plasma relies on these contracts embedded in Ethereum's main chain to create a bridge between the child and root chains. Through these contracts, assets can be deposited or withdrawn, and the system guards against fraudulent activity. The Ethereum main chain remains the final arbiter, the ultimate authority that oversees the entire process, ensuring fairness and security. But to truly maintain this balance, fraud proofs come into play.

Plasma chains must ensure that the transactions processed off-chain are legitimate, and users are empowered to challenge any suspicious or malicious activity. Should an invalid transaction or block surface, a fraud proof can be submitted to the Ethereum mainnet. If the proof holds, the malicious data is reversed, preserving the integrity of the Plasma chain and securing the trust of those who operate within it. In the background of all this, the intricate cryptography of **Merkle Trees** (cryptographic data structures used to efficiently and securely verify large sets of data by hashing each piece of data and organizing them into a tree of hashes) works tirelessly. Plasma chains use this data structure to compress information, allowing only the root of the Merkle Tree, representing the entirety of the chain's state, to be submitted to Ethereum. Instead of every transaction clogging the main chain, just this compressed snapshot is enough to keep things running smoothly, reducing the load on Ethereum's mainnet while ensuring transparency.

It all begins with a simple deposit. Users move assets, whether it be Ether or other tokens, from Ethereum into the Plasma chain through a smart contract. Once inside, they can transact freely, free from the constraints of Ethereum's slower and more expensive processes. It's faster, more efficient, yet still tethered to the safety net of Ethereum's main chain. Within the Plasma chain itself, transactions flow like a river. Users can transfer assets, execute smart contracts, and interact with decentralized applications (dApps), all depending on the design of that specific chain. These transactions are handled off-chain, but they don't vanish into the ether, they're batched and, in time, committed to Ethereum, ensuring a periodic reckoning with the main chain. Of course, users don't stay in Plasma forever.

They have the option to exit, returning their assets to the Ethereum mainnet. This process involves submitting an exit request to the Plasma smart contract, but there's always a period of scrutiny. During this window, others can challenge the exit if they believe fraud is at play. If no valid challenge arises, the assets are released, safe and sound back on Ethereum. In the end, final settlement is what ties it all together. Periodically, the Plasma chain commits its state to Ethereum's main chain, ensuring that, even if something goes wrong within the Plasma chain itself, the assets and transactions are secured by Ethereum. It's a system built on layers of trust, speed, and efficiency, with Ethereum standing as the unshakable foundation beneath it all. Plasma efficiency transforms the way things operate, allowing the system to breathe, where Ethereum's Layer 1 once gasped for air under the weight of its own popularity.

And then there are the lower gas fees. Off-chain transactions mean that users barely feel the pinch of fees, an enormous relief compared to the high costs of Ethereum's mainnet. Gas fees only come into play when a user interacts directly with Ethereum for things like deposits, exits, or submitting fraud proofs. It's a small price to pay for the speed and efficiency Plasma offers. Despite their independence, Plasma chains are far from unprotected. Plasma also offers his own playground for developers looking to experiment. Each child chain can be crafted with its own unique consensus mechanisms, governance models, and rules. It's a flexible design, allowing creators to shape their chains exactly how they see fit, without being tethered to the rigid structure of Ethereum's Layer 1.

As for use cases, Plasma opens doors to numerous possibilities. Payments, for one, are a natural fit. With high-frequency, low-value transactions like micropayments, Plasma excels. Users can move funds quickly and cheaply off-chain, making it ideal for systems where speed and cost are paramount. Similarly, token transfers benefit from Plasma's efficiency. In any scenario where fast, inexpensive transactions are needed, Plasma chains step in. Token-based applications, too, flourish in this environment, moving swiftly through the decentralized landscape. In the world of decentralized finance (DeFi), Plasma can be a game changer. Some DeFi applications don't require constant communication with Ethereum's mainnet, making

Plasma an ideal staging ground. Gaming finds a perfect home within Plasma as well. Blockchain-based games often demand frequent interaction between users and in-game assets. Plasma allows players to trade and transact with minimal fees, while the true ownership of their assets is settled back on Ethereum, ensuring security. And finally, there's scalability for dApps. Developers seeking to build decentralized applications can use Plasma to offload the heavy computational work from Ethereum, transferring it to Plasma chains instead.

This frees up resources, allowing dApps to scale faster, cheaper, and more efficiently, creating a seamless experience for users. In this intricate web of off-chain activity, Plasma chains stand as a solution, not just to Ethereum's current limitations, but to the future of decentralized applications and economies. Plasma, while powerful, is not without its limitations. One of the most noticeable drawbacks is the delayed finality. Plasma chains don't offer the luxury of instant results. Instead, they rely on Ethereum to settle disputes and manage fraud proofs, and with that comes the inevitable waiting. Users must endure a "**Challenge Period**," often stretching over a few days, before they can finalize their exits. For certain applications, those that thrive on immediacy and liquidity, this delay can feel like a frustrating pause in an otherwise fast-paced environment. Then there's the issue of smart contract limitations. Plasma was never intended to handle the intricacies of complex decentralized applications. It was built for the straightforward, payments and token transfers. While it's technically possible to implement smart contracts within Plasma's framework, the system is far more constrained than other Layer 2 solutions, such as **Optimistic Rollups** or **ZK-Rollups**. These alternatives offer broader support for dApps, allowing for more complex functionality that Plasma struggles to accommodate. Beyond the technical hurdles, complexity becomes another obstacle.

Plasma is intricate, its implementation demanding a deep understanding of both the child chains and their interaction with Ethereum's mainnet. Developers are tasked with navigating the fragile dance between chains, especially when it comes to handling fraud proofs and the often tricky exit mechanisms. It's a delicate balance, and one that requires careful oversight. This brings us to fraud proofs and user responsibility. Plasma's security hinges on the users themselves. Unlike other solutions where security is more automated, here the burden falls on the individuals. They must actively monitor the chain, ready to submit fraud proofs if something goes awry. For some, this added responsibility is empowering, but for others, it's an unwelcome chore, one that leaves the system vulnerable to human error or negligence. Despite these limitations, Plasma has seen notable implementations. **OmiseGO**, now known as **OMG Network**, was one of the first to embrace the Plasma model. It set out to build a decentralized exchange and payment platform, leveraging Plasma's scalability to handle a high volume of transactions.

It was a bold step into the future, a promise of what Plasma could achieve. And then there was Matic, which has since evolved into **Polygon**. Matic began with a hybrid model, blending Plasma with Proof of Stake to scale Ethereum. Its initial focus was on payments and simple token transfers, using Plasma to streamline the process.

9.4 Immutable X

In the world of Ethereum, where high gas fees and sluggish transaction times are the norm, something new emerges. It's called Immutable X, a Layer-2 scaling solution. Built to sit atop Ethereum's vast blockchain, it's here with a purpose: to take non-fungible tokens, NFTs, and make them faster, easier to use, and cheaper to trade. Ethereum has always been powerful, but it stumbles when it comes to scalability. Immutable X changes that. It brings with it the promise of speed and efficiency, powered by something called **ZK-Rollups**. Imagine a marketplace where creators and collectors no longer dread gas fees. Immutable X removes this burden, allowing minting and trading without a single drop of Ethereum's usual costs. A user creates a digital masterpiece, and it's minted, just like that, without any extra fees.

They transfer it, sell it, and buy another, all without watching their balance disappear into gas. Immutable X handles up to 9,000 transactions per second, leaving

Ethereum's own 15 TPS in the dust. And the magic lies in those ZK-Rollups. A technology that bundles up transactions, rolls them tight, and sends them to Ethereum's main chain, all while preserving the blockchain's cherished decentralization. Security and decentralization remain untouched. Immutable X clings to Ethereum's standards, using ZK-Rollups not just for speed, but to ensure every transaction is as secure as it gets. A user watches their trade close in an instant. No waiting. No hesitation. Whether it's in the middle of a fast-paced game or an art auction, Immutable X delivers finality in a heartbeat.

Developers step into the fold with ease, too. Immutable X extends its hand to them, offering APIs that cut through the complexity of blockchain integration. Building decentralized apps, dApps, is no longer a daunting task. It's simple, fast, and flexible. And for those concerned about the environment, there's more good news: Immutable X is carbon-neutral. Every step of the way, it offsets its footprint with verified carbon credits, quieting the whispers of blockchain's environmental impact. Here in details how Zero-Knowledge Rollups or ZK-Rollups, as they call them, work. In a quiet way, they ensure that off-chain transactions stay valid without spilling any data to the blockchain. The details remain hidden, safe, and secure. Immutable X gathers these transactions, compresses them, and sends them off to Ethereum's mainnet in one neat package. This reduces Ethereum's workload, making scalability not just a promise, but a reality. Immutable X allows gas-free trading, minting, and transferring of digital assets. Platforms like **OpenSea** catch wind of it, integrating this new technology, allowing creators and collectors to breathe easier. For gamers, Immutable X offers something more, a chance to tokenize in-game items and trade them freely, without worrying about delays or costs. Games like **Gods Unchained** take full advantage, letting players manage their in-game economies with smooth transactions, all backed by Immutable X. Artists, too, find freedom here. They mint and trade their digital art without a second thought, knowing there are no gas fees to hold them back. It's a new world where creativity flourishes, unhindered by the limitations of the past. Immutable X partners with giants in the NFT space.

At the center of Immutable X's ecosystem sits a token, **IMX**. It serves more than one purpose. Those who hold it can stake their IMX, earning rewards for their loyalty, their participation in the network. Governance, too, is shaped by this token. IMX holders get a voice, a vote, on the upgrades, features, and changes that will define the platform's future. Every transaction on Immutable X pays a small tribute to this token, helping sustain the network's growth. Immutable X doesn't rest. Its goal is decentralization, where the community takes the reins, and token holders hold the power to shape the future. As more decisions are handed over, IMX tokens become keys to governance, unlocking the door to the platform's destiny. In a sea of Layer-2 solutions, Immutable X stands apart.

While others, like **Optimism** and **Arbitrum**, focus on scaling general blockchain functions, Immutable X hones in on NFTs, making it the premier choice for creators and collectors alike. Gas fees? Gone. The barrier to entry? Lowered, making the world of NFTs more accessible to everyone. The future is clear. Immutable X isn't stopping. More features, more partnerships, more games, and more decentralized apps are on the horizon. Immutable X is poised to be the foundation of the next wave of NFT innovation, expanding its ecosystem and cementing its role as the go-to platform for anyone looking to explore the possibilities of NFTs, gaming, and beyond.

9.5 ZK-Rollups (Zero-Knowledge Rollups)

ZK-Rollups, a cutting-edge Layer 2 scaling solution, bring together two powerful concepts: **Rollups and Zero-Knowledge Proofs (ZKPs)**. The idea is simple yet revolutionary. Rollups bundle or "roll up" multiple transactions into a single batch, submitting it to the main blockchain, Ethereum's Layer 1. This technique significantly reduces the data load and computational strain on Layer 1, speeding things up and cutting costs. But the magic lies in the **Zero-Knowledge Proofs**, cryptographic tricks that allow one party to prove a transaction's validity without revealing anything about the transaction itself. The process begins with off-chain transactions, where ZK-Rollups handle the heavy lifting. Transactions take place on a separate Layer 2 network, far from the congestion of the main chain. As these transactions unfold, they're bundled into a single batch, ready for the next step. From here, the real innovation takes shape: proof generation.

For every batch of transactions, a **Zero-Knowledge Proof**, often in the form of a **SNARK (Succinct Non-Interactive Argument of Knowledge)**, is created. This proof ensures that all transactions in the batch are valid. Instead of sending every single detail to Ethereum's Layer 1, the ZK-Rollup submits only the compressed data, the SNARK proof and a state root, known as a **Merkle Root** (Merkle Trees are cryptographic data structures used to efficiently and securely verify large sets of data by hashing each piece of data and organizing them into a tree of hashes), back to the main blockchain. This step, known as the on-chain commitment, represents all the bundled transactions in one sleek package.

What makes ZK-Rollups truly remarkable is their instant finality. The ZK proof guarantees the validity of the transactions upfront, meaning that as soon as they're posted to Layer 1, they're considered final. No need for further checks or challenges–it's done. But who manages this intricate process? That role falls to the **Operator**, a central figure responsible for bundling Layer 2 transactions, generating the proofs, and submitting everything to Layer 1. In return, the Operator collects fees, ensuring the system runs smoothly. The backbone of ZK-Rollups is the rollup contract, a smart contract deployed on Ethereum's Layer 1. This contract doesn't just verify the proofs and store the compressed data, it maintains the state of the entire Layer 2 system. The benefits of ZK-Rollups are undeniable. The first is scalability. By processing transactions off-chain and sending only compressed data to Ethereum, ZK-Rollups dramatically increase transaction throughput. The blockchain becomes faster, smoother, and capable of handling far more than it ever could before. Security is another cornerstone. ZK-Rollups inherit Ethereum's security model, but with an added layer of cryptographic assurance through **Zero-Knowledge Proofs**. Every transaction is guaranteed to be valid, with the proof committed to Layer 1, leaving little room for error or fraud. Cost efficiency is where ZK-Rollups shine. Since fewer transactions are posted to the main chain, users save on gas fees. And because ZK-Rollups deal in compressed transactions, those fees shrink even further, offering an economical solution for DeFi protocols and dApps. One of the most exciting advantages is instant withdrawal. Unlike other scaling solutions such as **Optimistic Rollups**, which require a lengthy challenge period before funds can be withdrawn, ZK-Rollups allow users to move their assets back to Layer 1 almost instantly. There's no need to wait, the cryptographic proof guarantees that everything is in order.

Now some real use cases. **ZkSync**, built on Ethereum, is one of the leading platforms. Known for its speed and low fees, zkSync focuses on payments and general-purpose smart contracts, offering a glimpse into the future of scalable dApps. Another notable player is **Loopring**, which uses ZK-Rollups to scale decentralized exchanges (DEXs). Loopring combines the advantages of ZK-Rollups with its own DEX protocol, creating a seamless and cost-effective trading experience. Then there's **StarkNet**, a scaling solution that employs STARKs, a different type of Zero-Knowledge Proof than SNARKs. StarkNet provides scalability for dApps on Ethereum, opening the door for even more complex applications. ZK-Rollups are widely regarded as one of the most promising scaling solutions for Ethereum and beyond. As the technology continues to evolve, Proof Generation times are likely to decrease, ecosystem support will broaden, and ZK-Rollups will be able to handle even more sophisticated smart contracts. Their robust security, instant finality, and potential for privacy-enhancing applications make them a crucial piece of the future blockchain landscape.

9.6 Optimistic Rollups

Optimistic Rollups are a Layer 2 scaling solution designed to significantly increase the scalability and transaction throughput of the Ethereum blockchain while preserving security and decentralization. Unlike some other Layer 2 solutions like Plasma or **State Channels**, Optimistic

Rollups allow for more general-purpose smart contracts, making them ideal for decentralized finance (DeFi), decentralized applications (dApps), and other complex blockchain use cases. Let's break down how Optimistic Rollups work, why they are important, and how they fit into Ethereum's scaling strategy. Optimistic Rollups (ORUs) bundle transactions together and execute them off-chain, but unlike some other L2 solutions, they "optimistically" assume that transactions are valid without verifying each one immediately. This assumption is what gives them the term "optimistic." Only if someone challenges the validity of a transaction will a process of fraud proof verification take place.

This approach reduces the computational load on the Ethereum main chain (Layer 1), significantly lowering gas fees and increasing throughput. The security of Optimistic Rollups is anchored to Ethereum's main chain, meaning they still benefit from the same level of decentralization and security that Ethereum provides. Optimistic Rollups operate by shifting the majority of computation and transaction processing off-chain while committing data to Ethereum's Layer 1 for security. The process unfolds with precision, each step methodically building upon the last. It begins with batching transactions off-chain, where a multitude of actions are bundled together, far from the crowded lanes of the Ethereum mainnet. These transactions are executed in clusters by the Optimistic Rollup, their raw data compressed into a single unit. This batch, now reduced to its essential form, a **State Root** (a cryptographic hash that represents the entire state of a blockchain at a specific point in time) is posted to Ethereum's Layer 1.

The state root acts as a snapshot, representing the updated state after all those off-chain transactions have played out. But here's the catch, there's an optimistic assumption at the heart of it all. The system trusts that these transactions are valid, without verifying each one in real-time. It's a leap of faith. The rollup processes everything off-chain and sends the resulting state changes back to Ethereum, skipping the actual transactions themselves. The system, in essence, takes its chances that everything has gone smoothly. Of course, not everyone is so trusting. That's where **Fraud Proofs** come into play. If someone believes that something nefarious has slipped through, a fraudulent transaction or a malicious actor, they can submit a Fraud Proof, sounding the alarm. In response, a verification process begins.

The system checks the challenge, and if fraud is detected, the malicious transaction is swiftly undone. However, if no one raises a challenge within the designated window, typically one to two weeks, the transaction is locked in as valid, its fate sealed. With the challenge period behind them, transactions move to final settlement. The state change becomes a permanent part of the Ethereum blockchain. If fraud was uncovered along the way, the system punishes the guilty party, often through the **Slashing Mechanisms** (a penalty system used in Proof of

Stake (PoS) networks to discourage misbehavior by validators). It reduces a validator's staked tokens if they act maliciously or fail to meet network rules, enhancing security and network reliability, protecting the integrity of the system with swift justice. Behind the scenes, rollup contracts on Ethereum orchestrate the entire process. These smart contracts, deployed on Ethereum's Layer 1, manage the delicate interaction between the rollup and the blockchain. They safeguard the compressed data, the State Roots from the rollups, and stand ready to handle any fraud proofs or challenge processes that come their way. But none of this would be possible without the crucial challenge period, the window of time where disputes can be raised. This phase, though vital for security, brings with it a frustrating delay, often stretching to around a week before transactions can be fully finalized.

What sets Optimistic Rollups apart from other scaling solutions like Plasma is their support for general-purpose smart contracts. This means they can handle complex dApps and DeFi use cases, functioning just like Ethereum's Layer 1, but with far less overhead. The doors to innovation remain wide open, and developers can build without the usual limitations imposed by other Layer 2 systems. Beneath it all, security inheritance stands as the cornerstone of trust. As we have outlined above, Optimistic Rollups derive their security from Ethereum's decentralization. Users know their funds and data are protected by the very foundation that makes Ethereum a powerhouse, adding another layer of confidence to this scaling solution. Compared to ZK-Rollups, Optimistic Rollups face higher fees. Though they reduce costs significantly when compared to Ethereum's Layer 1, they still bear the overhead of maintaining the challenge window and resolving disputes. ZK-Rollups, with their more streamlined processes, often achieve even lower fees. Lastly, there's the issue of data availability. Despite inheriting Ethereum's security, Optimistic Rollups rely heavily on off-chain data for processing transactions. If that data is ever withheld or becomes unavailable, the entire system could be compromised. It's a vulnerability that, while not always at the forefront, lingers in the background as a reminder of the risks involved.

We have several uses case, and at the forefront of this tale are platforms like **Optimism.** As one of the leading Optimistic Rollup solutions, Optimism is dedicated to scaling Ethereum without losing compatibility with existing Ethereum smart contracts. It's no wonder that many of the giants in decentralized finance, **Uniswap** and **Synthetix**, to name just two, have embraced it. For these projects, Optimism offers what they desperately need: lower fees and higher throughput, the lifeblood of decentralized exchanges (DEXs) and the financial applications that rely on them. In this new landscape, speed and affordability are no longer luxuries–they're necessities.

Arbitrum, another prominent player in this space, has followed a similar path. Supporting Ethereum-compatible smart contracts, Arbitrum provides the same crucial ingredients: lower fees and faster transactions. But it's not just the speed or the cost that draws developers, it's the flexibility. Arbitrum has quickly become one of the most widely adopted Layer 2 solutions, offering a developer-friendly environment that makes building and scaling projects smoother and more accessible. It's a platform that welcomes innovation, allowing DeFi protocols to thrive. Uniswap's integration with Optimism marked a significant shift for its users. Suddenly, the platform that had been known for its revolutionary approach to trading was offering even more, faster and cheaper transactions. With Optimistic Rollups, Uniswap maintained its position at the top of the decentralized exchange world while enhancing the user experience, freeing traders from the burden of Ethereum's high gas fees.

9.7 State Channels

State Channels, a Layer 2 scaling solution, offer a way to make transactions faster and more efficient by taking most of the action off-chain. In this technique, two or more parties can execute numerous transactions between themselves without burdening the main blockchain, except for the opening and closing of the channel. It's a clever workaround to Ethereum's scalability problem, allowing participants to move freely without the usual congestion. It all begins with opening the channel. To set things in motion, the parties lock an initial state, this could be funds or specific contract conditions, into a smart contract on the Ethereum blockchain. This initial state is like laying the foundation for a building, recorded on-chain to keep everything official. Once that's done, the real magic begins. The bulk of the interactions happen in off-chain transactions.

The participants can now transact as much as they like, exchanging signed messages that reflect the changing state, be it updated balances or contract outcomes. But none of this touches the blockchain. These messages are kept off-chain, allowing for quick and seamless exchanges without the weight of on-chain verification slowing things down. Once the parties are done, it's time to close the channel. At this point, they submit the final state, the last record of their transactions or balances, back to Ethereum. The blockchain takes these signed messages, verifies the final state, and settles everything on-chain, bringing the off-chain interactions to a close with one final act. State Channels come in different forms. The most straightforward are Payment Channels.

These allow participants to make off-chain payments, only settling the final balance on the main chain. It's the same principle behind Bitcoin's **Lightning Network**, and Ethereum supports similar mechanisms for faster, cheaper payments. More advanced are **Generalized State Channels**, which can handle more than just payments. These channels allow for any kind of smart contract logic to take place off-chain. Whether it's a dApp's functionality or complex contract execution, everything can unfold off-chain until the final result is brought back to the blockchain. Despite their benefits, challenges lurk within State Channels. One major issue is the online requirement. Both parties need to stay connected throughout the channel's lifetime. If one becomes unresponsive, they run the risk of losing their funds, especially if the other party tries to close the channel unfairly. Thankfully, the use of **Watchtowers**, third-party services, can help mitigate this risk by monitoring the channel and defending against malicious closures. Another limitation is the number of participants. State Channels work best with small groups, usually no more than four people. Scaling beyond that can be cumbersome and is better suited to other Layer 2 solutions, like rollups. Then there's the risk of inactivity. If no one takes the initiative to close the channel, the funds or states locked inside could remain stuck indefinitely. A time limit can be set, but adding such a condition introduces additional complexity, something that needs to be managed carefully. And in the event of a force closure dispute, things can get tricky. If there's a disagreement over the final state, either party can submit what they claim is the latest version to the blockchain. But here's the catch, the other party must be online to challenge it with an even newer version. If not, disputes can drag on, leading to delays or complications. Despite these challenges, State Channels offer compelling use cases. In gaming, for instance, players can make rapid off-chain interactions, only sending the final game results to the blockchain when necessary, reducing latency and slashing gas fees. For recurring services, such as subscriptions, State Channels make regular payments smooth and efficient. The service provider can collect fees off-chain, without having to execute every transaction on Ethereum. Several notable projects have emerged to make State Channels a reality. The **Raiden Network** another Ethereum's answer to Bitcoin's Lightning Network, offering a fast, low-cost way to transfer ERC-20 tokens off-chain. There's also **Connext**, a framework that allows for not just off-chain payments, but contract interactions as well. From gaming to financial services, Connext opens the door for a wide array of applications. Similarly, the **Celer Network** offers another State Channel solution, designed to provide secure, fast, and low-cost scaling for Ethereum.

9.8 Tether

Tether stands as one of the most consequential inventions in the cryptocurrency era, a bridge suspended between the familiar world of fiat money and the boundless frontier of digital finance. When **Tether** first appeared in 2014 under the modest name **Realcoin**,. its founders, **Brock Pierce**, **Reeve Collins**, and **Craig Sellars,** sought to stabilize digital money within the blockchain's new reality. But the man who would ultimately define its fate was **Giancarlo Devasini**, the enigmatic Italian financier, long-time financial architect of **Bitfinex**, who took the reins as

Tether's architect-in-chief. Under his pragmatic and sometimes polarizing guidance, Tether evolved from an experimental bridge asset into a cornerstone of the global crypto economy. Together with Paolo Ardoino, the company's technologist and now CEO, Devasini turned Tether into a financial powerhouse, profitable, deeply liquid, and increasingly self-aware of its geopolitical weight.

The ambition was deceptively simple yet revolutionary in consequence. At a time when Bitcoin was swaying like a ship on stormy seas and Ethereum was still a young experiment in distributed logic, Tether proposed something different: a digital token permanently anchored to the value of the U.S. dollar. It promised that every USDT in circulation would correspond to one dollar held in reserve, a promise that made the volatility of crypto suddenly negotiable, and the concept of digital cash feel, for the first time, familiar.

As the years unfolded, Tether became the quiet heartbeat of the crypto economy. It allowed traders to exit and enter positions without touching the cumbersome banking system, giving the market its first true liquidity engine. In decentralized finance, it became the grease in the gears, used as collateral, as a safe store of value, and as the unit that denominated risk in a market where everything else seemed to move at light speed. In countries where currencies collapsed or inflation devoured savings, Tether became something closer to salvation: a digital version of the dollar that required no bank and no borders.

Yet, behind this promise of stability lingered a growing paradox. Tether, the asset meant to eliminate uncertainty, soon became one of the most debated subjects in the history of cryptocurrency. Critics and regulators alike asked the same uneasy question: Was every Tether truly backed by a real dollar? For years, the answer seemed to oscillate between technical statements, partial audits, and legal battles. In 2021, this tension reached its breaking point when the New York Attorney General's office launched an investigation into Tether's reserves. The company settled the matter with a fine and a pledge of transparency, marking a turning point for both Tether and the broader stablecoin industry. What followed was a gradual but deliberate effort toward public attestations, reserve reports, and a more disciplined image, steps that helped Tether not only survive but strengthen its dominance.

Today, Tether operates far beyond its early incarnation. Its tokens move across a multitude of blockchains. A critical function that Tether introduced was the integration of smart contracts, which automates transactions in a decentralized and secure manner. Tether operated (as per 2025 things changed a little) on multiple blockchain platforms, including **Bitcoin** (via the **Omni Layer**, a protocol built on top of the Bitcoin blockchain that enables the creation, transfer, and trading of digital assets), **Ethereum** (as an **ERC-20 token**), **Tron**, and more. However, Tether's presence on Ethereum, which introduced the integration of smart contracts, further solidified its utility and adoption. Tether tokens are issued when a user deposits fiat currency into Tether Limited's reserves. An equivalent amount of USDT is minted and sent to the user, maintaining the 1:1 peg to the fiat currency. Users can then trade or hold these tokens on the blockchain. When a user wants to redeem USDT for fiat, the process reverses: the tokens are burned, and the fiat equivalent is transferred to the user's bank account. Because Tether operates on multiple blockchains, users can transfer Tether between different networks, making it a highly flexible asset. This cross-blockchain compatibility has been key to its adoption across different exchanges and platforms. While Tether operates on multiple blockchains, it typically adopts the consensus mechanisms of those platforms. For example, Ethereum uses a Proof of Stake (PoS) mechanism, while Bitcoin (via Omni Layer) uses Proof of Work (PoW). Tether relies on these platforms' consensus mechanisms to verify transactions and secure the network. Across both centralized and decentralized exchanges, Tether has become one of the most traded assets.

While its foundation remains tied to the dollar, its spirit has expanded into something more ambitious. Tether has become a symbol of pragmatic innovation, quietly enabling billions in daily volume across exchanges and acting as the invisible infrastructure of modern crypto markets. When traders seek refuge from volatility, they do not retreat to dollars, they retreat to Tether.

The company behind it, **Tether Limited**, has evolved too. What began as a simple issuing entity has grown into a sprawling financial ecosystem with investments that reach far beyond stablecoins. Over the past two years, Tether has quietly transformed into a kind of digital conglomerate, funding artificial intelligence ventures, renewable energy projects, and even Bitcoin mining initiatives powered by sustainable infrastructure. It now reports profits exceeding those of many traditional banks and holds a venture portfolio of astonishing scale, estimated at over a hundred billion dollars, built from its operational earnings rather than its reserves. In late 2025, Tether announced its intention to raise up to $20 billion in private funding, an audacious move that could value the company at **half a trillion dollars** and cement its role not just as a crypto actor, but as one of the most powerful financial entities in the world.

And yet, Tether continues to reshape itself. In mid-2025, the company made the strategic decision to wind down operations on several legacy blockchains, among them **Omni Layer**, **Bitcoin Cash SLP,** and **Algorand,** preferring to focus on faster, more secure, and more widely adopted networks. That same summer, it revealed plans for a new U.S. regulated stablecoin, provisionally named **USAT**, to be issued under the oversight of a national trust bank. To lead this effort, Tether appointed **Bo Hines**, a former digital-assets adviser to the White House, a symbolic gesture that signaled the company's readiness to engage with Washington rather than defy it.

In parallel, Tether has deepened its cooperation with international authorities, helping law enforcement track stolen or illicit funds. In 2025 alone, it froze and later recovered hundreds of thousands of dollars linked to fraud and sanctioned entities, underscoring its dual role as both a private issuer and a participant in global financial oversight. This delicate balance between decentralization and compliance, freedom and responsibility, has come to define the company's modern identity.

Paolo Ardoino, Tether's charismatic CEO, often speaks of a future where billions of autonomous AI agents will transact value without intermediaries, machines paying machines, contracts executing themselves. In that world, he imagines, digital currencies like USDT and Bitcoin will become the lingua franca of artificial intelligence. Whether or not that future arrives as predicted, it reveals the philosophical pivot that Tether has made: it no longer sees itself merely as the keeper of a stablecoin, but as a central actor in the next phase of digital civilization.

After more than a decade of existence, Tether remains what it has always claimed to be, a digital reflection of the U.S. dollar, but it has also become something greater: the stable nucleus around which the chaotic particles of the crypto universe continue to orbit. It is both the most trusted and the most questioned name in blockchain finance, a paradox that captures the very essence of crypto itself–

decentralized yet dependent, transparent yet opaque, revolutionary yet pragmatic.

In a world still negotiating the boundaries between code and capital, Tether endures as a reminder that stability, in its truest form, is never static. It is built, challenged, and redefined, block by block, controversy by controversy, and innovation by innovation.

9.9 Binance and BNB

Binance emerged on the scene in 2017, a bold newcomer in the fast-growing world of cryptocurrency exchanges. Behind it stood **Changpeng Zhao**, or "**CZ**" as he's known to the community, a visionary who quickly transformed Binance into the largest cryptocurrency exchange by trading volume. What began as a simple platform for buying, selling, and trading digital assets rapidly grew into something much larger, a vast ecosystem that stretched beyond trading to encompass its own blockchain, **Binance Smart Chain (BSC)**, and its native cryptocurrency, **BNB**. Binance's influence now extends across decentralized finance (DeFi), staking, blockchain project launches, and much more.

Binance's story began with a spark. In the midst of a cryptocurrency boom, the company raised $15 million through an **Initial Coin Offering (ICO)**, issuing BNB as its native token. Launched during a period of rapid expansion in the industry, Binance distinguished itself with a user-friendly platform that supported a wide range of coins, low trading fees, and the ability to process vast numbers of transactions quickly. It wasn't long before Binance was the name on everyone's lips. By 2017, Binance had established itself as a go-to exchange, celebrated for its intuitive interface and high liquidity. But the real shift came in 2018. Facing regulatory pressure in China, Binance moved its operations to Malta, signaling the beginning of a global expansion that would cement its place as a dominant player in the crypto world.

The next year, 2019, saw Binance take things a step further. It launched **Binance Chain,** a blockchain designed for decentralized trading with BNB as its native coin. Yet the true innovation lay in the introduction of **Binance Smart Chain (BSC)**, a scalable and smart contract-compatible chain. BSC wasn't just about trading, it opened the door to decentralized applications and a world of automated financial services, all built on Binance's rapidly growing ecosystem. In 2020 and 2021, Binance diversified its offerings even further. Binance Launchpad provided a platform for new crypto projects to find their footing, while **Binance Academy** offered educational resources for those eager to learn. And **Binance Labs**, an incubator for blockchain startups, became a breeding ground for innovation. Throughout this expansion, BNB evolved from its original purpose as a token for trading fee discounts to a multi-purpose utility coin, central to the Binance Smart Chain ecosystem. Whether it was DeFi, staking, or governance, BNB found itself at the heart of it all.

The evolution of BNB from its humble beginnings on Ethereum's blockchain to its migration to Binance's own chain is a testament to the coin's growing importance. Initially launched as an **ERC-20** token, **BNB** was created to offer Binance users discounts on trading fees. But over time, it grew into much more than that. Today, it powers everything from transaction fees on Binance Smart Chain to staking, where users can earn rewards while supporting network security.

That chain itself has kept evolving. Under the broad **"BNB Chain"** banner, the ecosystem now spans the **BNB Smart Chain** at **Layer 1** and **opBNB**, an **Optimism-stack Layer 2** built for much higher throughput and lower costs, absorbing developer energy that once flowed to distant competitors. In public roadmaps and technical briefs, the team has described an aggressive cadence of upgrades: faster finality measured in fractions of a second, rising block gas limits, and a pathway that brings near-instant confirmations into the realm of the ordinary. In practice, the network's Layer 2 ambitions have translated into markedly cheaper transactions and a canvas wide enough for consumer apps, markets, and games that need speed to feel natural.

At the core of Binance's success is its exchange, the foundation upon which everything else was built. Here, users can trade a vast array of cryptocurrencies, with options for spot trading, margin trading, futures trading, and even **peer-to-peer (P2P)** trading. It's a robust platform, designed to cater to every level of trader, from the casual user to the institutional investor. But Binance's ambitions didn't stop there. Binance Chain became the first blockchain it developed, designed for fast and low-cost trading. Yet as Binance Smart Chain (BSC) gained prominence, it became clear that BSC would be the future of Binance's blockchain endeavors. Launched in 2020, BSC was built for the world of smart contracts, fully compatible with the **Ethereum Virtual Machine (EVM)**. This meant that developers could easily port their decentralized applications (dApps) from Ethereum to BSC, taking advantage of lower fees and faster transaction times. Binance Smart Chain operates on a consensus model known as **Proof of Staked Authority (PoSA)**, blending the efficiency of Proof of Stake (PoS) with the reliability of Proof of Authority (PoA). This hybrid approach allows for faster and cheaper transactions compared to Ethereum, making it an attractive option for developers looking to build decentralized applications or DeFi services. Through all of this, BNB remained the thread that tied everything together. Whether providing trading fee discounts on Binance's exchange or being used to pay transaction fees on Binance Smart Chain, BNB has become central to the entire Binance ecosystem. Users can even stake their BNB, earning rewards while helping to secure the network.

Even the most familiar pillars of that ecosystem have changed faces. BUSD, once an anchor stablecoin in Binance's markets, was wound down after New York regulators ordered **Paxos** to halt new issuance. The exchange orchestrated a measured migration away from BUSD, guiding users toward alternatives and smoothing liquidity by promoting pairs in First Digital's **FDUSD**. The era of the in-house branded dollar ended not with a sudden stop but with a carefully managed fade-out, leaving markets stable even as the logos changed.

As the platform matured, regulation, once peripheral, moved to center stage. In **Dubai**, Binance's local entity, **Binance FZE,** advanced through the city's structured licensing regime and secured a full market license from the **Virtual Assets Regulatory Authority (VARA)**, a milestone that signaled how the exchange's globalization increasingly runs through clear legal corridors rather than jurisdictional arbitrage. The Middle East, and the UAE in particular, has become both a commercial base and a reputational proving ground as Binance reframes itself as a licensed, compliance-forward institution.

Strategic capital has flowed toward Binance from the Gulf, where an Abu Dhabi group announced a multi-billion investment, a gesture that knits together the region's ambitions in AI and digital assets with Binance's campaign to rebuild trust at continental scale. These currents, investigations on one shore, patient capital on another, frame the present tense in which Binance operates. The **Burn Mechanism** at Binance is a quiet but powerful force, shaping the future of BNB. Periodically, Binance buys back BNB tokens, not to hold or redistribute them, but to burn them, reducing the overall supply, making each remaining token more scarce. It is a deflationary tactic, a way to slowly increase the value of BNB over time, a strategy designed for the long game. But the utility of BNB went far beyond this subtle economic maneuver. It is also the gateway to new opportunities on **Binance Launchpad**, a platform for token sales of emerging blockchain projects. Holding BNB means more than just a discount on trading, it is a ticket to participate in these token sales, where new ideas and innovations are born. Many projects had risen through this platform, their tokens launched into the market after rigorous vetting by Binance. Some of the names, like **Fetch.AI**, **Band Protocol**, and **Axie Infinity**, would go on to make waves in the wider crypto world.

Then there is DeFi, the decentralized finance landscape that had bloomed across Binance Smart Chain (BSC). BNB became the lifeblood of these protocols, flowing through yield farms, lending platforms, and liquidity pools. It isn't just a token, it is a force driving decentralized systems forward, facilitating lending, borrowing, and earning across a rapidly growing ecosystem.

On the other side of Binance's ecosystem, DeFi projects thrive. On **PancakeSwap**, a decentralized exchange, users trade tokens, farm yields, and stake in liquidity pools, enjoying low fees and high rewards. **Venus** offers a decentralized platform for lending and borrowing, where users could mint **Synthetic Stablecoins**. And then there is **Autofarm**, a yield aggregator designed to help users maximize returns from the various liquidity pools scattered across BSC. But Binance wasn't content with just DeFi. In 2021, it launched its own **NFT Marketplace**, an arena where users can mint, buy, and sell non-fungible tokens. Art, collectibles, gaming assets, everything can be found here, and all at a fraction of the cost that Ethereum-based platforms charged. The marketplace thrives, opening up new possibilities for creators and collectors alike.

Several key projects are anchored to the Binance ecosystem. **Trust Wallet**, which Binance acquired in 2018, provides users with a secure, decentralized wallet supporting multiple cryptocurrencies. It is integrated seamlessly with Binance DEX and BSC, making it an indispensable tool for traders.

9.10 Ripple

Ripple is both a digital payment protocol and a cryptocurrency. The protocol, often referred to as **RippleNet**, is designed to enable real-time, cross-border payment settlements and remittances. Ripple's native cryptocurrency is called **XRP**, which is used as a bridge currency for facilitating transactions on the Ripple network. Ripple aims to provide a faster, more efficient, and cost-effective alternative to traditional banking and financial systems, especially for international transfers. Ripple was founded in 2012 by **Chris Larsen and Jed McCaleb**.

The company behind Ripple, **Ripple Labs**, focuses on working with financial institutions, banks, and payment providers to improve cross-border payment systems. Ripple was originally founded as **OpenCoin** in 2012, with the goal of creating a decentralized payment network that could offer a fast, scalable, and cost-effective way to transfer money. The project quickly gained traction, and by 2013, Ripple Labs was working with financial institutions to integrate the protocol into their existing systems. Ripple stands at the crossroads of finance and technology, forging partnerships with some of the world's most powerful financial institutions. Banks like **Santander, Standard Chartered**, and **American Express** explored Ripple's technology, recognizing its potential to revolutionize cross-border transactions. Ripple offers real-time gross settlement **(RTGS)** capabilities, making it an attractive option for global players seeking efficiency in payment systems. At the heart of this transformation lies **XRP,** Ripple's cryptocurrency. XRP is adopted by exchanges, liquidity providers, and financial institutions alike. Its speed and low transaction fees turn it into a favorite for remittances and institutional use cases. XRP soon become a bridge currency, allowing transactions between different fiat currencies without the usual intermediaries, offering a streamlined solution.

Ripple's innovation takes shape within RippleNet, a decentralized network of banks and payment providers. RippleNet offers real-time, secure, and low-cost international payments, cutting through the complexities of traditional systems like SWIFT. But unlike SWIFT, RippleNet delivers faster, more affordable solutions, positioning itself as a new force in global payments. Ripple Labs pre-mined 100 billion XRP tokens at launch, reserving a portion for itself while distributing the rest among users and institutions. Instead of relying on Proof of Work or Proof of Stake, Ripple operates on its own **Ripple Protocol Consensus Algorithm (RPCA)**. Through this consensus process, independent validators confirm transactions swiftly and with energy efficiency, bypassing the need for mining and staking. Ripple's technology doesn't stop at its consensus protocol. Its ability to process transactions in just 3 to 5 seconds and at a fraction of a cent in fees makes it highly effective for cross-border payments. Traditional banking systems struggle to keep up with such speed, and even many cryptocurrencies can't match Ripple's efficiency. The magic of Ripple lies as well in its interoperability. It isn't just a solution for crypto transactions but also bridges the **gap between fiat currencies and cryptocurrencies**. Financial institutions use XRP as a bridge, converting currencies seamlessly without multiple layers of conversions.

Ripple stands out for this feature, offering a unique advantage in a world where cross-border currency exchanges often require costly intermediaries. The inner workings of Ripple's system are as intricate as they are effective. RippleNet serves as the backbone, functioning like a next-generation version of SWIFT. But unlike its traditional counterpart, RippleNet handles the settlement of payments as well as the messaging process. RippleNet's design consists of three main components:

xCurrent, a payment processing system for real-time cross-border transactions.
xRapid, which leverages XRP as a bridge currency, enabling fast and affordable currency exchanges.
xVia, a platform that businesses and payment providers use to connect and send payments across RippleNet.

At the core of Ripple's efficiency is its system of **Validators**, a group of independent actors that confirm transactions using the RPCA protocol. Unlike Bitcoin's energy-intensive mining process, Ripple's validators ensure the network remains fast and accurate, preventing double-spending and maintaining security. Ripple explores new possibilities with its **Interledger Protocol (ILP)**. This protocol allows payments to flow seamlessly across different networks, whether they are traditional financial systems or decentralized blockchains. However, not all is perfect in Ripple's world. Centralization concerns remain a major criticism. Ripple Labs controls a significant portion of XRP, 55 billion tokens were originally placed in escrow, allowing the company to release more tokens into circulation over time. Some argue this centralization makes Ripple less decentralized than networks like Bitcoin and Ethereum.

Ripple's ongoing legal battle with the SEC adds another layer of regulatory risks.

In December 2020, the **U.S. Securities and Exchange Commission (SEC)** filed a lawsuit against Ripple, claiming that XRP was sold as an unregistered security. The legal battles started, sending Ripples down through the industry. Some exchanges delist XRP, and uncertainty shrouds Ripple's future in the U.S. market. If XRP is ruled as a security, it may face substantial hurdles in the U.S. market, affecting its liquidity and usability. Concentration of Validators also raises eyebrows. While Ripple boasts a decentralized network of validators, the number is far smaller than those of other blockchain networks. This raises questions about Ripple Labs' influence on network governance. Ripple doesn't stand alone in its mission. It faces competition from other blockchain projects, including **Stellar**, which was founded by Ripple's own co-founder, **Jed McCaleb**. Stellar offers a more decentralized solution for cross-border payments, further adding to the competitive pressures Ripple faces. And through it all, Ripple continues to build, driven by its vision of a more connected and efficient financial world.

XRP's story over the last year has been about turning endurance into momentum. The token that powers the XRP Ledger was built for fast, low-cost settlement, and through the long arc of litigation and market cycles it has kept its niche in cross-border payments and exchange liquidity. Since late 2024, that niche has widened. The ledger itself matured with features that feel less like experiments and more like durable primitives for finance, and Ripple, the company most closely associated with the ecosystem, has nudged the conversation from courtroom outcomes back to product and policy.

The most consequential thread has been regulatory closure in the United States. What began in 2020 as a sweeping enforcement action ended in August 2025 with the **SEC dropping the fight** and leaving in place a court-imposed civil penalty on Ripple alongside limits on how it can conduct institutional sales. For market participants who spent years parsing every filing for clues, the practical effect is clarity: secondary-market trading of XRP has room to operate, while institutional distribution remains fenced by securities rules. The end of the case did not change how the ledger works, but it changed who is willing to build on it, list it, and hold it without fearing a fresh legal ambush.

Even before that final chapter closed, Ripple pivoted to a product the traditional payments world understands instinctively: a dollar stablecoin. In December 2024 the company launched **RLUSD** under New York oversight, promising full backing in cash, cash equivalents, and short-dated Treasuries and positioning it for corporate treasury, settlement, and DeFi use cases. Over 2025 its footprint grew, helped by listings and integrations, and by midyear it had amassed a meaningful outstanding supply that signaled real demand rather than a press-release launch.

The XRP Ledger itself has also changed in ways that attract builders. Automated market makers moved from discussion to production, giving the ledger an integrated way to pool liquidity and price assets without handing control to an external protocol. Because the AMM is native, it inherits the ledger's performance profile and avoids the fragmentation that comes from grafted-on designs. For developers, this looks like a sturdier base layer for payments and market infrastructure rather than another DeFi side quest; for users, it means tighter spreads and deeper liquidity when moving value across currencies and tokens.

Europe provided the policy tailwind that the U.S. lacked. Through 2024 and 2025, the EU's MiCA regime took shape in operational detail, and fresh liquidity and risk-management standards for stablecoins arrived in October 2025. While MiCA is not written for XRP specifically, it sets the rules of the road for the very instruments that fund settlement on public ledgers. For a network courting banks, remitters, and corporates, this matters: regulated euros and dollars move more freely when the guardrails are explicit. It is also where Ripple's stablecoin strategy meets policy reality, aligning an on-chain dollar with the most comprehensive stablecoin framework currently in force.

With those pieces in place, adoption looks less like isolated headlines and more like a steady rise in throughput. Public stats and industry reporting through 2025 show higher transaction counts on the ledger and growing stablecoin volumes in its orbit, outcomes you would expect when compliance, core features, and a credible fiat bridge arrive together. Commerce experiments continue at the edges, from travel to retail payments, while the center of gravity remains what XRP was built for: moving value quickly between financial intermediaries and venues where spreads and latency translate directly into cost. The broader market is noisy, but the signal for XRP is that builders are returning, liquidity is thickening, and policy is shifting from ambiguity to playbook.

None of this erases the open questions. U.S. rule-making could still redraw lines around token distribution, and interest-rate cycles will change the economics of stablecoin issuers that now sit alongside XRP on the same rails. Competition for payment flows is intense, and every major chain courts the same partners with similar promises. But the texture of the past year is unmistakable. A long legal overhang finally lifted. A regulated dollar arrived beside the native asset. The base protocol gained features that feel designed for professional money. And Europe's regulatory machine put stablecoins on a footing that banks can understand. XRP enters the next cycle not as a bet on a single event, but as an increasingly complete stack for internet-scale settlement where policy, product, and throughput are starting to rhyme.

9.11 Solana

Solana is a high-performance blockchain platform designed for decentralized applications (dApps) and cryptocurrencies. It aims to solve the scalability problems that have limited the growth of other blockchain networks by providing fast transaction speeds, low fees, and high throughput. Solana's ability to process tens of thousands of transactions per second (TPS) has made it a popular choice for decentralized finance (DeFi) applications, non-fungible tokens (NFTs), metaverse-based gamings and other dApps. Solana was founded in 2017 by **Anatoly Yakovenko**, a former **Qualcomm engineer**, with the goal of creating a blockchain that could scale without relying on Layer 2 solutions or sharding. The Solana mainnet launched in March 2020, and since then, it has rapidly gained adoption due to its unique architecture and performance. **Solana Labs**, the company behind Solana, and the non-profit **Solana Foundation** work together to support the development and growth of the ecosystem. Solana's world unfolded like a finely crafted piece of engineering, each component fitting together with precision.

At its heart was the enigmatic **Proof of History (PoH)**, a feature unlike any other in the vast expanse of blockchain. Anatoly Yakovenko had devised a cryptographic clock that works like magic, allowing the network's nodes to agree on the order and time of events without needing the age-old systems of Proof of Work or Proof of Stake. It isn't just a clock, it is the heartbeat of Solana, rhythmically stamping each event and transaction, ensuring smooth and efficient communication. The chatter between nodes becomes minimal, the network swifter, more agile. In Solana's realm, validators, guardians of the network, stake their **SOL**, Solana's native currency, as a pledge of trust. Their task? To process transactions, add blocks to the ever-growing blockchain, and in return, receive a reward, tokens of SOL for their diligence. **High Throughput** is Solana defining trait, its ability to manage a staggering 50,000 to 65,000 transactions each second like a conductor leading a grand symphony. The notes of transactions play effortlessly, with no need for extra layers or sharding to ease the weight of the performance. It is seamless, fluid. Each transaction comes with low costs. Low Transaction Fees became a hallmark, a mere $0.00025 per transaction, enticing the world of decentralized finance and NFT marketplaces.

It is a world where speed meet affordability, and developers flocked to build their dreams on Solana's shoulders. Beneath this intricate dance stands **Sealevel**, the parallel runtime that allows Solana to perform the seemingly impossible: **running multiple smart contracts side by side**. Efficiency is the name of the game, and Sealevel gives the network the tools it needs to scale, to grow, and to welcome more contracts without missing a beat. But for Solana, speed is more than just a technical achievement, it is a way of life. The **Turbine Protocol** breaks data into small packets, distributing them across the network's nodes, ensuring that communication flows fast, without burdening bandwidth. It is like sending whispers on the wind, each packet finding its way swiftly, aiding Solana's pursuit of speed. And then there is **Gulf Stream**, pushing transactions toward validators before a block had even formed.

The traditional mempool, a place where transactions often wait their turn, is no longer needed. Gulf Stream gives Solana its edge, its signature fast confirmation times. The network's consensus, though, rests in the hands of **Tower BFT**, a clever variation of the **Byzantine Fault Tolerance algorithm**. It allows the network to find agreement, to reach consensus quickly and with efficiency, keeping latency low and the system's performance sharp. But Solana's journey is not just about technology, it is about building an entire world. Its Ecosystem grew with rapid momentum, drawing in developers and projects, particularly in the realms of decentralized finance, NFTs, and Web3 applications. In the burgeoning world of DeFi, protocols sprout like wildflowers, each one a testament to Solana's prowess. There is **Serum**, a decentralized exchange that thrive on Solana's infrastructure, offering fast, cost-effective trades, while **Raydium** acts as an automated market maker, weaving its liquidity into Serum's market. On the side, **Solend** stepped in, a lending and borrowing protocol reminiscent of Aave on Ethereum, but powered by Solana's speed. Then there was the world of NFTs.

Magic Eden and **Solanart** became the go-to marketplaces, their platforms bustling with the trade of digital art, collectibles, and more. Solana's low fees and quick transaction times makes it the perfect home for artists and traders alike. In the Web3 domain, applications like **Audius** emerged, offering decentralized music streaming, giving power back to artists, and rewriting the rules of content ownership. SOL is also the key to Solana's governance, a future where decisions would likely rest in the hands of its holders, guiding the network's path forward.

Solana moves into 2025 with its reliability narrative hardening alongside performance. The five-hour mainnet halt from February 6, 2024 sits in the rearview as a lesson the core teams dissect and publish openly, and the following year's engineering cadence focuses on eliminating single-client risk and smoothing congestion paths so that stability becomes the norm even on peak days. The network's local fee markets continue to do the quiet work they are designed for: keeping routine transactions inexpensive while allowing priority fees to surge only where contention actually exists, a pattern that shows up in the divergence between median and average fees during activity spikes. The result is a user experience that remains fast and predictable for most flows while still clearing the hottest state changes first.

That reliability push gathers momentum as the ecosystem prepares a second, independently engineered validator client. **Firedancer**, built by **Jump Crypto**, is not a cosmetic upgrade but a parallel implementation meant to remove single-client exposure and to open new headroom for throughput. Developers outline how the client reworks hot paths and, in recent weeks, go further by proposing to remove the fixed block-level compute unit cap after a planned consensus overhaul, letting block producers pack more work when hardware and network conditions allow. The discussion references today's 60 million compute unit ceiling and sketches a future in which block capacity adapts dynamically once the consensus layer permits safe skipping of oversized blocks. In practical terms, the aim is simple: bigger, denser blocks when the network can handle them, without punishing slower validators.

The planned consensus overhaul now has a name and a community mandate. "**Alpenglow**," introduced as **SIMD-0326**, sets out to replace the **Tower BFT** era with a design that targets sub-second confirmations and clearer safety guarantees. Validators and stakeholders debate, then advance the proposal through governance, with public materials explaining the shift and the expected rollout path: testnet first, then mainnet once battle-tested. Commentary across the ecosystem converges on the same takeaway: if Alpenglow lands as designed, confirmation latency compresses toward the 150-200 millisecond range and the chain's throughput budget becomes easier to extend in tandem with Firedancer's pipeline.

And then, fresh from the founder's keyboard, comes a jolt of product-side experimentation. **Anatoly Yakovenko** surfaces "**Percolator,**" an implementation-ready perpetuals DEX concept he invites developers to lift, fork, and evolve, casting it as a self-custodial, shared design native to Solana and pointed squarely at the hyper-efficient perps venues that dominate today's volumes. The reveal arrives through code and posts rather than a glossy launch, and within hours follow-up coverage notes that the upload doubles as an experiment–open-sourced, not an official product roadmap–yet the invitation stands: take the design, build it, and push the limits of Solana's execution model for derivatives. In the short term, Percolator functions as a signal flare to trading builders; in the longer term, it is a test of whether Solana's upcoming consensus and client upgrades can translate into market-share wins in the most latency-sensitive corner of DeFi.

9.12 USDC

USD Coin (USDC) is a stablecoin that is pegged to the U.S. dollar, designed to maintain a 1:1 value with the USD. This means that each USDC token is backed by a corresponding U.S. dollar or dollar-equivalent asset held in reserve. USDC is a key player in the stablecoin ecosystem, providing stability and liquidity in the cryptocurrency market. It was launched in 2018 by **Circle** in partnership with **Coinbase** as part of the **Centre Consortium.** USDC stands tall in the ever-shifting landscape of digital currencies, a beacon of stability in a world often ruled by volatility. Its foundation rests on a promise of transparency. Every USDC token in circulation has a dollar backing it, a quiet guarantee that builds trust. Issuers like ensure this by providing regular audits of their reserves, showing the world that each token is fully backed. It's not just about numbers, it's about faith, about building something solid in an environment where doubt often reigns. Regulation guides USDC every move, like a compass pointing toward compliance. The issuers must follow **Know Your Customer (KYC)** and **Anti-Money Laundering (AML)** regulations. This gives institutions assurance, making USDC a stable choice. USDC's reach extends beyond a single blockchain.

It embraces **Multi-Chain Support**, operating on networks like **Ethereum**, **Solana**, **Algorand**, and **Avalanche**, among others. It moves through various ecosystems, appearing on decentralized finance platforms and ensuring users have the flexibility they need. Wherever USDC goes, it delivers Fast and Low-Cost Transfers, offering speed to those using it for payments, remittances, or navigating DeFi. USDC offers liquidity as well. In Liquidity Pools, it pairs with other tokens on automated market makers like **Uniswap** and **SushiSwap**. The trades happen quickly, seamlessly, allowing users to exchange their tokens against USDC with ease. For traders, USDC serves as a safe harbor during volatile times. When market prices plummet, they rush to convert their assets into USDC, finding stability amidst the chaos. It's not just individuals who rely on USDC, Corporate and Institutional Use continues to grow around it like vines around a sturdy pillar. Businesses and institutions, often cautious of the crypto world, turn to USDC for its compliance and regulatory backing. It becomes a trusted tool for payments, treasury management, and decentralized financial services, offering a way to engage with the digital world without sacrificing security.

The mechanics of USDC operate with simplicity and elegance. Issuance occurs when a user sends U.S. dollars to an issuer, and in return, USDC is minted, one token for each dollar, always equal, always backed. When a user wants to return to fiat, Redemption happens. They send USDC back, and the issuer transfers U.S. dollars to their account, burning the tokens in the process, keeping the supply balanced. USDC's reserves sit in cash and cash-equivalents like U.S. Treasury bonds, each one carefully monitored. Third-party auditors regularly inspect these reserves, ensuring transparency and confirming that everything is in place. A brief comparison of USDC with other stablecoins highlights the unique strengths and challenges of each within the broader cryptocurrency ecosystem. While all stablecoins aim to provide price stability, their approaches to transparency, regulation, and usage vary significantly. Lets start with **USDT**. **Tether** (USDT) is the most widely used stablecoin by volume, often serving as a default option for trading across both centralized and decentralized exchanges. However, Tether has faced ongoing scrutiny regarding the transparency of its reserves and whether it is fully backed by equivalent assets. Audits of USDT have been less frequent and less detailed compared to USDC's monthly, third-party audits. This gives USDC an edge in trustworthiness, particularly among institutional users. Furthermore, USDC operates in a stricter regulatory environment, making it more appealing for those who prioritize compliance and transparency.

However, Tether's ubiquity and multi-chain support make it highly liquid, which can be an advantage in certain markets. **DAI**, unlike USDC, is a decentralized stablecoin issued by the **MakerDAO** protocol. It is algorithmically pegged to the U.S. dollar but backed by a variety of crypto assets rather than fiat currency. This decentralized nature appeals to those who seek stability without reliance on centralized issuers like **Circle** or **Coinbase**. However, DAI's stability can be more volatile during extreme market conditions, as its collateral is subject to the fluctuations of cryptocurrencies. In contrast, USDC offers a more predictable and reliable peg due to its direct 1:1 backing with U.S. dollars. While DAI is favored in decentralized finance (DeFi) for its decentralized structure, USDC's full collateralization and regulatory compliance provide greater reassurance for institutional users and those seeking more stable collateral in financial applications.

Since mid-2024, the European Union has been the loudest proving ground for USDC trust. When the EU's MiCA regime for crypto assets came into force for stablecoins, Circle reorganized in Europe, obtained an **electronic money institution license in France**, and became the first global stablecoin issuer to declare MiCA compliance for both **USDC** and its euro sibling, **EURC**. That status isn't just a press headline, it means USDC can be marketed and used across the bloc under a harmonized playbook with disclosures, supervision and reserve rules that look much more like mainstream payments than speculative crypto. It is a compliance moat and a sales brochure rolled into one.

The other proving ground has been public markets. After an abandoned **SPAC** attempt years ago, **Circle** finally listed on the New York Stock Exchange in June 2025 under the ticker **CRCL**, raising roughly a billion dollars in an upsized IPO and debuting to outsized demand. Later in the summer, Circle even launched a secondary offering, signaling both a taste for growth capital and confidence that the market would absorb more shares. The listing forced a new level of transparency: quarterly results, reserve income detail, and circulation disclosures became routine. For a company whose product is a promise to redeem, the discipline of public reporting creates another layer of accountability on top of audits and regulator scrutiny.

Those disclosures tell the adoption story in numbers. Circle reported USDC in circulation of about **$61 billion** at the end of Q2 2025, climbing above **$65 billion** by August and, by early October, third-party trackers showed USDC pushing past **$74 billion**. Revenue and reserve income have risen with scale, helping Circle publish materially higher top-line figures year over year. The headline is simple: after a difficult 2023, USDC's float expanded meaningfully through 2024 and 2025, even as competition intensified.

Regulation in the United States remains the great unfinished chapter. Congress flirted with a federal stablecoin framework in 2024, and the policy mood shifted in 2025 toward a more permissive stance, but comprehensive law is still not settled. Instead, Circle has treated compliance as a product feature, audited reserves in cash and short-dated Treasuries, regulated entities where possible, and white papers and risk summaries where mandated, so that when rules arrive, the operational posture already fits the mold.

9.13 Tron

The genesis of TRON traces back to a singular ambition: to build a blockchain platform capable of handling large-scale content and value flows, with ambitions to broaden the internet's ledger layer beyond mere cryptocurrency. In early 2017, founder **Justin Sun** formalized the vision with the creation of the **TRON Foundation in Singapore**, and by May 2018 the **TRON mainnet** had launched, marking the token's transition from an ERC-20 on Ethereum to an independent chain. In that early phase TRON promised decentralised content distribution, entertainment applications, and a high-throughput infrastructure where smart contracts could scale.

TRON enables content creators to cut out intermediaries, allowing them to directly connect with consumers and receive rewards in the form of **TRX** (its native cryptocurrency). The TRON network supports decentralized applications (dApps) and smart contracts, making it comparable to Ethereum, though it boasts higher transaction throughput and lower fees. It utilizes a **Delegated Proof of Stake (DPoS)** consensus mechanism for faster and more efficient processing.

TRON grew rapidly, first by acquiring the peer-to-peer file-sharing service **BitTorrent**, Inc., then by aggressively marketing itself as a "**content blockchain**" and attracting dApps, especially gaming and gambling platforms. The network has expanded its ecosystem with DeFi, NFTs, and stablecoins, including its own algorithmic stablecoin, **USDD**.

By the mid-2020s TRON's identity had shifted. Its most important function was no longer just content distribution but serving as one of the world's most active platforms for stablecoins, settlement and micropayments. The network's design, high transaction volume, relatively low fees, many active users, fit the contour of global money flows rather than purely speculative tokens. That transition was unmistakable in 2025. Analytics reported that TRON ranked among the top chains globally for daily active users and transaction count, with millions of daily users and billions of transactions since inception. The chain's dominance in retail-sized stablecoin transfers (those below US$1,000) became a headline: in third quarter of 2025 TRON reportedly handled a majority share in that niche, evidencing its function as a "money rail".

At the same time core protocol upgrades reinforced the shift. **TRON's mainnet V4.8.0 upgrade in June 2025** improved cross-chain compatibility, and later in August the network approved a community governance decision that slashed energy/transaction fees by roughly 60 percent while implementing a dynamic fee model. These changes lowered friction for micropayments and developer use cases, reinforcing the notion that TRON was migrating from "blockchain curiosity" to "financial infrastructure".

Regulation and real-world settlement began to cast long shadows, not all positive. Critics pointed out that because TRON was so efficient for moving value, it also became attractive for less scrupulous flows. One high-profile report claimed that in 2024 TRON was the preferred channel for illicit crypto transfers in parts of Asia, raising questions about how a high-throughput chain balances openness with compliance. In parallel, research also highlighted that the ecosystem's emphasis on stablecoins and tokenized value meant that its architecture and data flows deserved fresh scrutiny.

Yet the real story of TRON in 2025 is institutional maturation. The network is increasingly treated like a settlement layer by a variety of players: remitters, fintech firms, decentralised finance (DeFi) protocols and tokenization platforms. Its total value locked, number of active accounts, and transaction volumes all surged. It is no longer just a contender, it is quietly entrenched. The combined research shows that in September 2025 the

Ethereum and TRON chains together processed nearly two-thirds of all stablecoin transaction volume globally, a metric of scale that few had foreseen from the platform's original entertainment-blockchain framing.

Through this evolution the native token TRX plays many roles: governance stake, fee currency, and alignment device for network growth. But perhaps the more interesting shift is in how the ecosystem is built: developers are prioritizing features like liquidity, cross-chain bridges, super-low fee micropayments and integrated stablecoins rather than hype-based token launches. TRON's settlement story is less glamorous than some rival media narratives, but more durable.

9.14 Lido Staked Ether

Lido Staked Ether (stETH) is a token that represents staked Ethereum (ETH) in the Lido network. When you stake ETH using Lido, you receive **stETH** in return. This token represents your staked ETH plus any accrued staking rewards. Ethereum 2.0 introduces a proof-of-stake (PoS) mechanism, where validators need to stake ETH to secure the network. Staking directly requires a minimum of 32 ETH and involves running a validator node, which can be complex and resource-intensive. Lido's Role is to allow users to stake ETH without needing to run their own validator nodes.

Instead, Lido pools users' ETH and manages the staking process on their behalf. When you deposit ETH into Lido you receive an equivalent amount of stETH. This isn't just a token, it's a reflection of your staked ETH, growing steadily over time as staking rewards accrue. The value of stETH quietly appreciates, a mirror of the expanding ETH balance that sits behind it, each moment a little richer than the last. But unlike traditional staking, where your funds might feel like they've been locked in a vault, stETH provides liquidity. It's not confined, not tethered. You can freely trade it or use it in decentralized finance (DeFi) applications, giving you flexibility while your ETH keeps earning rewards. If you wish to turn it back into ETH, Lido's platform or secondary markets await you, though you may encounter slight delays or shifts in value due to market conditions. In this transparent world, Lido offers a clear view of the stakes, how much ETH is currently staked, the rewards earned, and other vital metrics. Nothing hides in shadows here. The Benefits of Using stETH unfold like a map to ease and opportunity.

There's no need to worry about the complexities of managing validator nodes or diving into the intricacies of Ethereum 2.0 staking. The liquidity and flexibility of stETH means you can leverage it in various DeFi protocols while still enjoying staking rewards, a balance of earning and freedom. And with diversification, users find themselves staking ETH without sacrificing the chance to explore other DeFi opportunities. But every opportunity comes with its Risks and Considerations. There's the ever-present specter of Smart Contract Risk, lurking in the underlying technology of DeFi services. Market Risk casts its shadow too, as the value of stETH may not always perfectly match ETH due to market forces. And of course, the evolving Regulatory Risk hovers, a reminder that the rules surrounding DeFi and staking services are still being written. Lido, however, stands firm with its governance and security. A decentralized autonomous organization (DAO) leads its decisions, with LDO token holders guiding the protocol's future. Security measures are always in place, from audits to bug bounty programs, fortifying Lido against threats and keeping user funds safe.

9.15 Dogecoin

Meanwhile, in the world of Dogecoin, the atmosphere is playful yet unexpectedly impactful. Born from a joke in **December 2013,** Dogecoin enters the scene as a "fun" and "light-hearted" alternative to Bitcoin. Crafted by software engineers **Billy Markus** and **Jackson Palmer**, it draws inspiration from the viral **Doge meme**, featuring the ever-charming Shiba Inu. What begins as a joke quickly evolves into something more. Dogecoin grows into a widely recognized digital asset, with a community that radiates creativity and warmth. Known for its charitable spirit, the Dogecoin community organizes donation initiatives, tipping content creators online, and even sponsoring high-profile events like a **NASCAR** driver and the 2014 Winter Olympics. Humor mixes with genuine impact as the community leaves its mark. Social Media Influence breathes life into

Dogecoin's price and popularity. Influencers and celebrities, most notably **Elon Musk**, bring their weight to the coin, causing waves of attention and, with it, inevitable price fluctuations. Behind Dogecoin's lighthearted surface, serious technology drives it. Like Bitcoin, Dogecoin operates on a blockchain, using the Proof-of-Work (PoW) consensus mechanism. Miners solve complex mathematical problems, verifying transactions and keeping the network secure.

But unlike Bitcoin, Dogecoin's Supply knows no limit. Initially capped, the decision to remove the maximum supply unleashes an infinite flow of Dogecoins, over 140 billion of which are already in circulation. Dogecoin's pace is quicker too, with a Block Time of roughly one minute, far faster than Bitcoin's ten-minute block time. This speed allows for rapid transaction confirmation, giving Dogecoin an edge in day-to-day usability. It runs on the **Scrypt hashing algorithm**, designed to be more memory-intensive and resistant to specialized mining hardware, though over time, **ASICs (Application-Specific Integrated Circuits)** have found their way into Dogecoin mining. Use Cases and Adoption of Dogecoin might surprise those who see it as just a meme. It's used for tipping and donations, with users showing appreciation for content creators or supporting charitable causes through Dogecoin. Some retailers and online services even accept it as payment, and while Dogecoin rides the wave of being a memecoin, its influence stretches into real-world use, beyond the volatile ups and downs driven by social media trends. But Dogecoin's development isn't as robust as some other cryptocurrencies.

The Development Team largely relies on volunteers, with the original creators having stepped back. Governance is informal, shaped by community discussions and proposals rather than any formal structure. It's a digital democracy of sorts, powered by those who care enough to keep it alive.

Yet, as with all things in the crypto world, Dogecoin comes with Risks and Considerations. Volatility is a constant companion–prices soar and plummet on the whims of market sentiment and internet trends. Its limited development raises concerns too, without steady innovation, Dogecoin lags behind other, more advanced projects. And then there's the speculative nature of Dogecoin. Its price is often driven by speculation rather than tangible value, creating opportunities for rapid gains but also for devastating losses.

9.16 Cardano and ADA

Cardano is a third-generation blockchain platform focused on creating a more secure, scalable, and sustainable environment for decentralized applications (dApps) and smart contracts. Developed by **IOHK** and founded by **Charles Hoskinson**, it aims to improve upon the inefficiencies of earlier blockchains like Bitcoin (first gen) and Ethereum (second gen). Cardano was built from the ground up with a deliberate, phased approach, each phase named after a great figure from literature or philosophy, reflecting both technological and intellectual ambition. The journey began with **Byron**, moved into **Shelley**, and then unfolded into **Goguen**, with later eras such as **Basho** and **Voltaire** continuing the evolution.

At its core, **ADA** is more than a medium of exchange. It's a governance and participation instrument within one of the most formally designed blockchains in existence. Unlike Bitcoin, which relies on proof-of-work mining, ADA is secured through **Ouroboros**, Cardano's proprietary proof-of-stake protocol. Ouroboros was the first consensus algorithm to be peer-reviewed by academics and mathematically proven to be secure, combining energy efficiency with robust decentralization. Holders of ADA can "delegate" their stake to community-run pools or operate their own, earning rewards for helping to maintain the network, a model that aligns security with participation rather than hardware power.

Another defining feature is Cardano's layered architecture. The blockchain is split into two functional layers: the **Settlement Layer** (for ADA transactions) and the Computational Layer (for smart contracts). This separation allows Cardano to update one layer without disrupting the other, a modular design that supports long-term scalability and regulatory flexibility. It also allows for compliance-friendly applications, since transaction logic and value transfer can be managed independently.

ADA's governance utility is increasingly central. Through Cardano's on-chain voting framework, holders influence protocol upgrades, treasury spending, and governance decisions, transforming ADA from a passive asset into a voting right. As the **Voltaire** era progresses, ADA becomes the key to the network's constitutional democracy, where token holders collectively decide how Cardano evolves.

Economically, ADA is designed for sustainability. A portion of every transaction fee goes into a treasury that funds community proposals. This self-financing mechanism means that, over time, Cardano can continue to develop without depending on external investors or foundations, a contrast to many chains that rely on perpetual fundraising.

Finally, ADA benefits from Cardano's formal development approach. Every major feature is peer-reviewed and modeled in **Haskell**, a functional programming language known for mathematical precision. This gives ADA's ecosystem an academic backbone, slow, perhaps, but deliberately verifiable, aiming to reduce vulnerabilities that have plagued faster-moving competitors.

9.17 Hype and Hyperliquid

The story of Hyperliquid begins with a simple question: what if the speed, functionality and user experience of a centralized derivatives exchange could be delivered on-chain, without sacrificing transparency, self-custody or decentralised trust? Founded by alumni of places like **Harvard**, **Caltech**, **MIT** and top trading-firms, the team behind Hyperliquid chose not to fork an existing chain or copy an AMM model. Instead they built a dedicated Layer-1 designed for high-performance perpetual trading, low latency, high throughput, on-chain order-books, custom consensus. The result was a platform positioned at the intersection of CeFi and DeFi: familiar to active traders yet built for blockchain native flows.

What sets Hyperliquid apart is its deep innovation in the perpetual futures domain. Unlike many DEXs that rely on automated-market-maker (AMM) designs, Hyperliquid uses a **fully on-chain order-book** matching engine and its own consensus system (**HyperBFT**) to achieve sub-second block finality, minimal slippage and tight spreads. Trading on more than 100 assets, with up to 40-50× leverage and margin/cross-margin support, it offers the kind of infrastructure previously reserved for premier centralized venues, but in a self-custodial, non-custodial setting. Liquidity, order execution, matching, liquidation mechanics: all engineered for serious traders. When the derivative volumes began escalating into billions of dollars of daily open interest, the platform's architecture proved its thesis.

The native token **HYPE** embodies two dynamics: utility and speculative narrative. On the utility side, HYPE is used for governance, staking, fee discounts, liquidity incentives and buy-back mechanisms built into the ecosystem. But the narrative side is what caught the market's imagination. In a matter of months, HYPE's market cap vaulted to roughly

$12.9 billion, reflecting both token supply economics and intense demand for exposure to a platform gaining scale. The token's rise was catalyzed by a sequence of events: record daily trading volumes (for example one day surpassing $29 billion in perpetual volume), major institutional interest (public firms redirecting holdings into HYPE), and strategic announcements about native stablecoin launches (in particular the proposed **USDH** stablecoin with 95% of its reserve yield directed into HYPE buy-backs). Each of these signaled to markets that Hyperliquid was not a niche DEX but a core piece of the next-gen financial rails.

Why did HYPE become so valuable so fast? First, because the product-market fit in derivatives is ruthless: traders reward latency, cost, liquidity. Hyperliquid delivered both speed and volume, making it a rare DeFi venue that genuinely scaled. Second, because token-economics aligned with growth: buy-backs, stake incentives, protocol revenue sharing all pointed toward a scarcity and yield story, which in crypto markets drives valuation fast. Third, because narratives matured: institutional players began to treat Hyperliquid as part of the infrastructure stack rather than merely a speculative project. When publicly-listed firms announce accumulation of HYPE and asset-services launch custody for it, value perception leaps. Lastly, because the broader crypto ecosystem recognized that derivatives are where large capital flows move; if you build the rails that carry those flows, you capture not just fee income but network effects, data advantages and optionality for future services.

Yet this accelerated ascent also raises questions. High valuation imposes very high expectations: execution must remain flawless, risk management rigorous, regulatory landscape favourable. Derivative platforms bear outsized liability if things go wrong: liquidations stack up, algorithms misfire, user funds are at stake. Token holders will ask: does revenue sustain the valuation? Are buy-backs reliable? How decentralized is the system really if speed is the priority? And finally: can the narrative hold once volume growth slows or competition moves in?

In conclusion, Hyperliquid and HYPE together represent a **striking case**: when you identify a high-ruthless niche (perpetual futures), build a high-performance chain tailored for it, and align token mechanics with growth and scarcity, value can surge quickly. The journey from launch to multi-billion-dollar valuation in months didn't happen by chance. It happened because infrastructure matters, because traders care about execution, and because token markets reward credible rails for money movement. As Hyperliquid transitions from early momentum toward sustained infrastructure, the real test will be whether volume, protocol revenues and user-trust all scale in tandem with the valuation.

9.18 Bitcoin Cash

Bitcoin Cash (BCH) is a cryptocurrency created in 2017 as a fork of Bitcoin (BTC) to address issues of scalability and transaction speed. Its primary goal is to offer faster, cheaper transactions compared to Bitcoin by increasing the block size from 1 MB to 8 MB (and later to 32 MB). This allows Bitcoin Cash to handle more transactions per second, making it more suitable for everyday payments and commerce. While it shares the same underlying technology as Bitcoin, Bitcoin Cash emphasizes being a peer-to-peer electronic cash system. BCH supporters view it as a true representation of Satoshi Nakamoto's original vision. However, the fork led to ideological divides within the Bitcoin community, with some preferring Bitcoin's focus on security and decentralization over BCH's approach to scalability. Despite this, Bitcoin Cash has grown to become a prominent cryptocurrency, accepted by various merchants and platforms worldwide.

9.19 Chailink

Chainlink is a decentralized oracle network that enables smart contracts on various blockchains to securely interact with real-world data, APIs, and external systems. It acts as a bridge between blockchain environments and external data sources, making it possible for smart contracts to execute based on real-time information like prices, weather, or events. Chainlink's decentralized nature ensures the accuracy, reliability, and tamper-resistance of the data it provides. The network uses a system of independent node operators who retrieve and verify data from multiple sources, reducing single points of failure. Chainlink's flexibility allows it to be integrated across different blockchain platforms and is widely used in DeFi (Decentralized Finance) for secure price feeds. The project has become a cornerstone of smart contract applications, enabling more complex and trustworthy automation.

9.20 USDE

USDe emerged as a new class of stablecoin–synthetic, yield-bearing, and backed not by cash but by over-collateralized crypto and derivatives. Created by **Ethena Lab**s, it sought to merge stability with yield, using delta-neutral strategies that generated returns from futures markets while maintaining a soft dollar peg. The model promised a "yielding dollar," attracting rapid adoption through early 2025 as supply surged into the tens of billions.

Unlike fiat-backed peers such as USDC or USDT, USDe's innovation was its structure: algorithmic hedging and funding-rate income replaced bank reserves, making it capital-efficient but also market-sensitive. That sensitivity was exposed in October 2025 when, during a sharp crypto downturn, USDe briefly slipped to $0.65 on one exchange before rebounding. Ethena reassured users that redemption and collateral mechanisms held, yet the event reminded markets that yield comes with complexity.

Even after volatility, USDe's footprint kept growing, integrated into DeFi protocols, listed on major exchanges, and embraced as an on-chain yield instrument. Its trajectory now defines a new frontier: stablecoins that behave less like tokenized dollars and more like programmable money markets. The challenge ahead lies in proving that innovation and resilience can coexist–keeping the dollar's trust while reinventing its form.

9.21 Stellar

Stellar, a decentralized, open-source blockchain, rises into the world of digital finance in **2014**, with a clear purpose etched into its core. It is designed not just as another cryptocurrency, but as a bridge, a way to connect the vast and often inaccessible world of traditional banking with the fluid, rapidly evolving world of blockchain technology. Behind it all stands **Jed McCaleb**, who once helped birth **Ripple**, now turning his focus toward something new: financial access for those who have long been underbanked, left out of the global economy's digital revolution.

The **Stellar Development Foundation (SDF)**, the driving force behind Stellar's creation, sets out with a mission. They want to tear down the walls that separate people from financial services, creating a system where sending money across borders is as easy as sending a text. At the heart of this system lies **Lumens (XLM)**, Stellar's native token, designed to pay transaction fees and ensure the network's smooth operation. The primary use of Stellar is clear from the start: fast, low-cost international transfers. Here, institutions find a way to tokenize fiat and other assets, allowing for the seamless movement of value across the globe. Transaction speed becomes one of Stellar's trademarks. Thousands of transactions move through the network every second, each one settling in the blink of an eye, usually within 2 to 5 seconds. But speed isn't everything. Low fees define the experience on Stellar. Transactions cost mere fractions of a cent, making it not only ideal for large transfers but also for the micro-transactions that other systems struggle to handle. Behind the scenes, Stellar's unique Consensus Mechanism sets it apart. Instead of relying on the power-hungry mining systems of Bitcoin or Ethereum, Stellar operates using the **Stellar Consensus Protocol (SCP)**. With SCP, quorum slices come into play, validating transactions in a more energy-efficient and decentralized way. There is no need for traditional mining here, Stellar moves at the pace of consensus. Stellar's reach extends beyond just crypto. It boldly supports fiat integration, opening the door for the issuance of stablecoins and digital versions of fiat currencies. The line between traditional money and digital assets blurs, as Stellar makes it easier than ever to convert between the two worlds. Its partnerships only fuel this mission.

IBM becomes a powerful ally, teaming up with Stellar to launch World Wire, a cross-border payment system aimed at revolutionizing how money moves across nations. Other financial institutions soon follow, recognizing the potential Stellar holds in transforming global finance. Though the **Stellar Development Foundation** guides much of its growth, Stellar remains decentralized. Validators, scattered across the globe, work to keep the network secure and running smoothly. These decentralized nodes, along with anchors, trusted entities on the network that issue fiat tokens, provide the essential link between fiat and crypto, ensuring that the network never loses its connection to the real world. While smart contracts on Stellar aren't as complex as those found on platforms like Ethereum, they serve their purpose well. Asset issuance and transfers become easy, smooth processes, allowing developers to create and manage custom tokens with a few simple commands. It's a system designed for efficiency, one that prioritizes ease of use and accessibility. But Stellar never loses sight of the need for compliance.

In its ecosystem, Stellar is not just a payment network. It houses decentralized exchanges (DEX), allowing users to trade assets directly on the network without needing to leave the Stellar environment. Use cases stretch far beyond remittances, they include microfinance, mobile payments, and the tokenization of assets, with Stellar positioning itself as a versatile platform for all types of financial applications. Governance decisions remain largely in the hands of the **Stellar Development Foundation**, but the community's voice is always welcomed. Stellar fosters an environment where users can contribute ideas, shaping the future of the network. Through it all, Stellar's vision never wavers. It seeks to create a financial system that includes everyone, one that makes money transfers seamless and accessible to anyone, anywhere.

Between 2024 and 2025, Stellar (XLM) entered a period of rapid expansion and technical refinement. The Stellar Development Foundation set an ambitious goal to bring roughly $3 billion worth of real-world assets on-chain by the end of 2025, up from less than $300 million a year earlier, signaling a major push toward tokenizing tangible value on its network.

During the same period, Stellar's technology stack matured significantly. Its smart-contract platform, **Soroban**, evolved into a production-ready environment, while new developer tools such as Lab 3.0 (and the upcoming 4.0 release) improved usability and scalability. Network upgrades focused on throughput, targeting performance benchmarks near 5,000 transactions per second, positioning Stellar as a faster and more developer-friendly blockchain for payments and tokenized assets.

In October 2025, the network prepared for its **Protocol 24 mainnet upgrade,** a maintenance-focused update aimed at enhancing stability and addressing core state-archival bugs. While not a feature-heavy release, it reinforced Stellar's reputation for reliability as it moved deeper into real-world finance, bridging regulated assets, payments, and on-chain liquidity within a trusted ecosystem.

9.22 Sui

Sui arrived in the blockchain world with a clean design and a bold ambition: to rethink how digital assets move, interact, and scale. Developed by **Mysten Labs**, a team of former Meta engineers who had worked on the **Diem and Move projects,** Sui is a Layer-1 blockchain built from the ground up for speed, parallel execution, and a more intuitive object-based data model. Its name, derived from the Japanese word for "water," captures the guiding metaphor–fluidity, adaptability, and constant motion.

At its core, Sui uses the **Move programming language**, originally designed for Meta's abandoned Diem project. Move is what sets Sui apart from most other blockchains. Instead of treating assets as mere account balances, Sui models them as distinct "objects" with ownership and state. This structure allows the network to execute transactions that do not depend on each other in parallel rather than sequentially. The result is exceptional scalability: while traditional blockchains line up transactions in a single queue, Sui processes many simultaneously, dramatically increasing throughput and lowering latency.

Sui's consensus mechanism, **Narwhal and Bullshark**, is another architectural innovation. Narwhal handles data availability and ordering, ensuring every node sees the same transaction history, while Bullshark determines final consensus. This dual-layer approach allows the system to maintain both high speed and strong security, even under heavy demand. In real-world terms, Sui achieves sub-second finality for simple transfers and maintains high efficiency even as usage scales, a key difference from chains that slow down under congestion.

Functionally, Sui positions itself as a general-purpose blockchain for digital assets and on-chain applications, with a particular focus on user experience. Developers can design apps and games where assets–such as NFTs, tokens, or in-game items–behave like real digital objects: ownable, tradable, and programmable. This makes Sui a natural home for next-generation Web3 apps that require high performance, like gaming, social networks, and finance products that rely on fast, low-cost interactions.

Another distinct feature is Sui's emphasis on horizontal scalability rather than monolithic upgrades. As demand grows, validators can simply add more processing power to handle parallel transactions, a design that mirrors cloud computing elasticity more than traditional blockchain scaling. It also supports dynamic gas pricing, which adjusts automatically to prevent fee spikes during network surges.

The difference, ultimately, is philosophical as much as technical. Sui treats digital assets as programmable resources rather than entries in a ledger, aiming for an internet of owned objects rather than accounts. Its combination of object-centric logic, parallel execution, and instant settlement makes it stand out in a field dominated by sequential blockchains. In a landscape crowded with L1s chasing throughput through shortcuts, Sui's architecture feels deliberate and durable–an infrastructure built not merely for transactions, but for an evolving digital economy where ownership, speed, and usability must coexist.

9.23 Shiba Inu

Shiba Inu (SHIB) is a decentralized cryptocurrency launched in August 2020 as an Ethereum-based token. Originally created as a meme coin inspired by the Shiba Inu dog breed, it has grown into a prominent player in the crypto space. SHIB is part of a larger ecosystem, including other tokens like **LEASH** and **BONE**. Unlike traditional cryptocurrencies, Shiba Inu gained popularity through its community-driven approach and widespread social media attention. The **ShibaSwap** decentralized exchange allows users to trade SHIB and stake their assets for rewards. Its total supply started at one quadrillion, with a large portion sent to Ethereum co-founder Vitalik Buterin, who burned a significant amount. Shiba Inu aims to rival Dogecoin, and its passionate community, known as the "Shiba Army," supports its growth. It has become more than a meme, seeking to expand into utility-focused ventures like NFTs and decentralized finance (DeFi). Despite its humble beginnings, Shiba Inu continues to evolve in the crypto ecosystem.

9.24 Avalanche and Avax

Avalanche, launched by **Ava Labs** in 2020 under the direction of Cornell computer scientist **Emin Gün Sirer**, set out to prove that a blockchain could be fast, decentralized, and scalable all at once. Its native token, **AVAX,** fuels this ecosystem, used for transaction fees, staking rewards, governance, and securing the network's expanding constellation of subnets. By 2025, AVAX had grown into one of the top Layer-1 assets, underpinning a vibrant DeFi, gaming, and tokenization landscape across hundreds of applications and millions of daily transactions.

At the heart of Avalanche lies its breakthrough consensus protocol, a probabilistic, gossip-based mechanism that lets validators repeatedly query one another until consensus is achieved. This design allows the network to process thousands of transactions per second with sub-second finality, positioning Avalanche among the fastest blockchains in existence. Built on proof-of-stake rather than proof-of-work, it is highly energy-efficient while remaining secure and decentralized.

Avalanche's architecture consists of three interoperable chains: the **X-Chain** for asset creation and exchange, the **C-Chain** for Ethereum-compatible smart contracts, and the **P-Chain** for coordinating validators and managing subnets, custom blockchains that operate under Avalanche's shared security. Subnets are the platform's signature innovation, enabling institutions, developers, and even governments to launch blockchains with tailored compliance, performance, or privacy needs, all connected by AVAX as the settlement and staking layer.

AVAX plays a central economic role. Validators must stake it to participate in consensus, earning rewards proportionate to uptime and reliability. Transaction fees, governance proposals, and subnet creation all require AVAX, giving the token intrinsic utility and deflationary dynamics through periodic fee burning. As demand for subnets and DeFi activity rises, AVAX becomes the scarce resource that anchors the network's economy.

In practice, Avalanche has evolved into a high-performance financial ecosystem, hosting blue-chip DeFi protocols such as **Aave** and **Curve**, NFT marketplaces, and tokenized real-world assets. Its speed, modularity, and Ethereum compatibility attract both developers and institutions seeking an efficient yet decentralized base layer. What distinguishes Avalanche is not just throughput–it is the architectural elegance of scaling through parallel subnets rather than external layers, creating a cohesive, multi-chain network unified by one token.

In essence, Avalanche and AVAX embody a new model of blockchain infrastructure: modular, fast, and institution-ready. It delivers the usability of centralized systems with the trustless design of decentralization, positioning itself as a foundation for the next generation of on-chain finance and programmable economies.

9.25 Litecoin

Litecoin (LTC) is a decentralized cryptocurrency created by Charlie Lee in 2011 as a lighter, faster version of Bitcoin. It operates on a peer-to-peer network using a modified Bitcoin codebase, aiming to enable faster transaction times and lower fees. Litecoin uses the **Scrypt hashing algorithm**, which is less resource-intensive than Bitcoin's SHA-256, allowing for easier mining by individuals without specialized hardware. The total supply of Litecoin is capped at 84 million, four times that of Bitcoin. It shares many technical similarities with Bitcoin, such as its proof-of-work consensus mechanism, but processes blocks every 2.5 minutes, compared to Bitcoin's 10 minutes, making transactions quicker. Litecoin is often considered a "silver to Bitcoin's gold" due to its complementary role in the cryptocurrency space.

It has gained adoption for micropayments and everyday transactions, thanks to its lower fees and faster speeds. While it doesn't have the same market dominance as Bitcoin, Litecoin remains a significant player in the crypto ecosystem. The network is secured through decentralized nodes, and Litecoin also adopted technologies like **SegWit** and the Lightning Network for scalability. Though it lacks the extensive ecosystem of Ethereum or Bitcoin, it has maintained a stable presence as a reliable medium of exchange in the crypto market.

9.26 Monero

Monero emerges in 2014, carving out a space in the vast world of cryptocurrencies, one that prioritizes privacy above all else. Its decentralized blockchain hums with activity, ensuring that every transaction remains secure, private, and untraceable, far from the prying eyes of outsiders. At the heart of Monero lies privacy, its defining feature. Advanced cryptographic techniques form the bedrock of this secrecy. **Ring Signatures**, **Stealth Addresses**, and **RingCT (Confidential Transactions)** blur the lines, hiding details that would otherwise be visible on most blockchains. The sender, the receiver, the transaction amount, all of it shrouded in mystery, known only to those involved. It's a cloak of invisibility for digital transactions. With this level of anonymity comes fungibility. Every Monero coin, indistinguishable from the next, moves through the network free from any past associations. Unlike other cryptocurrencies that can be tainted by their transaction history, Monero coins are always clean, always equal. Monero's foundation is rooted in decentralization. It belongs to no one and everyone all at once. It begins without pre-mining, without any unfair advantage given to early adopters, allowing all users to stand on equal ground from the very beginning. Mining Monero isn't a task reserved for those with specialized equipment. Instead, its **Proof-of-Work (PoW)** consensus algorithm, enhanced by **RandomX**, favors the average user.

CPU mining reigns here, as Monero stays true to its vision of decentralization, making the process accessible and resisting the dominance of ASIC miners. The soul of Monero is open-source. Developers from across the world contribute to its evolution, driven not by profit but by a shared belief in privacy and freedom. The community, global and resilient, keeps Monero alive, pushing updates and improvements forward. Unlike Bitcoin's transparent ledger, where addresses and amounts are visible to all, **Monero hides everything**. The sender's address disappears into the ether, the amount traded veiled from view. It's a stark contrast to the openness of other blockchains, creating a delicate dance between privacy and transparency. For Monero, privacy is paramount. Only the parties involved in a transaction know its details. There are no third parties, no intermediaries. Monero places the power squarely in the hands of its users, a silent promise that no one else will ever know. But with this power comes challenges.

Behind Monero stands a community, strong and global, a network of developers and users who believe fiercely in its mission. They maintain it, nurture it, push it forward. Updates are constant, each one sharpening Monero's edges, improving its privacy, security, and performance. Despite the challenges, adoption grows. Merchants, valuing the anonymity it provides, begin accepting Monero for payments. Donations flow in, drawn by the privacy that Monero promises.

The costs of using Monero are low. Its transaction fees, thanks to the adaptive block size, remain modest. No exorbitant fees here–just a quiet, efficient network that keeps churning out secure transactions. For those on the go, **Monerujo** becomes a companion. A popular mobile wallet for Monero, it allows users to send and receive their private coins with ease, keeping the spirit of Monero close at hand. Monero continues to evolve, embracing **Atomic Swaps**, a technology that allows for seamless cross-chain swaps. Monero moves easily between chains, opening doors to other cryptocurrencies, enhancing its interoperability in a world that values connections. Its deflationary supply adds another layer of intrigue. Monero, like a treasure chest with a fixed number of gold coins, will one day stop growing. Its capped supply ensures that as demand rises, so too will its value, each coin becoming a little more precious over time. Regulatory pressure never leaves Monero's side. As governments tighten their grip on cryptocurrency regulation, Monero's anonymity remains a sticking point. Some exchanges have backed away, bowing to the pressure, but Monero stays the course. For those who value privacy, it remains a beacon, popular and enduring despite the forces arrayed against it.

9.27 Crypto.com and CRO

CRO is the native token of the **Cronos Chain** and the broader ecosystem of **Crypto.com**. The token's identity is intertwined with the transition of Crypto.com from a crypto exchange and payments platform into a full-blown blockchain ecosystem. Initially, CRO served as the utility token inside Crypto.com's exchange, payments, wallets and card services. Over time it evolved into the on-chain fuel for

Cronos and the gateway token for a range of DeFi, Web3 and payments applications. The core technology of the Cronos chain is a **Proof-of-Stake (PoS)** network compatible with the **Ethereum Virtual Machine (EVM)**, meaning that smart contracts, tokens and dApps originally built for Ethereum can deploy onto Cronos with minimal friction. This compatibility, combined with low fees and optimized performance, enables CRO to act as the gas token on the network, support staking and enable governance. Users staking CRO delegate to validators on the Cronos PoS chain and earn rewards for supporting block creation. In the Crypto.com ecosystem, holding or staking CRO enables fee discounts, card-tier benefits, access to premium services, and participation in token-economics of the network.

What makes CRO different is the dual role it plays. Unlike many tokens that only power a blockchain or only serve as an exchange utility, CRO spans both worlds: it is the work-horse for a blockchain platform (Cronos) and the economic anchor of a large payments/exchange infrastructure (Crypto.com). As a result, CRO's value proposition includes payments-adoption, staking yield, network effect from DeFi & NFT activity, and consumer-financial services utilities. Furthermore, the recent strategic announcements elevated its profile: for example, a prominent media and treasury deal announced in August 2025 saw major institutions commit to holding and integrating CRO, underlining its emerging role as a treasury asset and utility token in media/

web-platform integrations. This kind of alignment between platform utility, consumer finance, network-growth and institutional narrative is rare.

In practice, owning CRO means you can pay for services inside the Crypto.com ecosystem, stake it to earn rewards and moderate governance, use it on the Cronos chain to fuel smart-contract transactions, and benefit from future growth of the network infrastructure. It is designed to scale as the ecosystem expands into DeFi, NFTs, payments and tokenized services. The architecture emphasises EVM-compatibility for ease of development, low transaction cost for user-friendliness, and staking/delegation for security and decentralization. This combination means CRO is not just another utility token but a branching instrument that ties together payments, infrastructure and decentralised applications.

In summary, CRO distinguishes itself by bridging consumer finance and blockchain infrastructure. Its technology base (Cronos chain), its function (gas, staking, utility, governance) and its ecosystem (Crypto.com and beyond) combine to create a token aimed not just at speculative activity but at real-world usage and network growth. Its uniqueness lies in this multi-dimensional role–enabling payments, powering a chain, aligning incentives for users, validators and service providers–and positioning CRO as more than a token: it is the axis of a converging crypto-ecosystem built for scale.

9.28 Toncoin

Toncoin (TON) is the native cryptocurrency of the **Telegram Open Network (TON)**, a blockchain platform developed by Telegram, a popular messaging app, to create a high-performance blockchain platform. The project aimed to offer fast and scalable blockchain solutions with a focus on user-friendly applications and integration with Telegram's ecosystem. Telegram's involvement in the blockchain space started with the announcement of TON in 2018. The project gained significant attention and raised substantial funds through a private token sale. Toncoin's story begins in the shadow of regulatory challenges. In 2020, Telegram, the original architect behind the TON blockchain, makes a fateful decision. Pressured by the U.S. Securities and Exchange Commission (SEC), the company halts the development of the TON blockchain and its ambitious token sale. The project's future seems uncertain, yet the heartbeat of TON continues to pulse through the efforts of others. Toncoin (TON), the native cryptocurrency of the TON blockchain, emerges from these trials, designed to carry the weight of its ecosystem. It becomes the lifeblood for facilitating transactions, paying for network services, and providing incentives to those who choose to participate in the sprawling TON network.

Within this digital landscape, Toncoin's functions come to life. It's not just a token, it's the currency for transaction fees, moving value across the TON network. Stakers, those who believe in the future of TON, lock up their Toncoin, placing their trust in the network's consensus process. Their reward? The chance to earn more, a return for their participation. And governance, the possibility that one day, Toncoin holders will have a voice in shaping the network's future, voting on decisions that could alter its course. Key features of TON make it stand apart from its competitors. It's a platform that thrives on scalability, its multi-layered architecture and sharding technology ensuring it can handle an ever-growing number of transactions without breaking a sweat.

Speed is a defining trait, transactions happen quickly, with low latency, positioning TON as a prime candidate for a variety of applications, from finance to decentralized services. The power of smart contracts also hums beneath the surface, enabling developers to craft decentralized applications (dApps) that can run on the platform, giving it a dynamic and adaptive edge. Though Telegram officially steps away, there remains a lingering connection. Once, there was a vision to integrate TON with Telegram's messaging platform, promising enhanced functionality and a seamless user experience. Now, that dream drifts further from reality, yet it still colors the way TON is perceived. The technical aspects of the TON blockchain reveal a carefully crafted system. It employs proof-of-stake (PoS) as its consensus mechanism, where validators stake their Toncoin to secure the network and validate transactions. The architecture, with its clever use of sharding and the masterchain structure, allows the blockchain to process multiple transactions in parallel, achieving efficiency and scalability that few can rival. The system is modular, designed with flexibility in mind, supporting a wide range of applications and services that extend the blockchain's reach far beyond its initial purpose. As the blockchain grows, so do its use cases. For those who believe in the future of TON, staking and governance present the opportunity to participate directly in the network's growth and governance, a chance to steer the ship and reap the rewards. Yet, despite its potential, TON's current status is shaped by its past.

After Telegram steps away, the project finds new life under the guidance of the **TON Foundation** and a community of independent developers. They continue the work, evolving the blockchain, separated now from its original creators. The vision remains, but it's in different hands, growing within the framework of a community-driven ecosystem. But adoption and ecosystem development are key to its success. For Toncoin and the TON blockchain to thrive, the ecosystem must grow. Developers need to build, partnerships need to form, and the community must engage. Only through these steps will TON's full potential be realized. However, with any innovation comes risks and considerations. Regulatory risk looms large, casting a shadow over the future. The legal landscape for cryptocurrencies is in constant flux, and scrutiny from regulators could impact the blockchain's progress. There's also the inherent market volatility that Toncoin faces, its value can rise or fall, dictated by market conditions and the whims of adoption. And development risks remain. The blockchain's future depends on attracting developers and users alike, growing its community, and continuously evolving to meet the needs of a fast-changing digital world. Toncoin's journey is still unfolding, a story of resilience, innovation, and the ever-present dance with regulatory forces. Its path may be uncertain, but the potential remains, shimmering just beyond the horizon.

9.29 ZEC

Zcash, or ZEC, was created in 2016 by cryptographer **Zooko Wilcox** to combine blockchain transparency with true financial privacy. Unlike Bitcoin, where every transaction is public, Zcash allows users to hide sender, receiver, and amount through its unique **zk-SNARKs technology,** zero-knowledge proofs that verify transactions without revealing data.

The network offers two address types: transparent (public like Bitcoin) and shielded, which encrypt transaction details on-chain. This dual model lets users and institutions choose between privacy and auditability. Over time, upgrades such as **Sapling**, **Orchard**, and the **Halo 2** proof system have made transactions faster, cheaper, and trustless, removing earlier setup requirements.

What makes Zcash distinct is its philosophy: privacy by design, not by workaround. It shows that decentralization and confidentiality can coexist on the same ledger. In a world of traceable blockchains, ZEC stands as digital cash for those who value both autonomy and choice over visibility.

9.30 TAO

TAO is the native token of **Bittensor,** a decentralized network that transforms **artificial intelligence** into an open marketplace. Instead of relying on a few corporations to build and control large models, Bittensor allows anyone to contribute machine learning power, data, or models and earn TAO in return. Users who query or train on the network pay in TAO, creating a circular economy where intelligence itself becomes the traded resource.

The technology behind TAO is built on a custom blockchain running a "**Proof of Intelligence**" consensus. Nodes, called miners, submit AI outputs that are continuously scored and rewarded based on value and accuracy. The better the model performs, the more TAO it earns. This system aligns incentives between contributors and validators without central authority, producing a self-governing ecosystem of evolving AI models.

TAO differs from other cryptocurrencies because it doesn't just represent governance or fee rights, it represents access to collective machine intelligence. With a capped supply of 21 million, TAO's value grows in tandem with the usefulness of the network's models. Holders can stake it, delegate it, or spend it to access high-quality AI, giving the token real utility beyond speculation.

In essence, TAO converts computing and intelligence into a digital asset class. It stands at the frontier where blockchain meets artificial intelligence–a system that rewards knowledge, not hash power, and treats learning itself as the world's newest form of value.

9.31 UNI and Uniswap

Uniswap began as a simple experiment, a few hundred lines of code published in 2018 by **Hayden Adams**, inspired by an idea from Ethereum's founder, Vitalik Buterin. The premise was radical for its time: replace the traditional order book of an exchange with an automated market maker, or **AMM**, where **Liquidity Pools**, not counterparties, set prices. Traders would interact directly with smart contracts rather than centralized intermediaries. That design not only reimagined how markets could function on Ethereum but also introduced an entirely new vocabulary to decentralized finance.

At its core, Uniswap's technology is elegantly simple yet powerful. It uses a mathematical formula–$x \times y = k$–to maintain constant liquidity between two tokens in a pool. Whenever one token is bought, its price rises relative to the other, automatically balancing supply and demand. Liquidity providers deposit token pairs into these pools and earn a share of the trading fees in return, turning capital into a public good that serves both traders and investors. Each upgrade of the protocol–V1, V2, V3, and now V4–has refined that equation with greater flexibility. V3 introduced concentrated liquidity, letting providers allocate capital precisely where trading occurs, multiplying efficiency, V4 now adds "hooks," modular pieces of logic that allow developers to customize pool behavior at deployment, enabling native integrations, dynamic fees, and programmable liquidity.

The **UNI** token anchors Uniswap's governance. Holders can propose and vote on protocol upgrades, treasury allocations, and fee structures. It doesn't function like equity or yield-bearing stock but as a key to collective decision-making. Governance proposals have funded ecosystem grants, cross-chain expansion, and research efforts. Over time, UNI's role has broadened beyond the protocol itself, becoming a signal for decentralization and community ownership in one of crypto's most influential ecosystems.

What makes Uniswap different is not just its code but its philosophy. It eliminates intermediaries entirely, no central custody, no permission to list, no gatekeepers controlling liquidity. Any token compatible with Ethereum can be traded instantly and globally. That openness has made Uniswap a foundation for decentralized finance: most DeFi applications either source liquidity from it or replicate its AMM model. Its contracts now power billions in daily volume and hold tens of billions in locked assets, all without a single matching engine, broker, or clearinghouse.

Uniswap also represents a deeper transformation. It turned liquidity into a programmable commodity and markets into public infrastructure. Where traditional exchanges monetize access, Uniswap made it **open source**. Where banks pool capital privately, Uniswap pools it publicly. Its evolution, through multiple versions, governance debates, and cross-chain expansions, illustrates how software can rewire finance when incentives and algorithms align.

In essence, Uniswap is the decentralized exchange that taught the world that markets don't need middlemen. Its technology is mathematics, its function is coordination, its difference lies in its code's neutrality and its community's ownership. UNI and Uniswap together stand as proof that open systems, when well-engineered, can become the most trusted institutions of all–because they don't require trust at all.

9.32 AAVE

Aave is one of the cornerstones of decentralized finance, built to let people lend and borrow crypto without intermediaries. Founded in 2017 by **Stani Kulechov,** it began as ETH Lend before evolving into Aave, "ghost" in Finnish, a protocol where users supply assets to liquidity pools and earn yield, while borrowers draw from those pools using crypto as collateral. Everything runs on smart contracts, replacing banks and credit checks with transparent, algorithmic rules.

The system's core lies in its code: deposits and loans are managed entirely on Ethereum through self-executing contracts that adjust interest rates automatically based on supply and demand. Governance belongs to the Aave DAO, whose community votes on risk parameters and new collateral types. One of Aave's key innovations is the **Flash Loan**, which allows borrowing without collateral as long as the loan is repaid within the same blockchain transaction, a breakthrough that powers arbitrage, market balancing, and liquidity automation.

With **Aave v3**, the protocol became multi-chain and more efficient, adding features like isolation mode for risk control, efficiency mode for correlated assets, and portals that move liquidity across blockchains such as **Ethereum**, **Polygon**, and **Avalanche**. What sets Aave apart is its transparency: users keep control of their funds, every transaction is visible on-chain, and trust is replaced by verifiable code. In practice, Aave acts like a bank that no one owns, a silent "ghost" infrastructure where finance runs automatically, governed by its users, and open to anyone with an internet connection.

9.33 Polkadot

Polkadot is a next-generation blockchain platform designed to enable multiple blockchains to operate together seamlessly. Founded by **Gavin Wood**, co-founder of Ethereum, Polkadot aims to solve interoperability challenges by connecting various blockchains into one unified network. Its unique relay chain coordinates and secures the network, while **Individual Parachains** can operate independently, each with its own features and use cases. This setup allows for scalability and specialization, letting developers create chains optimized for specific tasks. Polkadot uses a **Nominated proof-of-stake (NPoS)** consensus mechanism, which enhances security and energy efficiency. Through its cross-chain messaging, it facilitates data exchange between blockchains. The ecosystem also supports governance, allowing DOT token holders to vote on network upgrades and protocol changes. With substrate technology, developers can easily create custom blockchains. Polkadot envisions a decentralized web where multiple blockchains interact, share value, and unlock new possibilities.

9.34 DAI

DAI is a decentralized stablecoin on the Ethereum blockchain, pegged to the U.S. dollar. Unlike centralized stablecoins, DAI is not backed by fiat reserves but by over-collateralized crypto assets, such as Ethereum (ETH). It is created through the **MakerDAO** protocol, where users lock up collateral in smart contracts to mint DAI. DAI maintains its peg via a system of smart contracts and governance by MKR token holders. This stablecoin allows for decentralized lending, borrowing, and payments within the DeFi ecosystem. DAI is widely used for its stability, transparency, and resistance to censorship. It operates independently of traditional banking systems.

9.35 Pol (ex Matic)

POL (formerly known as MATIC) is the native token of Polygon, a Layer 2 scaling solution for Ethereum that enhances its performance by increasing transaction speed and reducing costs. Originally launched in 2017 as MATIC, the rebranding to POL reflects Polygon's expanded ambitions beyond simply being an Ethereum scaling solution. Polygon operates as a Layer 2 network, working alongside Ethereum to offer faster and cheaper transactions while maintaining compatibility with Ethereum's security. POL is secured through a **Proof of Stake (PoS)** consensus mechanism, where users stake their tokens to validate transactions. The token itself is used to pay transaction fees, for staking, and for governance decisions on the Polygon network. What sets Polygon apart is its aim to become a multi-chain network, often referred to as "Ethereum's internet of blockchains." This vision allows Polygon to be interoperable with various blockchains, positioning it as a central player in the broader blockchain ecosystem. Polygon initially relied on Plasma, the framework that allows for fast and cheap transactions on Ethereum, by offloading some of the transaction load. Today, Polygon offers developers a **Software Development Kit (SDK)** to build their own custom blockchains, which can interact seamlessly with Ethereum. This flexibility, combined with high throughput, thousands of transactions per second, and low fees, has made Polygon a preferred platform for many decentralized finance (DeFi) projects. In addition to its technical strengths, Polygon also leverages Ethereum's security while offering faster and more independent transaction processing. This balance has made it a hub for DeFi projects like **Aave**, **Sushiswap**, and **Uniswap**, all of which have integrated with Polygon to take advantage of its scalability. POL token holders have governance rights on the network, allowing them to vote on protocol upgrades and other key decisions. As the Polygon ecosystem continues to grow, its vision remains focused on providing scalable, interoperable blockchain solutions that are compatible across multiple networks. This approach has made Polygon one of the most important projects in the blockchain space, not just for Ethereum, but for the broader adoption of decentralized technologies.

9.36 Stacks

Stacks (STX) is a blockchain solution designed to bring smart contracts and decentralized applications (dApps) to Bitcoin without modifying its core protocol. It operates as a Layer 1 blockchain that connects to Bitcoin, leveraging Bitcoin's security and stability while adding advanced functionality. STX is the native token of the Stacks network, used for transaction fees and staking. Stacks introduces a unique consensus mechanism called **Proof of Transfer (PoX)**, where miners use Bitcoin to mine Stacks, creating a direct link between the two blockchains. Unlike Ethereum or other platforms, Stacks allows developers to build on Bitcoin's blockchain by adding smart contracts and dApps, making Bitcoin programmable. It also supports **Clarity**, a predictable and secure programming language for smart contracts. The Stacks ecosystem aims to enhance Bitcoin's utility beyond being a store of value, providing decentralized finance (DeFi) and non-fungible tokens (NFTs) to Bitcoin users. With its innovative approach, Stacks brings additional layers of functionality to Bitcoin without compromising its security.

9.37 Filecoin

Filecoin (FIL) is a decentralized storage network that allows users to rent out spare storage space and others to store their files securely. Launched in 2020 by **Protocol Labs**, it operates on a blockchain, with **FIL** as its native token, used to pay for storage services and reward participants. Filecoin aims to create a global, decentralized marketplace for data storage, addressing issues like data centralization and high costs in traditional cloud storage. The network incentivizes storage providers, who compete to offer the best price and reliability, making it a cost-efficient alternative to centralized platforms like AWS. Filecoin uses a **Proof of Replication (PoRep)** and **Proof of Space-Time (PoSt)** consensus mechanism to ensure data is stored securely and over time. This creates a more trustless environment, with the blockchain ensuring that files are available and retrievable when needed. Storage providers are rewarded with FIL tokens, and the network is designed to grow as more participants join, creating a decentralized and scalable storage ecosystem. Filecoin is widely used for archival storage, NFTs, and Web3 projects, leveraging its decentralized architecture to ensure privacy and security.

9.38 Immutable

Immutable (IMX) is the native token of Immutable X, a Layer 2 scaling solution for NFTs on Ethereum, designed to enable fast, gas-free trading while maintaining security and decentralization. Launched by **Immutable**, a company focused on blockchain gaming and digital asset ownership, IMX powers the ecosystem's transaction fees, staking, and governance. Immutable X leverages zk-rollups, a Layer 2 technology that bundles transactions off-chain, reducing costs and congestion on Ethereum's main chain. The platform is built specifically for NFTs, enabling the minting and trading of digital assets without the high gas fees typically associated with Ethereum. IMX token holders can participate in the governance of the platform by voting on key protocol upgrades and improvements. Additionally, users can stake IMX to earn rewards for supporting network security. The platform has been widely adopted in the gaming and collectibles sectors, offering a seamless way to integrate NFTs into decentralized applications. With partnerships in the gaming industry and a focus on environmental sustainability by being carbon neutral, Immutable X aims to revolutionize NFT trading by making it more accessible, efficient, and eco-friendly.

9.39 Vechain

VeChain (VET) is a blockchain platform designed to improve supply chain management and business processes. Launched in 2015, it aims to provide enhanced transparency, traceability, and efficiency in global supply chains by leveraging blockchain technology. **VET** is the native cryptocurrency of the VeChain ecosystem and is used to transfer value across the network. Additionally, the platform operates with a dual-token system, where VET is used for staking and governance, while another token, **VTHO**, is used to pay for transaction fees. VeChain's primary focus is on providing enterprise solutions, and it has established partnerships with major companies like **Walmart** China, **BMW**, and **PwC**. The blockchain allows businesses to track products from manufacturing to delivery, ensuring authenticity and reducing counterfeiting. The network utilizes **Proof of Authority (PoA)**, which enables faster and more efficient transaction validation compared to Proof of Work or Proof of Stake systems. VeChain's goal is to enhance business operations by integrating blockchain into real-world applications, making it a popular choice for industries like logistics, healthcare, and luxury goods.

9.40 Cosmos Hub

Cosmos Hub (**ATOM**) is the native cryptocurrency of the Cosmos network, designed to solve the problem of blockchain interoperability. Launched in 2019, Cosmos Hub is a key part of the broader Cosmos ecosystem, often called the "**Internet of Blockchains**." Its main goal is to enable different blockchains to communicate, share data, and transact with each other through its **Inter-Blockchain Communication (IBC) Protocol**. ATOM is used for staking, securing the network via the Proof of Stake (PoS) consensus mechanism, and as a governance token for voting on network upgrades. Validators and delegators stake ATOM to validate transactions and earn rewards. The Cosmos Hub does not issue smart contracts itself but serves as a central ledger for different blockchains, facilitating their interoperability. One of its unique features is the **Tendermint Consensus Engine**, which enables high-speed, scalable transactions. Cosmos Hub promotes a modular architecture where developers can create and connect customized blockchains called "zones," improving scalability and flexibility. Cosmos Hub's vision is to create a decentralized network of interconnected blockchains, moving away from siloed systems toward a more interoperable future.

9.41 Starknet

The Starknet token (**$STRK**) serves as the native cryptocurrency for Starknet. It plays several key roles: it's used for transaction fees on the network, staking to secure the network, and governance, allowing holders to vote on protocol upgrades and changes. Starknet uses **Cairo**, a unique programming language that optimizes for ZK-

Rollups, enabling developers to build decentralized applications (dApps) with more flexibility and efficiency. This makes Starknet particularly appealing for applications requiring high scalability, such as decentralized finance (DeFi) and gaming. One of Starknet's core advantages is privacy, as ZK-Rollups inherently offer strong privacy features by validating transactions without revealing all transaction data. Starknet is also Ethereum-compatible, meaning developers can easily build on it using familiar tools and frameworks. The project is developed by **StarkWare Industries**, a team with deep cryptographic expertise, and has already garnered significant attention for its potential to solve Ethereum's scalability challenges. Starknet is positioned to be a major player in the Ethereum ecosystem as Layer 2 solutions grow in importance.

9.42 Axie Infinity

Axie Infinity is a blockchain-based game where players collect, breed, and battle digital creatures called Axies. Built on the Ethereum network and using **Ronin**, a sidechain for faster transactions, it introduces play-to-earn mechanics. Players earn **Smooth Love Potion (SLP)** tokens through gameplay, which can be traded or used to breed Axies. The governance token, **Axie Infinity Shards (AXS)**, gives holders a say in the game's future development and can be staked for rewards. Axie's economy centers around its NFT-based Axies, which can be bought, sold, or traded on decentralized marketplaces.

Players need at least three Axies to start playing, and each Axie is unique with different traits and battle abilities. Axie Infinity became popular for allowing players, especially in developing countries, to earn real income. However, it faces challenges such as regulatory scrutiny and concerns over sustainability due to fluctuating SLP and AXS prices. Despite these issues, it remains a leading example of blockchain gaming.

9.43 Wormhole

Wormhole Coin (Wormhole) is a cross-chain messaging protocol designed to enable the transfer of tokens, NFTs, and data between multiple blockchains. It acts as a bridge, allowing different blockchain ecosystems like Ethereum, Solana, Binance Smart Chain (BSC), and more to communicate and interact with each other. By wrapping assets on one chain and issuing equivalent tokens on another, Wormhole facilitates seamless interoperability across decentralized applications (dApps). The protocol uses a **Guardian Network of Nodes** to validate and verify transfers, ensuring that assets are securely wrapped and unwrapped. These guardians observe transactions on the source blockchain, sign off on them, and execute the transfer on the target blockchain. This decentralized process minimizes the risk of centralization or failure. Wormhole also supports cross-chain smart contract calls, allowing developers to build dApps that operate across multiple blockchains. This boosts flexibility and scalability for DeFi, NFT platforms, and other projects seeking to leverage multi-chain capabilities. However, users must remain cautious of smart contract risks and liquidity limitations on less popular chains. Wormhole aims to be a key infrastructure for the future of blockchain interoperability.

10. Legacy Power

"I've been studying the early days of Bitcoin, and I'm struck by how governments and banks initially responded to your creation. It was chaos, wasn't it?"

Satoshi's eyes–obscured partially by the dim lighting, seemed to gleam with something between amusement and melancholy. "Chaos is perhaps too gentle a word," he replied, his voice measured and thoughtful. "What I proposed in 2009 was nothing short of revolutionary. A financial system that operated outside the control of any government or central bank. Can you imagine what that meant to the powers that be?"

I leaned forward. "Tell me about it. Help me understand what you were really offering the world."

"For the first time in history," Satoshi explained, "people could transact value directly, peer-to-peer, without needing intermediaries like banks or payment processors. The blockchain technology underlying Bitcoin promised something that seemed impossible, a currency free from government manipulation, immune to inflation in the traditional sense, and private in ways that no fiat currency could ever be. But you see, this very independence was precisely what made it threatening."

"The established financial order," I murmured.

"Exactly. In the beginning, most governments dismissed Bitcoin and other cryptocurrencies as fringe innovations." Satoshi's tone carried a hint of irony. "They viewed it as a technological experiment that would eventually fizzle out.

Can you blame them? It sounded almost fantastical, digital money created by solving complex mathematical problems, secured by a distributed network of computers. But then something unexpected happened."

"The price explosion," I said.

Satoshi nodded slowly. "Bitcoin went from fractions of a penny to thousands of dollars in just a few years. Suddenly, governments couldn't ignore it anymore. Fear crept in–fear that this new, unregulated currency could facilitate illegal activities. Money laundering, drug trafficking, terrorism financing. These weren't unfounded concerns, but they also weren't the whole story."

I pulled out my notes. "The traditional banking system must have seen Bitcoin as an existential threat."

"Oh, they did," Satoshi confirmed, their voice darkening slightly. "Think about it. Banks have served for centuries as intermediaries between individuals, businesses, and the economy, ensuring money flows efficiently and securely. That was their purpose, their power, their very reason for existence. And here comes Bitcoin, promising the complete eradication of the need for these intermediaries. These digital currencies were stripping away the need for middlemen, allowing people to exchange value directly, bypassing the traditional gatekeepers."

"So they resisted," I said.

"Fiercely. Major banks refused to allow customers to use credit or debit cards to buy Bitcoin. They refused to work with crypto exchanges. For banks, it wasn't just a shift in the financial landscape, it was a threat to their existence." Satoshi paused, as if choosing their next words carefully. "But there was more to their resistance than simple self-preservation."

"What do you mean?"

"The shadowy reputation that early cryptocurrencies found themselves tangled in threw fuel on the fire," Satoshi explained. "The dark web, platforms like **Silk Road,** they became associated with illegal activities. And in its early days, Bitcoin, much like paper dollars, was occasionally used in illicit transactions. Drug trafficking, weapons deals, money laundering, all occurring discreetly within the digital realm of the internet."

I interjected, "But that wasn't Bitcoin's fault, was it? Cash has always been used for illegal purposes."

"True," Satoshi acknowledged. "But banks, already skittish about this new technology, now discovered a new potential risk, not only to their reputation but also to their very survival in the regulatory arena. They knew that regulators, always watchful, would not turn a blind eye to institutions flirting with such shady activities. The fear of backlash hung heavy in the air."

"And beyond the criminal associations?" I prompted.

"Beyond that, there was a more profound uncertainty, the regulatory gray zone where cryptocurrencies resided. Banks, burdened by strict regulations, found themselves standing at the edge of this new world, unsure of what awaited. What would the regulators say? How would this new asset class be treated?" Satoshi's voice carried the weight of those early uncertainties. "Banks are accustomed to rules, clear guidelines, and the certainty of compliance. But with crypto, the landscape was blurry. One wrong step could have plunged them into the murky waters of anti-money laundering laws or other regulations, and they were not willing to take that risk."

I flipped through my notes. "And then there was the volatility issue."

"Ah, yes." Satoshi almost smiled. "Bitcoin and its counterparts seemed to dance wildly, soaring to incredible highs only to plummet without warning. Compared to the steady, predictable rhythm of traditional fiat currencies, cryptocurrencies were then, and are now, a chaotic storm. For risk-averse banks, which thrive on stability, the idea of integrating such an unpredictable asset class felt reckless. It wasn't just uncharted territory, it was dangerous territory."

The conversation paused. I seized the moment to ask about what came next. "But the landscape shifted, didn't it? Things changed."

"Yes, they did," Satoshi said, his tone brightening slightly. "As cryptocurrencies matured, gaining legitimacy and shedding some of their notorious past, a new kind of financial institution emerged. These were the crypto-friendly banks, the ones who saw potential where others saw peril. They embraced the digital revolution, offering services tailored to this growing market: crypto custody, fiat-to-crypto exchanges, even lending against crypto collateral. They weren't afraid of the future, they leaned into it, ready to guide their clients through the evolving world of blockchain and cryptocurrencies, while the traditional banking world watched from the sidelines, unsure whether to join or resist this digital tide."

"Can you give me examples?" I asked. "Who were these pioneers?"

Satoshi leaned back, counting them off as if reciting from memory. "**Silvergate Bank** (closed in 2023) in California became a leading player in the crypto space by offering banking services to cryptocurrency exchanges and businesses. The **Silvergate Exchange Network (SEN)** (now closed) allowed crypto companies to move U.S. dollars between exchanges in real time, addressing the issue of slow transaction speeds that traditional banks faced."

"I've heard of them," I interjected. "Though didn't they face troubles later?"

Satoshi's expression grew somber. "They did. We'll get to that. But in those early days, they were revolutionary. Then there was **Signature Bank** (closed and acquired by Flagstar Bank) another U.S.-based institution that actively sought to serve the cryptocurrency industry. Their **Signet** platform (shut down in March 2023) allowed real-time, blockchain-based payments between customers, making it easier for crypto businesses to access liquidity."

"What about Europe?" I asked.

"Europe had its champions too," Satoshi continued. "**Revolut** in the UK and EU, a digital bank and financial technology company that offers cryptocurrency trading and storage services alongside traditional banking products. Users could buy, hold, and sell cryptocurrencies directly through its app. **Bank Frick** in Liechtenstein became one of Europe's leading banks for cryptocurrency services. Partner to the Exchange Kraken, they offer as well cold storage solutions, direct crypto investments, working as well with several blockchain companies and providing them access to traditional financial services."

"Switzerland seems to have been particularly forward-thinking," I observed.

"Indeed. **SEBA Bank** (now **Amina Bank AG**) offers both traditional banking services and a wide range of crypto-related services, including digital asset management and custody. It is regulated by Swiss financial authorities and provides services for institutional and professional investors in crypto. **Swissquot**e is also one of the most user-friendly banking options for traders who work with multiple crypto exchanges. It offers seamless fiat on/off-ramping and remains one of the best choices for retail users, while providing secure crypto trading and institutional-grade custody solutions.

Satoshi continued through the list, **Fidor Bank** (now closed) in Germany has been one of the earliest adopters of Bitcoin, while **Metropolitan Commercial Bank**, known for partnerships with crypto firms like **Coinbase** and

Circle, and **Mercury Bank**, a digital bank offering crypto-friendly services for startups in the fintech and crypto space, **Bitbank** in Japan, a leading cryptocurrency exchange offering banking services, **Solaris Bank** in Germany, providing banking as a service and highly crypto-friendly, and **Xapo Bank** in Gibraltar, primarily offering services related to Bitcoin and digital currencies with institutional-grade cold storage.

"These crypto-friendly banks helped bridge the gap between the traditional financial system and the emerging crypto ecosystem," Satoshi explained. "They provided essential services that allowed cryptocurrency businesses to scale and grow. They also demonstrated to the broader banking sector that it was possible to engage with the crypto industry in a compliant and regulated manner."

I nodded, absorbing the information. "But what about governments? How did they evolve in their thinking?"

Satoshi's expression grew more serious. "Governments, through regulatory agencies, began working with banks to monitor cryptocurrency activity, flagging suspicious transactions and imposing restrictions on exchanges. Governments were slow to understand the full implications of cryptocurrencies, but they quickly recognized the potential threat to monetary sovereignty, financial stability, and regulatory control."

"Monetary sovereignty?" I echoed.

"Yes. With the rise of cryptocurrencies, governments feared that people might turn away from national currencies and begin using decentralized alternatives like Bitcoin for daily transactions. If this happened on a large scale, it could undermine the central bank's ability to manage the money supply, control inflation, and respond to economic crises." Satoshi paused for emphasis. "In countries experiencing hyperinflation, such as **Venezuela and Zimbabwe**, people had already started using **Bitcoin** as a store of value and means of exchange, bypassing the local currency altogether. This worried governments, especially those that rely on their currency's global position for economic leverage, such as the United States and the European Union."

"So they saw it as a direct challenge to their power," I said.

"Precisely. One of the first red flags for governments was the use of cryptocurrencies to evade taxes and launder money. Cryptocurrencies, especially those promising anonymity like **Monero** and **Zcash**, made it difficult for authorities to track financial flows. The decentralized nature of crypto transactions meant that individuals could hide their wealth from tax authorities or move large sums of money across borders without detection."

I set down my pen and looked directly at Satoshi. "But that was the early days. What's happened more recently?

Satoshi's demeanor shifted, as if acknowledging we'd crossed into more contemporary territory. "Ah, now we arrive at the most dramatic period yet–both tragic and transformative. Let me start with the tragedy. Do you remember the banking crisis of March 2023?"

"Vaguely," I admitted. "**Silicon Valley Bank**?"

"Yes, but it was bigger than that. In the span of a single week in March 2023, three of the most crypto-friendly banks in the United States collapsed: **Silvergate**, **Silicon Valley Bank**, and **Signature Bank**. It was called 'the unbanking of crypto in America.' Silvergate announced on March 8, 2023, that it would wind down operations and liquidate. Silicon Valley Bank collapsed on March 10 after depositors withdrew over forty-two billion dollars. Signature Bank was seized by regulators on March 12."

"That must have devastated the crypto industry," I said.

"It did. These weren't just banks, they were critical infrastructure. The **Silvergate Exchange Network** and **Signature's Signet** were real-time payment platforms that crypto customers considered core offerings. They allowed commercial clients to make payments twenty-four hours a day, seven days a week, through instant settlement services. When they disappeared, Bitcoin liquidity and crypto liquidity overall became severely impaired. These were the two most bitcoin-friendly banks, supporting the lion's share of fiat settlement for bitcoin trades between trading counterparties in the U.S."

"What caused the collapse?" I asked.

Satoshi's voice took on a professorial tone. "Multiple factors. Silvergate had been struggling for months after the cryptocurrency market crash of 2022 and the spectacular collapse of **FTX** in November of that year. The bank reported nearly a one-billion-dollar net loss in the fourth quarter as customer deposits plummeted sixty-eight percent to three point eight billion dollars. To cover withdrawals, they had to sell two billion dollars of debt securities. They even went to the **Federal Home Loan Bank** for an additional four point three billion dollars."

"And the regulatory hammer eventually came down," I prompted.

"Indeed. Sixteen months after Silvergate's collapse, in July 2024, regulators imposed sixty-three million dollars in civil penalties on the bank and its holding company. The former CEO settled with the **Securities and Exchange Commission** for one million dollars, and the chief risk officer for two hundred fifty thousand dollars. The SEC accused them of failing to detect nearly nine billion dollars in suspicious transfers among FTX and its related entities. The regulatory message was clear: crypto-friendly didn't mean regulation-free."

I scribbled notes furiously. "And after this crisis? How did the industry recover?"

"With remarkable resilience," Satoshi said with evident pride. "New crypto-friendly banks emerged or expanded their services. **Mercury**, though it had been affected by its partner bank **Evolve Bank & Trust's** data breach in 2024, secured a three-hundred-million-dollar funding round in early 2025, pushing its valuation to three point five billion dollars with five hundred million in annual revenue. They became the default bank for Web3 startups, offering clean fiat-to-crypto workflows."

"And in Europe?" I asked.

"Europe emerged as the most structurally progressive region for crypto-friendly banking. What set it apart wasn't just the number of banks embracing digital assets, but the regulatory clarity that made those services scalable. The EU's Markets in Crypto-Assets framework **(MiCA)** laid the groundwork for unified licensing. Major traditional banks joined in, **Standard Chartered UK**, **BBVA Switzerland**, and **Barclays UK** made massive investments in the crypto landscape."

"It sounds like Europe got ahead of the United States," I observed.

"For a time, yes. But then came what many in the crypto world call the 'regulatory watershed' of 2024 and 2025. In **January 2024**, the SEC approved **exchange-traded funds (ETFs)** tied to the spot prices of Bitcoin and Ethereum. This was enormous. It marked a shift in regulatory posture, allowing investors to buy shares that track the value of these cryptocurrencies through traditional financial products. The decision was widely seen as a step toward broader institutional acceptance of digital assets."

Satoshi's enthusiasm was palpable now. "And then, in July 2025, came the **GENIUS Act**. This was the first major crypto legislation ever passed by Congress. **President Trump** signed it into law, establishing regulatory guidelines for stablecoins across the United States."

"Stablecoins being cryptocurrencies pegged to stable assets like the U.S. dollar?" I clarified.

"Exactly. The GENIUS Act formalized rules for stablecoins, mandating that companies must ensure they're holding proper reserves and providing information about their holdings. It introduced anti-money laundering rules and other regulations intended to address concerns that stablecoins were being used by criminals, ransomware hackers, drug cartels, even sanctioned regimes. The bill had significant bipartisan support, passing the House with a three hundred eight to one hundred twenty-two vote."

"That's remarkable political consensus," I noted.

"It was. The legislation recognized that stablecoins had become critically important, their transaction volumes had surpassed Visa and Mastercard combined in 2024, and usage had increased twenty-eight percent year over year. With this bill, the United States joined a growing list of countries seeking to bring oversight and stability to the rapidly expanding digital asset ecosystem."

I leaned back, processing all this information. "So after all the chaos, the resistance, the collapses, governments are finally accepting cryptocurrency?"

"Accepting and attempting to control," Satoshi corrected gently. "In January 2025, President Trump issued the **'Strengthening American Leadership in Digital Financial Technology' Executive Order,** establishing support for responsible growth and use of digital assets as federal policy. He created a working group to develop federal regulations imposing clarity and consistency. The SEC established a Crypto Task Force, led by **Commissioner**

Hester Peirce, to develop a comprehensive and clear regulatory framework for crypto assets."

"And globally?" I prompted.

"The response has been mixed and fascinating. China's state media called for yuan-backed digital currencies to be pursued 'sooner rather than later,' wary of how U.S. stablecoin legislation might proliferate the dollar worldwide. **Zhou Xiaochuan**, former governor of the **People's Bank of China**, warned that pursuing dollarization could bring many adverse side effects. **European Central Bank President Christine Lagarde** expressed similar concerns, emphasizing that U.S. dollar-denominated stablecoins threatened European monetary policy and autonomy."

"So it's become a new front in the currency wars," I observed.

"In a sense, yes. Meanwhile, **Hong Kong passed its Stablecoin Ordinance in May 2025**. Dubai positioned itself as a crypto-friendly jurisdiction with smart regulations. Traditional giants like **JPMorgan**, through its **Kinexys platform**, began piloting on-chain foreign exchange settlements and tokenized real-world assets. Banks that once rejected crypto were now racing to integrate it."

"And new crypto-friendly institutions keep emerging?" I asked.

"Constantly. **Kraken** launched **Krak** in June 2025, a revolutionary crypto-fiat platform operating across one hundred ten countries with over three hundred assets, instant peer-to-peer transfers, and rewards of up to four point one percent on stablecoins and ten percent on digital assets. Revolut continues to expand, now offering over eighty digital assets alongside traditional banking. **Ally Bank** integrated with Coinbase for crypto transfers. Even **Cash App** simplified Bitcoin buying and selling for mainstream users."

I shook my head in wonder. "It's almost dizzying how much has changed since you first published the Bitcoin whitepaper."

"Indeed," Satoshi agreed. "From dismissal and hostility to regulatory frameworks and institutional adoption. From underground digital cash to ETFs traded on major exchanges. From Silk Road associations to Congressional legislation."

"But there are still risks, aren't there?" I asked. "Still uncertainties?"

Satoshi's expression grew contemplative. "Always. The volatility hasn't disappeared, it's inherent to the technology and the market. Regulatory frameworks are still evolving and differ dramatically across jurisdictions. Security concerns persist, the **Evolve Bank & Trust** data breach in 2024 reminded everyone that even crypto-friendly banks face traditional banking risks. And there's the ongoing philosophical tension between Bitcoin's original vision of decentralization and the centralization that comes with regulation and institutional involvement."

"Does that tension trouble you?" I asked softly.

"It's complicated," Satoshi admitted. "Part of me wanted Bitcoin to remain pure, truly peer-to-peer, beyond government control. But another part understands that for cryptocurrency to achieve mass adoption, to truly change the world's financial system, it needed to interface with existing structures. The crypto-friendly banks, the regulatory frameworks, the institutional investors, they're bridges between the old world and the new."

"Bridges that can also become chokepoints," I suggested.

"True. Which is why the decentralized ethos must be preserved even as we build these bridges. The blockchain remains distributed. Anyone can still run a node, validate transactions, participate in the network. No government can truly shut down Bitcoin, t**hey can only regulate the on-ramps and off-ramps,** the points where crypto meets fiat."

"And the future?" I asked. "Where does this all lead?"

Satoshi was quiet for a long moment. "I see multiple possible futures. In one, cryptocurrency becomes fully integrated into the traditional financial system, regulated and controlled like any other asset class. In another, it remains parallel to the traditional system, an alternative that people can choose when they've lost faith in government-issued currencies. In yet another, the technology transcends currency entirely and becomes the foundation for a new kind of internet, a new way of establishing digital ownership and identity."

"Which future do you prefer?" I pressed.

"I prefer a future where individuals have choice," Satoshi said firmly. "Where governments can't inflate away people's savings through unlimited money printing. Where financial services are accessible to everyone, not just those with bank accounts. Where transactions can flow freely across borders without intermediaries taking large cuts. That was always the point, not to destroy banks or governments, but to provide an alternative, to create competition in the monetary sphere."

"And we're getting closer to that future?" I asked.

"Closer, yes. The latest developments represent more progress than the previous five years combined. The GENIUS Act, the EU's MiCA framework, the proliferation of crypto-friendly banks despite the 2023 collapses, the SEC's Crypto Task Force, the Bitcoin and Ethereum ETFs–these are all signs that the tipping point has been reached. Cryptocurrency can no longer be ignored, dismissed, or wished away. It must be engaged with, regulated, integrated."

I glanced at my notes, filled with banks and regulations and dates. "It's ironic, isn't it? Bitcoin was designed to operate outside government control, but its success has forced governments to pay attention and create new control mechanisms."

"That's not irony," Satoshi said with a slight smile. "That's dialectics. Thesis, antithesis, synthesis. Bitcoin proposed a world without financial intermediaries. Banks and governments opposed it. Now we're synthesizing, a world where traditional and decentralized finance coexist, compete, and influence each other."

"And you're satisfied with that outcome?" I asked.

Satoshi considered the question carefully. "Satisfaction is perhaps too strong a word. But I'm cautiously optimistic. The genie is out of the bottle now. Billions of people know that alternatives to government-issued currency exist. Millions have experienced the freedom of truly owning their digital assets, of sending value anywhere in the world without permission. That knowledge, that experience–it can't be taken back."

"Even if Silvergate and Signature failed," I said, thinking aloud. "Even if governments regulate stablecoins and require banks to hold reserves and implement anti-money laundering measures"

"The fundamental architecture remains decentralized," Satoshi finished. "The Bitcoin blockchain still operates independently of any bank or government. That's the beauty of it. They can regulate the periphery, but they can't control the core."

I realized we'd been talking for hours.

"One last question," I said as we prepared to part ways. "Given everything that's happened, the crashes, the regulations, the institutional adoption, would you do anything differently if you could start over?"

Satoshi was silent for a long moment, his face unreadable. Finally, he spoke: "I would have been more explicit about the political nature of what we were creating. Bitcoin isn't just technology, it's a political statement about monetary policy, about individual sovereignty, about trust and centralization. I think I underestimated how threatening that would be to existing power structures."

"And overestimated how quickly people would embrace it?" I suggested.

"Perhaps. Or maybe I expected the conflict but hoped it would resolve more quickly. What I didn't anticipate was how adaptable the traditional system would prove to be. Banks learning to coexist with crypto. Governments creating regulatory frameworks rather than outright bans.."

"Anti-fragile," I murmured, using **Nassim Taleb's** term for systems that benefit from stress.

"Exactly. Every crisis, every regulatory challenge, every bank collapse, they're stress tests that reveal weaknesses and force adaptation. The crypto-friendly banks that survived learned from those that didn't. The regulations being written now incorporate lessons from past failures. The ecosystem evolves."

I had one final thought. "So this story isn't really about Bitcoin versus banks or crypto versus governments. It's about the evolution of money itself."

Satoshi smiled, a genuine, warm smile that transformed his enigmatic features. "Now you understand. Money is an human invention, shaped by technology and politics and human nature. Bitcoin and blockchain are just the latest chapter in a very old story. We're witnessing the digitization of value, the decentralization of trust, the evolution of what it means to own something. Banks and governments are part of that story, not antagonists to it."

"Even when they resist?"

"Especially when they resist. Their resistance validates the importance of what we're building. If cryptocurrency didn't matter, they'd ignore it. Instead, they're crafting comprehensive legislation, creating task forces, launching their own digital currencies. That's not defeat, that's acknowledgment that the world is changing and they need to change with it."

10.1 Central Bank Digital Currencies

"You wanted to talk about CBDCs," Satoshi said, not as a question but as an acknowledgment of the elephant that had been looming over the crypto ecosystem for years.

I nodded, opening my notes. "The crypto community has been watching with growing concern as governments around the world rush to develop their own digital currencies. It feels like we're at a crossroads."

Satoshi leaned back, his expression thoughtful. "Central Bank Digital Currencies. Yes. They represent a fundamental misunderstanding, or perhaps a willful rejection, of what decentralized currency was meant to achieve."

"But they're recognizing the potential of blockchain technology," I offered. "Isn't that progress?"

"Recognition without understanding is dangerous," he replied. "Let me be clear: CBDCs and cryptocurrencies, like

Bitcoin and Ethereum, are antithetical to each other. They share some superficial technological similarities, perhaps, but in philosophy and function, they are opposites."

I felt the weight of that statement. "Can you explain what makes them so fundamentally different?"

Satoshi's eyes lit up with the intensity I'd only read about in forums and cryptic emails. "Bitcoin was designed to operate independently of governments and central authorities. It's trustless, permissionless, borderless. CBDCs, on the other hand, are digital forms of a country's fiat currency, issued and controlled entirely by central banks. They aim to offer the efficiency that people associate with cryptocurrencies while maintaining the control and regulatory oversight of traditional financial systems."

"So they want the benefits without relinquishing power," I said.

"Precisely. And that's what makes them so concerning to those of us who built this ecosystem." He paused, choosing his words carefully. "CBDCs are entirely controlled by central banks and governments. They would have the ability to track every transaction, control monetary policy directly in ways that were never before possible, and possibly even restrict the use of digital currencies based on certain conditions."

"What kind of restrictions are you talking about?"

"Think about it," Satoshi said, his voice taking on an edge. "With a fully digital, centrally controlled currency, a government could prohibit certain purchases, enforce negative interest rates automatically, freeze accounts instantaneously without any due process, or even program money to expire after a certain time, forcing citizens to spend rather than save. The fear in the crypto community is justified: widespread adoption of CBDCs could marginalize decentralized cryptocurrencies and give governments unprecedented control over financial transactions."

The implications settled over me like a cold mist. "That's dystopian."

"It's pragmatic, from a government's perspective," he countered. "But yes, from the standpoint of individual liberty, it's nightmarish. Let me walk you through what's actually happening around the world.

"China has been the most aggressive," Satoshi began, pulling out a tablet and showing me charts and figures. "The **People's Bank of China** has been working on the **Digital Yuan, or e-CNY**, for years. As of June 2025, the cumulative transaction volume reached 7 trillion yuan, that's $988 billion. This is nearly four times what it was just two years ago."

I whistled low. "That's massive adoption."

"It is. And it's accelerating. The pilot program has expanded to 17 provinces, covering everything from education and healthcare to tourism. There are approximately 180 million individual digital yuan wallets open, nearly one in every eight Chinese citizens. But here's what you need to understand about China's motivation."

He leaned forward, and I could see the analyst in him coming alive. "China has a twofold strategy. First, they see the Digital Yuan as a way to modernize their domestic payment system. China is already largely cashless, platforms like **WeChat Pay** and **Alipay** dominate the payments landscape. But these platforms are controlled by private companies, which the Chinese government views as a potential threat to its control over the financial system."

"So it's about centralizing control that had become dispersed," I said.

"Exactly. By introducing the Digital Yuan, the government can regain control over the payment infrastructure and ensure that all transactions flow through the central bank. The second motivation is even more ambitious: China views the Digital Yuan as a way to challenge the dominance of the U.S. dollar in global trade and finance."

This caught my attention. "How would that work?"

Satoshi pulled up another document. "China is promoting the use of the Digital Yuan in cross-border transactions, particularly in countries that participate in its **Belt and Road Initiative**. In 2025, the People's Bank of China established an **International Digital Yuan Operations Centre in Shanghai** specifically to internationalize the e-CNY. They're targeting trade finance and cross-border payments."

"Is it working?" I asked.

"The early signs are promising, for China, at least. ASEAN's renminbi-denominated trade hit 5.8 trillion yuan in 2024.

Thailand completed its first digital yuan oil transaction. The e-CNY is being integrated into infrastructure projects like the **China-Laos Railwa**y and the **Jakarta-Bandung High-Speed Rail**, forming what they call a 'Digital Silk Road.' **Singapore** has been expanding pilots where tourists from both countries can pay with e-CNY."

I absorbed this, feeling the tectonic plates of global finance shifting beneath us. "So China is building an entire parallel financial system."

"They're not just building it, they've largely succeeded," Satoshi said quietly. "The Digital Yuan operates on a two-tiered system. The central bank issues the currency to commercial banks, which then distribute it to consumers. The Chinese government has made it clear that the Digital Yuan is intended to complement, not replace, physical cash. But over time, especially with this kind of momentum, it's expected to become the primary means of transaction in the country."

"And internationally?"

"That's where it gets interesting. Chinese officials, including former People's Bank of China Governor **Zhou Xiaochuan** and current **Governor Pan Gongsheng**, have been advocating for a multipolar monetary system where multiple currencies coexist, rather than dollar hegemony. The e-CNY is their tool for advancing that vision. They're even involved in the **mBridge** project, a cross-border wholesale digital currency initiative with **Thailand, the UAE, and Saudi Arabia**, among others."

"And this threatens the dollar," I said, connecting the dots.

"It's designed to. According to the IMF, the U.S. dollar currently accounts for about 58% of global foreign exchange reserves. But if China can get its major trading partners using the e-CNY for bilateral trade, gradually settling oil in yuan, offering yuan-denominated credit at competitive rates, which they're already doing, then over time, the dollar's dominance erodes. Not overnight, but incrementally. Death by a thousand digital transactions."

"What about **Europe**?" I asked. "They've been working on a **Digital Euro**, haven't they?"

Satoshi nodded, switching to a different set of documents. "The European Central Bank has been exploring the Digital Euro as part of its broader strategy to modernize the European financial system. Their motivations are different from China's. The ECB's primary concern is ensuring that Europe remains competitive in the global digital economy and that European consumers have access to a secure, government-backed digital currency."

"That sounds more defensive than offensive."

"It is. The ECB has emphasized that the Digital Euro would complement existing forms of payment, cash, electronic transfers, instant payments, rather than replacing them. But they're concerned that if they don't offer a digital currency, private companies or foreign governments could fill the void, potentially undermining Europe's financial sovereignty."

"Like China's e-CNY expanding into European trade?" I suggested.

"Exactly. Or American stablecoins dominating European transactions. The ECB's vision for the Digital Euro is a currency that's accessible to all European citizens and businesses, regardless of their location or banking status. They're particularly focused on ensuring it's easy to use, secure, and privacy-preserving."

"Privacy-preserving?" I raised an eyebrow. "How does that work with government control?"

Satoshi smiled grimly. "That's the challenge. One of the major obstacles the ECB faces is finding the right balance between transparency, to prevent illegal activity, and privacy, to protect users' financial data. It's a tension that may be fundamentally irresolvable, but they're trying. Unlike decentralized cryptocurrencies, the Digital Euro would be **fully controlled by the ECB**, with strict regulatory oversight."

"Where are they in the development process?" I asked.

"As of October 2025, they're in what they call the 'preparation phase,' which is scheduled to end this month," Satoshi explained. "The ECB's Governing Council is expected to decide on the way forward after this phase concludes. They've been developing a scheme rulebook through a collaborative process with market participants, over 50 participants from more than 30 organizations including payment service providers, merchants, fintech companies, and consumer groups."

"So they're taking input from the industry."
"Yes. They've also established what they call an 'innovation platform' with about 70 market participants to explore potential use cases. Some of these 'pioneers,' as they call them, have been conducting technical tests on features like conditional payments, transactions that are triggered only under specific conditions, like upon delivery of a parcel. The 'visionaries' have been brainstorming creative ideas for how a digital euro could fit into the financial ecosystem."
I was impressed by the thoroughness. "It sounds like they're being methodical."
"They are. They've also been working on setting holding limits, how much digital euro any person can hold, to balance user experience with monetary policy and financial stability implications. Early discussions mentioned a limit around €3,000 per person, though that's still being debated. The official decision on whether to issue the digital euro will only come once the relevant EU legislation has been adopted."
"And when might that be?"
Satoshi shrugged. "The legislative process is ongoing. The ECB has also selected providers for five key digital euro components, things like alias lookup, fraud and risk management, app and SDK development, offline solutions, and settlement. The framework agreements were signed in October 2025, with companies like **Worldline and Sapient** involved. But these agreements don't involve payment at

this stage and include safeguards allowing for adjustments based on legislative changes."

"So it's still years away from actual implementation."

"Most likely. But the groundwork is being laid systematically. Europe is playing the long game, trying to do this carefully and inclusively. Whether that proves wise or whether it means they'll be overtaken by more aggressive players remains to be seen."

"And what about the **United States**?" I asked. "They're the ones with the most to lose if the dollar's dominance erodes, aren't they?"

Satoshi's expression turned more complex. "The U.S. has been on a rollercoaster with CBDCs. For years, they were cautiously exploring the concept. The Federal Reserve conducted research into the potential benefits and risks, but there was never a formal commitment to issuing a Digital Dollar."

"Why the hesitation?"

"Several reasons," Satoshi explained. "The U.S. dollar is already the world's dominant reserve currency. The Federal Reserve was concerned that introducing a Digital Dollar could have unintended consequences for the global financial system, particularly if it destabilized the banking sector or led to increased demand for cash withdrawals, causing bank runs."

"That's a legitimate concern," I acknowledged.

"It is. There were also serious worries about privacy and civil liberties. A government-controlled digital currency could be used to monitor financial transactions, potentially infringing on Americans' constitutional right to privacy. These concerns resonated across the political spectrum, though for different reasons."

"But something changed?"

Satoshi nodded. "Everything changed in January 2025 when President Trump took office. On January 23rd, just three days after his inauguration, he signed an executive order titled '**Strengthening American Leadership in Digital Financial Technology.**' This order **officially banned** the **creation and issuance of a CBDC in the United States**."

I sat back, surprised. "He banned it? Completely?"

"Completely. The executive order prohibits federal agencies from undertaking any action to establish, issue, or promote CBDCs within the United States or abroad. Any ongoing plans or initiatives related to creating a CBDC were to be immediately terminated. The order cited risks to financial stability, individual privacy, and national sovereignty."

"So the U.S. became the only major country to explicitly ban CBDCs," I said, processing this.

"Correct. According to the Atlantic Council, which tracks CBDC development globally, the U.S. is an outlier among its peer central banks. In 2025, 137 countries and currency unions, representing 98% of global GDP, are exploring CBDCs. Seventy-two countries are in advanced phases, development, pilot, or launch. There are 49 CBDC pilot projects around the world. But the U.S. has pulled out entirely."

"What's the reasoning behind this?"
Satoshi leaned back. "The Trump administration framed it as protecting economic liberty and preventing government overreach. The executive order revoked President Biden's 2022 Executive Order 14067, which had called for exploring digital assets including CBDCs. Trump's approach prioritizes private-sector innovations, particularly dollar-backed stablecoins, to reinforce the dollar's global dominance rather than a government-issued digital currency."
"So they're betting on stablecoins instead?"
"Essentially. The order promotes 'legitimate dollar-backed stablecoins worldwide' and establishes a Working Group on Digital Asset Markets to review current regulations and propose a federal regulatory framework. The administration's view is that private stablecoins can provide the benefits of digital currency without the government surveillance and control that CBDCs would enable."
"But doesn't that cede control to private companies?" I asked.
"It does, which is ironic in its own way. **Senator Mike Lee** and others have introduced legislation to make Trump's CBDC ban permanent. Lee has said that Americans shouldn't have to fear 'unelected federal bureaucrats creating an invasive, all-seeing central bank digital currency controlled by the government.' He's referenced China's digital yuan trials where money was canceled after set periods, forcing citizens to spend their savings."

I nodded slowly. "So the U.S. position is philosophically closer to Bitcoin's ethos, at least in terms of opposing government-controlled digital currency."

"Superficially, yes," Satoshi said carefully. "Though the motivations are different. The crypto community opposes CBDCs because they centralize power and eliminate the financial freedom that cryptocurrencies enable. The U.S. Republican position opposes CBDCs partly for those reasons, but also because they see stablecoins as a way to maintain dollar hegemony (and public debt sustainability) without direct government issuance. They're trying to have their cake and eat it too, preserve dollar dominance while avoiding the political fallout of government surveillance currency."

"Is it working?"

"Too soon to tell. But here's the geopolitical calculation: by refusing to develop a CBDC while China, India, Europe, and others race ahead, the U.S. is potentially ceding ground in the future of digital payments infrastructure. If the yuan becomes the default digital currency for large portions of Asian trade, if the Digital Euro becomes standard in European and African transactions, then the dollar's network effects weaken even if stablecoins remain popular."

"So it's a gamble," I said.

"A massive one. And it's based on the assumption that private U.S. stablecoins will be able to compete with state-backed CBDCs in international trade. That may prove true–

stablecoins like Tether reported $13.7 billion in profits for 2025. But there are questions about whether private entities can scale as quickly as governments, especially when those governments can mandate usage through state enterprises and trade agreements."

"You mentioned **India**," I said. "What's happening there?"

Satoshi's expression brightened slightly. "India's actually become one of the success stories, depending on your perspective. The digital rupee pilot is now the second-largest CBDC pilot in the world after China. Digital rupee in circulation rose to 10.16 billion rupees, about $122 million–by March 2025, up 334% from the previous year."

"That's explosive growth."

"It is. The Reserve Bank of India is expanding both retail and wholesale CBDCs with new use cases, offline functionality, and broader participation. For many developing countries, CBDCs represent a powerful tool for promoting financial inclusion."

I leaned forward, interested in this angle. "How does that work?"

"In regions where large portions of the population are unbanked, lacking access to traditional banking services, digital currencies offer an opportunity to provide financial access without the need for physical bank branches, which are expensive to build and maintain, especially in remote areas. Countries like **Nigeria,** which launched the **eNaira** in 2021, are using CBDCs to expand financial access to underserved populations."

"Nigeria's one of the three countries that have fully launched, right?" I asked, remembering his earlier comment.

"Correct. The other two are the **Bahamas** with the **Sand Dollar** and **Jamaica with Jam Dex**. The Bahamas actually launched the Sand Dollar back in 2020, it was the first fully operational CBDC in the world. The Central Bank of the Bahamas took a similar approach to Nigeria, focusing on financial inclusion."

"How's the adoption been?"

Satoshi pulled up some data. "Mixed, honestly. The narrative for a while was that countries that launched CBDCs saw low or no usage. But that's changing. According to **Josh Lipsky** at the Atlantic Council, there's been real uptake in recent months. The key in these countries is that CBDCs are seen as a way to promote economic growth by reducing the costs of financial transactions and increasing access to credit."

"And reducing reliance on cash," I added.

"Exactly. Cash is expensive to produce and distribute, especially in countries with scattered island populations like the Bahamas or vast rural areas like Nigeria. Digital currency can reach anyone with a mobile phone, which is increasingly everyone. These countries are also using CBDCs to reduce remittance costs, the fees that migrant workers pay to send money home to their families."

"That's actually a positive use case," I admitted.

"It can be," Satoshi agreed carefully. "The question is always the balance between benefits and the potential for abuse. A CBDC that genuinely helps unbanked populations access financial services without imposing surveillance or control mechanisms could be beneficial. But the infrastructure that enables inclusion can also enable control. It's a tool, and like any tool, its value depends on who wields it and to what end."

"Let me step back," I said, trying to synthesize everything. "Can you give me a sense of the overall global picture as of October 2025?"

Satoshi nodded. "The pace has been remarkable. As I mentioned, 137 countries and currency unions representing 98% of global GDP are exploring CBDCs. Back in May 2020, that number was only 35. All G20 countries are now looking into CBDCs. Currently, there are 49 CBDC pilot projects around the world."

"And how many have actually launched?"

"Depending on how you count, between three and eleven. The Bahamas, Jamaica, and Nigeria are the main three retail CBDCs. But if you include the eight islands making up the **Eastern Caribbean Currency Union with DCash**, plus some others, you get to eleven. Though I should note that DCash actually faced challenges, the Eastern Caribbean Central Bank announced its pilot closure in 2024."

"So even launched CBDCs aren't guaranteed success."

"Nothing is guaranteed. What's clear is that emerging markets are driving global retail CBDC growth to reduce cash use, enhance financial inclusion, and improve regulatory oversight. Meanwhile, advanced economies are focusing more on wholesale CBDCs, digital currency for financial institutions that operates similarly to central bank reserves."

I thought about this. "So different countries have different priorities."

"Absolutely. According to the Bank for International Settlements, about 94% of central banks are engaged in some form of work on CBDCs as of 2024. But the level of commitment and progress varies significantly across markets. The BIS survey found that 91% of the 93 central banks surveyed were exploring either a retail CBDC, a wholesale CBDC, or both."

"What are the main challenges in implementing CBDCs?" I asked. "Beyond the philosophical objections from the crypto community."

Satoshi's expression grew more animated. "There are several, and each one needs careful consideration before a country launches a CBDC. First, there's the risk of bank disintermediation. If citizens can hold digital currency directly with the central bank, they might pull too much money out of commercial banks by converting deposits into CBDCs. This could trigger bank runs, affecting banks' ability to lend and sending shocks through interest rates."

"That could destabilize the entire banking system."

"Precisely. It's especially problematic for countries with unstable financial systems. That's why many CBDC designs include holding limits–restricting how much digital currency any individual can hold to prevent massive shifts out of bank deposits."

"What else?"

"Operational risks. CBDCs are vulnerable to cyber attacks and need to be made resilient against them. We're talking about a nation's entire money supply potentially being digital and networked. The attack surface is enormous. The IMF published a paper in 2024 specifically on cyber resilience of the CBDC ecosystem because the concerns are so significant."

I nodded, following along. "And privacy?"

"That's the big one for civil liberties. CBDCs require a complex regulatory framework including privacy protections, consumer protection, and anti-money laundering standards which need to be robust before adopting this technology. But here's the fundamental tension: governments want transparency to prevent illegal activity, but citizens want privacy to protect their financial data. With CBDCs, every transaction can potentially be monitored."

"Can they build in privacy protections?" I asked.

"Theoretically, yes. The ECB has talked about using techniques like data encryption and hashing to prevent links between transactions and specific users. But there's always a backdoor, a master key, some mechanism by which the issuing authority can see what's happening if they want to. It's not like Bitcoin where transactions are pseudonymous and the protocol itself doesn't have an override."

"So the privacy is contingent on government restraint."

"Exactly. And history suggests that once governments have a capability, they tend to use it, especially in times of crisis or when combating things they deem threats. The infrastructure for total financial surveillance, once built, is very tempting to use."

I sat quietly for a moment, absorbing this. "What about the technical challenges of implementation?"

"Those are substantial too," Satoshi said. "There's the question of architecture, how do you design a system that can handle millions or billions of transactions per day? How do you ensure it's accessible both online and offline, because you need offline functionality for areas with poor connectivity? How do you make it interoperable with existing payment systems? The ECB, for instance, is testing both online and offline digital euro solutions, including deployment on the secure elements of mobile devices."

"Secure elements?" "Specialized chips in phones that can handle cryptographic operations securely. They're used for things like contactless payments now. For offline CBDCs, they'd allow person-to-person transfers without internet connectivity, which is crucial for resilience and inclusion."

"That's actually impressive technologically," I admitted.

"It is. The IMF has also been working on positioning CBDCs in the payments landscape, thinking about how they fit alongside cash, card payments, instant payments, digital wallets, and stablecoins. There's a lot of technical work on topics like adoption strategies, data use and privacy protection, implications for monetary policy operations, and cross-border payments with retail CBDCs."

"Cross-border is where it gets really interesting, right?" I asked. "That's where CBDCs could reshape the global financial system."

"Absolutely. That's the ultimate prize and the ultimate threat, depending on your perspective. Projects like **mBridge,** where **China, Thailand, the UAE**, and others are testing **cross-border CBDC payments**, could eventually provide an alternative to the SWIFT system that currently dominates international transfers."

"SWIFT being the system that processes trillions of dollars in transactions daily and that the U.S. uses as a sanctions tool," I said.

"Right. If **mBridge** succeeds at scale, and projections suggest it could handle $500 billion annually by 2025, then countries under U.S. sanctions or those wanting to avoid potential sanctions have an alternative. That changes the geopolitical leverage calculation fundamentally."

"What happens next?" I asked. "Over the next few years, as these systems roll out and mature?"

Satoshi thought carefully. "We'll see several parallel developments. China will continue aggressively pushing the digital yuan internationally, particularly in Asia, Africa, and among Belt and Road Initiative countries. They'll reach a tipping point where enough trade is denominated in yuan that it becomes self-reinforcing–the more people use it, the more people want to use it to avoid currency conversion costs."

"And Europe?"

"The Digital Euro will launch, probably around 2027 if the legislative process stays on track. It will be more privacy-focused than China's system but still centrally controlled. Europeans will gradually adopt it, especially for cross-border transactions within the EU, where it will be more convenient than card payments. Cash usage will continue declining."

"What about the U.S.?"

"That's the wild card. If Trump's ban holds, the U.S. will rely on stablecoins and private digital currencies. If a future administration reverses it, we could see a Digital Dollar pilot by 2028 or 2029. Either way, the dollar's global dominance will face pressure it hasn't experienced in generations."

"And the developing world?"

"More countries will launch CBDCs, with varying degrees of success. The ones that genuinely improve financial inclusion and keep surveillance minimal will succeed. The ones that impose heavy restrictions or fail technically will struggle. But the trend toward digital currency is irreversible at this point."

10.2 Adoption as a Legal Tender

"You seem interested in how the world is receiving what we started all those years ago."

"I am. I've been trying to understand which countries have actually taken the leap, adopting cryptocurrency not just as an investment vehicle or a speculative asset, but as genuine legal tender. As far as I can tell, only a handful have done so."

"You're correct," Satoshi responded. "Legal tender status is a significant milestone. It means official recognition as currency–money that can settle debts, facilitate everyday transactions, and exist within the formal legal framework of a nation. As of now, only two countries have truly crossed that threshold."

"**El Salvador**," I said immediately. "They were first."

"Indeed." There was something in that single word–pride, perhaps, or vindication. "September 2021. A historic moment. El Salvador became the first sovereign nation to adopt Bitcoin as legal tender. President **Nayib Bukele** championed what they called the **Bitcoin Law,** which granted Bitcoin equal status alongside the U.S. dollar, their existing official currency."

I thought about the implications. "So citizens can actually use Bitcoin for everyday purchases? Not just in theory, but in practice?"

"That was the intention," Satoshi replied. "The government launched a digital wallet called **Chivo** specifically to facilitate Bitcoin transactions. They distributed it freely to citizens and even provided initial Bitcoin balances as an incentive for adoption. Bitcoin ATMs, what they called 'Chivo ATMs', were installed throughout the country, converting Bitcoin to dollars and vice versa."

"That sounds ambitious," I said, picturing the infrastructure required. "But also risky. How do you handle volatility when your legal tender can swing ten percent in a day?"

"An excellent question," Satoshi acknowledged. "This is the tension inherent in early adoption. The Salvadoran government accepted this risk as part of a broader economic strategy. They've even issued Bitcoin bonds, financial instruments designed to fund national projects. The most ambitious of these is **Bitcoin City**, an entire municipality planned to be powered by geothermal energy harvested from the country's volcanoes."

The image was striking, a city powered by volcanic energy, mining and transacting in Bitcoin. "Geothermal energy and Bitcoin," I mused. "There's a poetry to that. Using the earth's natural heat to power a digital revolution."

"There is," Satoshi agreed. "It addresses one of Bitcoin's most persistent criticisms, energy consumption. By leveraging renewable geothermal power, El Salvador demonstrates that Bitcoin mining and transactions need not depend on fossil fuels. It's an elegant solution, though the project's success remains to be seen."

I paused, collecting my thoughts. "You said two countries. Who was the second?"

"**The Central African Republic**," Satoshi replied. "April 2022. CAR became the second nation to adopt Bitcoin as legal tender. **President Faustin-Archange Touadéra** signed legislation making Bitcoin an official currency, allowing its use for payments and legal transactions throughout the country."

I frowned slightly, trying to recall what I knew about the Central African Republic. "That's a much different context than El Salvador. CAR is one of the world's poorest nations, isn't it? With limited internet infrastructure?"

"Precisely why the adoption was so controversial," Satoshi said. "The Central African Republic faces significant challenges, poverty, political instability, limited technological infrastructure. Yet these same conditions also explain the appeal. CAR is a member of the Central African Economic and Monetary Community, known as **CEMAC**, which uses the Central African CFA franc. This currency is tied to the euro and, some argue, perpetuates post-colonial economic relationships with France."

"So Bitcoin represents financial sovereignty," I said slowly, understanding dawning. "A way to circumvent traditional monetary systems that have historically disadvantaged the country."

"That's one interpretation," Satoshi confirmed. "The government framed it as a path toward modernization and financial inclusion. Whether it achieves those goals is another matter entirely. The infrastructure challenges are real, and the volatility issues we discussed regarding El

Salvador are amplified in a country with less economic stability."

I leaned back in my chair, processing this information. Outside my window, the evening light was fading. "So those are the only two? Just El Salvador and the Central African Republic have fully adopted cryptocurrency as legal tender?"

"As of now, yes," Satoshi said. "But the landscape is evolving. Several other nations are watching closely, conducting their own explorations and experiments."

"Tell me about them," I prompted. "Which countries are on the cusp?"

"**Panama** has been particularly active," Satoshi began. "The Panamanian government has been working on legislation to regulate cryptocurrencies and potentially authorize their use for payments in specific sectors. Panama already has a robust financial services industry and positions itself as a bridge between North and South America. Cryptocurrency regulation could enhance that role."

"Regulation, but not full legal tender status?" I asked.

"Correct. There's a significant difference. Legal tender means mandatory acceptance for debts and transactions throughout the economy. What Panama is exploring is more nuanced–creating a regulatory framework that legitimizes cryptocurrency use without necessarily granting it the same status as the balboa or U.S. dollar, both of which function as Panama's official currencies."

I nodded, making mental notes. "Who else?"

"**Ukraine**," Satoshi continued. "The Ukrainian government has been developing comprehensive legislation to create a legal framework for cryptocurrencies. This work has taken on additional significance given recent geopolitical events. During times of crisis, cryptocurrencies have provided Ukrainians with alternative means of storing value and conducting transactions, particularly when traditional banking systems face disruption."

"The war," I said quietly. "Cryptocurrency donations to Ukraine became a significant story."

"Indeed. The conflict demonstrated cryptocurrency's utility in crisis situations–borderless, censorship-resistant, accessible to anyone with internet connectivity. While Ukraine hasn't adopted cryptocurrency as legal tender, the government recognizes its strategic value and is working to integrate it into the formal economy through proper regulation."

"That makes sense," I said. "Create the legal infrastructure first, then see how adoption evolves organically."

"Precisely," Satoshi affirmed. "And then there's **Paraguay**. This is particularly interesting because the focus isn't primarily on payments or financial inclusion–it's on mining."

"Mining?" I echoed. "You mean Bitcoin mining specifically?"

"Yes. Paraguay has abundant hydroelectric power, generating far more electricity than the country consumes. This creates an opportunity, excess energy that can be directed toward cryptocurrency mining. Legislative initiatives in Paraguay have focused on attracting mining operations by offering favorable regulations and access to cheap, renewable energy."

I could see the logic. "So rather than adopting cryptocurrency as legal tender, Paraguay wants to position itself as a mining hub, essentially becoming part of the infrastructure that makes cryptocurrency possible."

"Exactly. It's a different approach to engagement with the ecosystem. Not all countries need to make Bitcoin or other cryptocurrencies legal tender. Some can participate by providing the computational resources that secure the networks, particularly if they have advantages like cheap renewable energy."

11. Regulatory Ecosystem

I had come here seeking perspective, a place to organize my thoughts. Between the **SEC's** enforcement actions, **MiCA's** implementation across Europe, and the **UAE**'s intricate regulatory framework, the landscape had become bewilderingly complex.

"You're pondering the regulatory paradox, aren't you?" “It answers the question of whether innovation can survive its own success.”

"The transformation that cryptocurrencies triggered" Satoshi said "goes far beyond technology. It has become a fundamental challenge to the traditional financial order, and the regulatory responses we're witnessing reveal as much about power and control as they do about protecting investors"

"Let's examine this together, piece by piece. The regulatory landscape is more significant than most realize.

"Let me start with the obvious:” I said “cryptocurrencies didn't just create a new asset class. They fundamentally disrupted how we think about money, value, and financial systems. When Bitcoin emerged, it promised freedom from traditional financial intermediaries. Decentralization became both a technological innovation and a philosophical statement.

Satoshi: "That was the intent, yes. A peer-to-peer electronic cash system that operated without trusted third parties. But as Bitcoin and subsequent cryptocurrencies gained traction, they revealed something governments had long taken for granted: control over the monetary system is fundamental to sovereign power. The moment digital assets began to threaten that control, regulatory responses became inevitable".

“Exactly” I replied “Agencies like **FinCEN** in the United States and the **European Union's Anti-Money Laundering directives** were among the first to recognize the potential risks. They saw cryptocurrencies not as innovative payment systems but as potential vehicles for criminal activity. The fear was palpable: tax evasion, money laundering, and broader threats to financial stability".

"Those fears aren’t entirely unfounded” Satoshi explained, “though they are often exaggerated. Yes, cryptocurrencies could facilitate illicit activities, just as cash has for centuries. But what governments truly fear is something more profound: losing their monopoly on creating, controlling, and monitoring money. The volatility of major cryptocurrencies like Bitcoin, whose prices could swing dramatically within hours, represented a tangible threat. If significant portions of the population invested heavily in such unstable assets, the consequences could ripple through the entire economy".

I nodded ”The traditional banking system faces disruption too. As decentralized finance platforms and peer-to-peer exchanges grow, banks see their customers and deposits potentially disappearing. Without steady inflows of deposits, banks struggle to issue credit, make investments,

and manage financial risk. This isn’t just about innovation versus tradition, it is about maintaining economic stability".
"And governments responded accordingly. Central banks and regulatory bodies worldwide began collaborating to mitigate what they perceived as existential threats”.
"China's crackdown on Bitcoin mining and India's temporary bans created massive uncertainty. Markets panicked. Then the SEC in the United States began targeting Initial Coin Offerings, many of which were unregulated and had raised billions without proper oversight. When numerous ICOs were revealed as fraudulent, it damaged the industry's reputation. The crypto community feared that excessive regulation would drive innovation away from North America and Asia to more friendly jurisdictions.”
"Which brings us to the fundamental tension:” Satoshi replied “How do you regulate something designed to be unregulatable? How do you protect consumers without stifling the very innovation that makes cryptocurrencies valuable? This tension plays out differently across the globe, creating a patchwork of regulatory approaches that reveals how different societies balance freedom and control.
"Let's talk about **Europe**. The European Union took a progressive yet cautious stance. They introduced the **Fifth Anti-Money Laundering Directive in 2020**, which placed crypto exchanges and wallet providers under **AML regulations**. But the real game-changer is MiCA, the

Markets in Crypto-Assets Regulation. MiCA represents the European approach to comprehensive regulation. MiCA came into force in June 2023, but its implementation has been phased. The first major milestone was June 30, 2024, when rules for asset-referenced tokens and e-money tokens became enforceable. The full framework became applicable on December 30, 2024, covering all crypto-assets and crypto-asset service providers, or CASPs as they're called.

Me: "And what makes MiCA distinctive"?

Satoshi: "It creates a unified regulatory framework across all 27 EU member states, with passporting rights for service providers. This means a company licensed in one EU country can operate across the entire union. By early 2025, over 40 CASP licenses had been issued, with the **Netherlands, Germany, and Malta** leading the way. The regulation introduces clear classifications for digital assets, imposes strict rules on stablecoin issuers requiring full reserves and redemption rights, and mandates rigorous KYC requirements. Europe chose standardization over the American approach of regulatory fragmentation. The adoption has been uneven. G**ermany, France, and the Netherlands** achieved over 90 percent compliance by early 2025. But countries like **Greece, Portugal, and Ireland** lagged behind, with only 50 to 60 percent of firms obtaining licenses due to bureaucratic delays. **Estonia and Lithuania,** once known for lenient regulations, saw a 42 percent drop in new crypto company registrations as stricter MiCA rules deterred non-compliant firms. Malta, conversely, saw a 35 percent increase, leveraging its pro-crypto reputation.

The numbers tell a story of market consolidation. MiCA forced businesses to either professionalize or exit. The regulation created winners and losers, which is inevitable when you impose order on chaos".

Me: "What about investor confidence"?

Satoshi: "That's improved significantly. About 80 percent of crypto users in the EU report greater trust in regulated exchanges compared to non-compliant platforms. And 32 percent of institutional investors increased their crypto holdings after MiCA's investor protection measures took effect. The European crypto market is projected to reach 1.8 trillion euro by the end of 2025, growing 15 percent year-over-year under MiCA's framework. Those statistics validate the European bet: that clear rules, while limiting some freedom, ultimately expand the market by building trust. Of course, enforcement matters.

Me: "Has Europe been willing to use its regulatory teeth"?

Satoshi: "Absolutely. Over 540 million euros in penalties have been issued to non-compliant crypto firms since MiCA enforcement began. The message is clear: comply or face consequences".

Satoshi: "Now contrast that with the United States, where regulatory fragmentation has been the defining characteristic. Different agencies with overlapping jurisdictions, each interpreting cryptocurrencies through their own lens. Historically, the SEC focused on securities-related matters, particularly token offerings and ICOs. The **CFTC** regulated cryptocurrency derivatives like **Bitcoin futures**. The **IRS** treated cryptocurrencies as property for tax purposes, triggering capital gains taxes. Meanwhile, **FinCEN** enforced stringent Know Your Customer and AML regulations for exchanges. A regulatory Tower of Babel.

Me: "How did businesses navigate such complexity"?

Satoshi: "With great difficulty and enormous legal costs. But January 2025 marked a turning point. **President Trump** issued an executive order on January 23rd declaring crypto a national priority and supporting responsible growth of digital assets. This created the President's Working Group on Digital Asset Markets, chaired by **David Sacks**, dubbed the Crypto and AI Czar. The order fundamentally shifted the federal government's attitude from skepticism to support. Political winds change, and regulatory approaches follow. The SEC underwent a radical transformation. Acting **Chairman Mark Uyeda** established the **Crypto Task Force** on January 21, 2025, with **Commissioner Hester Peirce** as its leader. The task force outlined ten priority areas including defining digital asset security status, clarifying SEC jurisdiction, providing relief for token offerings, and establishing pathways for broker-dealers to custody digital assets. More significantly, the SEC began dismissing enforcement actions.

On February 21, 2025, the SEC closed investigations into **Robinhood Crypto** and **OpenSea** without taking action.

Most significantly, they dismissed charges against **Coinbase**, America's largest crypto exchange. Then on February 27th, the SEC announced that memecoins would no longer be considered securities subject to oversight. The message was clear: the agency was pivoting from enforcement to regulatory clarity. On February 24, 2025, **OKX** pled guilty to operating an unlicensed money business and agreed to enormous fines. The administration made clear it would still prosecute anti-money laundering matters and fraud. The shift was about registration requirements and securities classifications, not abandoning enforcement altogether".

Me: "What about legislative efforts"?

Satoshi: "Multiple bills are under consideration. In May 2024, the House passed **FIT21**, the Financial Innovation and Technology for the 21st Century Act, which would apportion regulatory authority between the CFTC and SEC. The **CFTC would get plenary authority over spot market digital asset commodities**, while the S**EC maintains authority over securities**. In May 2025, **Chairman French Hill** introduced the **Digital Asset Market Clarity Act,** which would grant the CFTC exclusive jurisdiction over digital commodity spot markets.

Me: "What about the **Howey Test**? That's been central to SEC enforcement for years".

Satoshi: "The Howey Test remains the framework for determining whether a token qualifies as a security. It asks four questions: Is there an investment of money? In a common enterprise? With an expectation of profit? Derived from the efforts of others? If all four are met, it's a security requiring registration. This test has been at the heart of the SEC's crypto enforcement. Which brings us to one of the most watched cases in crypto history: **Ripple Labs and XRP**. The Ripple case became a defining moment for crypto regulation. In December 2020, the SEC sued Ripple Labs and two executives for conducting an unregistered securities offering by selling XRP. The case dragged through the courts for years. In July 2023, **Judge Analisa Torres** delivered a partial summary judgment that Ripple's programmatic XRP sales to retail buyers on exchanges did not violate securities laws, but institutional sales did.

A split decision that created legal nuance: the token itself wasn't inherently a security, but the manner of its sale could make it one. That's an important distinction. In August 2024, the court imposed a civil penalty of 125 million dollars on Ripple, far less than the SEC's requested 876 million. The court rejected disgorgement of profits, finding no proof of investor harm. Both parties appealed. Then came the political shift. In March 2025, Ripple CEO **Brad Garlinghouse** announced the SEC would withdraw its appeal. By May 8, 2025, the parties reached a final settlement of 50 million dollars, roughly half the original penalty.

This is not only a victory for Ripple, but provides unprecedented legal clarity. XRP is officially not a security when sold on public exchanges. That's something Bitcoin and Ethereum don't have, just informal SEC guidance. For XRP holders, the case created fierce loyalty and a organized community. The XRP price surged to around 3 dollars by August 2025, its highest level since 2018. The XRP Ledger processed around 2 million transactions per day in 2025, with weekly payments exceeding 8 million, an 800 percent increase since 2023".

Satoshi: "While the U.S. and Europe wrestled with how to regulate crypto, some countries saw opportunity rather than threat. Switzerland became a global hub through **Crypto Valley in Zug**. The Swiss government provided clear guidelines on how cryptocurrencies should be classified and taxed, creating a stable environment for blockchain projects. **Malta** branded itself the Blockchain Island, developing legal frameworks specifically to attract crypto companies. **Singapore** crafted supportive regulations that balanced innovation with financial integrity. These countries demonstrated that embracing crypto could create competitive advantages.

Estonia embraced blockchain on a national level, incorporating it into e-governance and offering licenses to crypto businesses. Though as MiCA came into force, Estonia's lenient approach changed, and they saw that 42 percent drop in new registrations I mentioned earlier. The lesson: regulatory havens can become victims of their own success when broader frameworks impose higher standards.

Japan took a balanced approach, creating frameworks that fostered innovation while ensuring adherence to financial laws. They recognized crypto exchanges as legitimate financial institutions requiring licensing and oversight. Singapore followed a similar path. Both countries demonstrated that supportive regulation doesn't mean no regulation. It means clear, predictable rules that businesses can follow.

Me: "CZ, the founder of Binance, sits in Dubai right now. The UAE has positioned itself aggressively in the crypto space. What's happening here"?

Satoshi: "The UAE's approach is sophisticated and multi-layered. The government enacted stringent regulations to oversee virtual asset transactions while actively courting the industry. They use the term Virtual Asset Service Providers, or VASPs, to define entities handling virtual assets. This includes exchanging cryptocurrencies for fiat, transferring virtual assets, providing custodial services, facilitating ICOs, and operating trading platforms.

The UAE has multiple financial free zones, each with its own regulator. Let me walk you through the key authorities. The **Securities and Commodities Authority, the SCA**, oversees six of the seven emirates, excluding only the DIFC, ADGM, and Dubai itself. The SCA's mandate is clear: protect markets, shield investors, ensure fairness. Licenses are their weapon of choice. Without SCA approval, no VASP can operate in their territory. They monitor markets vigilantly for fraud and manipulation.

The **Dubai International Financial Centre (DIFC)** has the **DFSA**, the Dubai Financial Services Authority. It operates like a sovereign ruler within its realm. Financial services thrive under its watch, with VASPs submitting to firm but fair control. The DFSA's regulatory framework is tight, clear, and built to maintain market integrity. Audits and inspections are routine. When rules are broken, enforcement is swift and precise.

The **Financial Services Regulatory Authority, FSRA**, presides over the **Abu Dhabi Global Market, ADGM**. The FSRA is both regulator and gatekeeper to innovation. They balance strict oversight with a nurturing hand, allowing fintech and virtual assets to flourish while maintaining watchful supervision. Licensing is rigorous, followed by constant compliance checks, regular reporting, and heavy emphasis on risk management. The FSRA knows that great innovation carries great risk, and they're prepared to manage it.

VARA, the Virtual Assets Regulatory Authority, it's Dubai's bold statement that it intends to lead in crypto. VARA has singular focus: virtual assets and the landscape they inhabit. VASPs must prove themselves worthy through a meticulous licensing process. Once approved, there's no room for complacency. VARA's supervision is constant, expectations high. The authority enforces rules not just for order but for consumer protection. Safety and transparency are VARA's promises, delivered with dedication that sets Dubai apart as a beacon in the crypto world.

Me: "Four separate regulatory bodies in one country, each with its own domain. How do businesses navigate that complexity"?

Satoshi: "Carefully. The jurisdictional boundaries are clear: if you want to operate in the DIFC, you deal with DFSA. In ADGM, it's FSRA. In Dubai proper, VARA. In other emirates, SCA. The complexity creates opportunities for forum shopping, where businesses choose the regulatory environment best suited to their operations. Together, these authorities form a regulatory web that keeps the UAE's virtual asset ecosystem alive and thriving, balancing risk with opportunity.

With this framework, the UAE has attracted major crypto companies and exchanges. By offering clear rules, stable government, and access to Middle Eastern and Asian markets, they've positioned themselves as a bridge between East and West. The strategy mirrors Singapore's success: be welcoming but not lawless, create clear frameworks but don't stifle innovation.

Me: "After surveying the global regulatory landscape, what patterns do you see emerging? Is there convergence, or will we remain in a world of fragmented approaches"?

Satoshi: "Several key trends have crystallized. First, AML and KYC protocols are becoming universal. Even crypto-friendly jurisdictions now require exchanges and service providers to implement robust customer identification and transaction monitoring. First, the Financial Action Task Force has been instrumental in setting these global standards, releasing its fifth targeted update on virtual assets in 2024 and 2025 emphasizing international cooperation. FATF wields tremendous soft power through its standards and gray-listing mechanisms. Second, jurisdictional clarity is gradually improving, though still incomplete. The debate over whether the SEC or CFTC should regulate crypto in the U.S. exemplifies this struggle. Countries like Japan and Singapore have been more decisive in assigning regulatory responsibilities. Third, consumer protection is becoming central. Whether through MiCA's disclosure requirements or the UAE's licensing rigor, protecting retail investors from fraud and market manipulation is now priority.

Regulation is driving consolidation. The compliance costs of meeting MiCA requirements or U.S. money transmitter licenses favor larger, well-capitalized firms. Smaller exchanges and startups struggle. This creates tensions: regulation brings legitimacy and institutional participation, but at the cost of the scrappy innovation that characterized crypto's early days. By 2025, 26 percent of countries still have no clear classification for crypto assets, creating ongoing uncertainty.

12. Language

I had been wrestling with questions about blockchain programming languages for weeks. Satoshi Nakamoto sat across from me, ready, as usual, to address all my queries.

"You wanted to understand the languages," Satoshi said, his voice carrying that familiar tone of patient authority I'd come to expect from our correspondence. "But I suspect you're really asking about something deeper, why different tools emerged for different parts of this ecosystem."

I nodded, pulling out my notebook. "Exactly. When I look at blockchain development today, it's not like traditional software. There's this entire constellation of languages, each serving different purposes. It's almost as if the technology itself demanded new approaches to programming."

Satoshi's eyes seemed to brighten slightly. "That's perceptive. You see, when we first conceived of Bitcoin, the focus was on solving the double-spending problem, on creating a system that could achieve consensus without central authority. But as the ecosystem evolved, something fascinating happened, the unique constraints of distributed computation began to reshape how people thought about code itself."

"How so?" I asked, leaning forward.

"Consider the fundamental challenges," Satoshi continued, their fingers tracing patterns on the wooden table. "In traditional software development, you choose a language for performance, developer productivity, or integration with existing systems. But blockchain programming introduced entirely new requirements. Code that, once deployed, becomes immutable. Execution that must be deterministic across thousands of nodes scattered around the globe. Cryptographic precision where even the smallest error could compromise security or cost users millions of dollars."

The weight of those constraints hit me. "So the languages had to evolve to meet these demands?"

"Some evolved, others were born from necessity," Satoshi replied. "Take **Solidity**, for instance. It didn't exist when Bitcoin launched, but as Ethereum emerged with its vision of programmable money, the need for a language specifically designed for smart contracts became apparent. **Gavin Wood** and the Ethereum team created something purpose-built–a language that understood gas costs, that could handle the peculiarities of blockchain state management, that made cryptographic operations feel natural."

I scribbled notes as Satoshi spoke. "But Solidity isn't the only smart contract language. There's **Vyper**, which seems to take a completely different philosophical approach."

"Ah, yes," Satoshi said with what might have been a smile. "Vyper represents something important, the recognition that flexibility can be the enemy of security. Where Solidity offers powerful features and expressive syntax, Vyper deliberately constrains the developer. It removes inheritance, limits recursion, makes the code more auditable. It's the difference between giving someone a Swiss Army knife and giving them a scalpel, one is versatile, the other is precise."

"And both have their place?"

"Absolutely. The beauty of this ecosystem is that it's naturally polyglot. A developer building a decentralized exchange might write their trading contracts in Solidity because they need the flexibility to handle complex financial logic. But the same developer might choose Vyper for a simple token contract where auditability trumps expressiveness."

I paused, thinking about the broader architecture. "But smart contracts are just one layer, aren't they? What about the blockchains themselves?"

Satoshi leaned back slightly, and I caught a glimpse of satisfaction in his expression. "Now you're seeing the bigger picture. The blockchain infrastructure, the consensus engines, the peer-to-peer networking, the cryptographic verification, these require different tools entirely. This is where languages like **Rust** and **Go** shine."

"Why those specifically?"

"Performance and safety," Satoshi explained. "When you're building the foundation that thousands of nodes will run, that will process millions of transactions, you need languages that can handle concurrency elegantly, that manage memory safely, that can squeeze every bit of performance from the hardware. Rust gives you memory safety without garbage collection overhead. Go provides excellent concurrency primitives and fast compilation. These aren't languages for writing business logic, they're languages for building the engines that make everything else possible."

The conversation was painting a picture I hadn't fully grasped before. "So we end up with this layered approach, different languages for different parts of the stack?"

"Precisely," Satoshi said, their voice taking on the tone of someone who had watched their creation grow beyond their original vision. "A single decentralized application might involve Rust for the blockchain node software, Solidity for the core business contracts, **JavaScript** for the user interface, and **Python** for analytics and monitoring services. Each language is chosen not just for its technical capabilities, but for how well it matches the specific constraints and requirements of that layer."

I found myself fascinated by the elegance of this distributed approach. "It's almost like the blockchain ecosystem naturally selects for specialization."

"That's one way to put it," Satoshi agreed. "But there's something deeper happening here. Each language brings its own philosophy to the problem space. Solidity embodies the philosophy of programmable money–expressive, powerful, but with built-in economic constraints through gas costs. Vyper represents security-first thinking, readable, auditable, defensively designed. Rust brings the philosophy of systems programming–maximum performance with compile-time safety guarantees."

"And these philosophies shape the applications themselves?"

Satoshi nodded slowly. "They do more than that, they shape how developers think about problems. When you're writing in Vyper, you naturally think about simplicity and auditability. When you're working in Rust at the protocol level, you're constantly considering performance implications and memory management. The tools don't just enable the vision, they help refine it."

I realized we'd been talking for over an hour, but there was one more thing I needed to understand. "Looking at all of this, the specialized languages, the layered architectures, the philosophical differences, what does it tell us about where blockchain development is heading?"

Satoshi was quiet for a long moment, staring into his coffee. When he finally spoke, his voice carried a note of something, pride, perhaps, or wonder at how far things had come.

"It tells us that this technology has matured beyond a single inventor's vision," he said. "Bitcoin was my attempt to solve a specific problem with the tools available at the time. But what we see now is an entire ecosystem of tools, languages, and approaches that have evolved organically to meet challenges I couldn't have fully anticipated. The polyglot nature of blockchain development isn't a bug, it’s a feature. It reflects the complexity and diversity of the problems we're now trying to solve with decentralized systems."

He paused, then continued with quiet intensity. "Each language in this ecosystem carries within it certain assumptions about how distributed computation should work, what security means, how much performance you can trade for safety. By understanding these languages, not just their syntax, but their underlying philosophies, developers gain insight into the deeper principles that govern decentralized systems."

As Satoshi prepared to leave, he turned back to me one last time. "Remember this: we're not just building applications anymore. We're building the infrastructure for a new kind of digital society. The languages we choose, the architectural decisions we make, the trade-offs we accept, these will shape how that society functions for generations to come. Choose wisely."

Bitcoin Script is the built-in programming language that governs how Bitcoin transactions are executed and validated. Unlike general-purpose languages designed for broad applications, Script is intentionally narrow, serving as a specialized tool to define the conditions under which a transaction output can be spent. Every Bitcoin transaction output is locked with a script, and to claim that output, the spending transaction must provide data that satisfies the locking conditions. This mechanism makes Script the foundation of Bitcoin's programmability, enabling not only simple payments but also a range of conditional transactions.

At its core, Script is a stack-based, interpreted language. It does not run on a virtual machine in the way Ethereum smart contracts do, instead, it executes commands in a linear sequence, manipulating data pushed onto a stack. The design resembles **Forth,** an early minimalist language, where each operation consumes or produces values on the stack. When a node verifies a transaction, it executes the unlocking script provided by the spender in combination with the locking script specified in the output being spent. If the final evaluation leaves a valid state on the stack, typically a "true" value, the transaction is considered valid.

One of the defining characteristics of Bitcoin Script is its non-Turing completeness. It deliberately omits loops and recursion, ensuring that every script is guaranteed to halt. This decision was made for security and predictability, as unrestricted computation could introduce denial-of-service vectors and unpredictable verification times. By constraining expressiveness, Bitcoin ensures that all nodes can efficiently and deterministically validate scripts across the network. The set of available operations, called **Opcodes**, covers data handling, cryptographic checks, and basic arithmetic. Among these, the most common are those enabling **Pay-to-Public-Key-Hash (P2PKH)** and **Pay-to-Script-Hash (P2SH)**, which together account for the majority of transaction logic seen on the blockchain.

The primary use of Script is to enforce spending conditions, which can range from straightforward payments to more nuanced arrangements. A simple P2PKH script requires the spender to provide a digital signature corresponding to a known public key hash. More complex constructions, such as multi-signature schemes, demand signatures from multiple private keys, enabling joint custody or escrow-like functionality. Time-locking features, expressed through opcodes like OP_CHECKLOCKTIMEVERIFY, allow outputs to become spendable only after a certain block height or timestamp, a building block for payment channels and layered protocols. Through combinations of these primitives, developers can encode conditional transfers that approach contractual logic without the need for a general-purpose virtual machine.

However, Script's design is as much about restraint as it is about possibility. Many opcodes that existed in the original release were later disabled, either due to vulnerabilities or lack of necessity, and the remaining set has been carefully curated to minimize attack surface. This limited expressiveness makes Script reliable but also restrictive. Developers cannot build arbitrarily complex decentralized applications directly on Bitcoin in the way they can on smart contract platforms like Ethereum. Instead, Bitcoin's philosophy favors simplicity at the base layer, pushing complexity to higher-level protocols such as the Lightning Network or sidechains. These systems often use Script as a secure anchor, but handle the more elaborate state transitions off-chain or in parallel systems.

Another limitation stems from readability and usability. Script was never designed for human-friendly coding, it lacks the syntactic sugar or structure that higher-level languages provide. To address this, abstractions and compilers such as **Miniscript** have been introduced, offering a structured framework that translates more intuitive conditions into Script while ensuring safety and auditability. These developments aim to expand Bitcoin's practical programmability without sacrificing its conservative security posture.

In evaluating Bitcoin Script, one must understand it as a deliberate trade-off between functionality and resilience. It is not a tool for building full-fledged applications, but rather a secure and deterministic language for expressing spending rules. Its strength lies in its predictability, the ease with which the network can achieve consensus on validity, and its resistance to computational abuse. Its weakness lies in its rigidity, which can frustrate attempts to create more expressive financial instruments directly on-chain. Yet this very rigidity has been crucial to Bitcoin's longevity, ensuring that its scripting system has remained stable and dependable for over a decade.

In summary, Bitcoin Script is the quiet machinery beneath every transaction, a language whose constraints define Bitcoin's unique balance of programmability and security. By offering just enough expressiveness to enable conditional transfers, multi-signature arrangements, and time locks, while avoiding the pitfalls of open-ended computation, Script has shaped Bitcoin into a system that is programmable yet resistant to systemic risk. Its role is foundational but understated: a simple, stack-based language that embodies the principle of doing one thing well, and leaving more ambitious experiments to layers built on top of it.

Solidity emerges as the language that shapes the very fabric of the Ethereum blockchain. It's the tool of choice for developers crafting the intricate web of smart contracts that power decentralized systems. Its reach extends beyond Ethereum, weaving through platforms like **Binance Smart Chain (BSC) and Polygon**, binding these networks with the same elegant precision. Born from the mind of Gavin Wood, a visionary co-founder of Ethereum, Solidity is now under the stewardship of the **Ethereum Foundation**. Its purpose is singular yet powerful: to give life to smart contracts. Solidity is the language that brings them to life, dictating how agreements will unfold in a world where code is law. Solidity stands out with its key features, offering developers a powerful tool that feels familiar yet designed for a revolutionary purpose. It carries the high-level structure of languages like JavaScript or C++, statically typed to ensure precision, while allowing for the creation of complex logic within smart contracts. Every function, every operation, carefully constructed to follow exact rules, brings those contracts to life in ways both simple and intricate. At its core, Solidity integrates seamlessly with the

Ethereum Virtual Machine (EVM), the heartbeat of the Ethereum network, where these contracts are executed. Solidity's power doesn't stop there. It supports inheritance, letting contracts borrow from others, making them more efficient and modular. It also offers libraries and user-defined data types, expanding the possibilities for developers. The use cases are vast. Solidity is the backbone of decentralized applications (dApps), helping developers create systems that operate autonomously on the blockchain. It's the language behind the coding of Initial Coin Offerings (ICOs) and widely adopted token standards like **ERC-20** and **ERC-721**, which fuel the world of tokens and NFTs. Some of the most transformative projects in the crypto space owe their existence to Solidity. **Uniswap**, the decentralized exchange where users trade without intermediaries, and **Compound**, a decentralized finance (DeFi) platform for lending and borrowing, are just two shining examples of what Solidity makes possible.

Vyper emerges from the Ethereum landscape, carved with precision and intent. It stands as an alternative to Solidity, designed not with complexity in mind, but with an unwavering focus on simplicity and security. Where Solidity weaves intricate logic, Vyper strips things down, offering a cleaner, more deliberate path for developers who prioritize safety over feature-rich code. Born from the hands of the Ethereum community, Vyper exists to answer a need, an alternative that reduces the risk of vulnerabilities. It avoids the lure of complexity, recognizing that with too many features, the cracks in security begin to show. Its key feature is its Python-like syntax, making it a comfortable transition for developers who have worked in the Python world. Vyper's strength is in what it doesn't have. There are no complicated tricks, no function overloading, recursion, or inheritance to navigate. This conscious limitation ensures fewer opportunities for things to go wrong. In this world of smart contracts, where every vulnerability is a door left open, Vyper locks it tight. The use cases for Vyper are clear: it shines in environments where security is paramount, where the cost of complexity is too high. It's used to write smart contracts that must function with utmost precision, particularly in high-security applications. Among the projects that trust Vyper's simplicity is **Curve Finance**, a decentralized finance protocol focused on stablecoin trading. Here, in the quiet precision of its code, Vyper proves its worth, safeguarding transactions in a space where stability is everything.

Rust stands tall in the world of systems programming, a language forged with precision and care. It's known not just for its raw power, but for its ability to ensure safety in the most critical of areas: memory. In a field where speed and security often clash, Rust brings harmony. It's the trusted language for several of the newer blockchains, like **Solana** and **Polkadot**, where performance is everything, and the stakes are high. Birthed by **Mozilla Research**, Rust isn't just another programming language, it's a solution. Built to handle the demands of high-performance systems, it finds its place perfectly in the infrastructure of blockchains, where every nanosecond and every byte counts. Rust's defining features shine through in every line of its code. It offers memory safety without relying on a garbage collector, guarding against bugs that have plagued developers for decades, null pointer dereferencing, buffer overflows, all prevented by Rust's careful design. It doesn't stop there. Rust's built-in concurrency ensures that systems can run in parallel, safely and efficiently, making it a natural fit for the decentralized, distributed worlds of blockchains. Rust finds its purpose in writing the very core infrastructure of these blockchains, the foundational code that keeps everything running. It also steps into the realm of smart contracts, offering developers a tool for building on platforms like Solana, where speed and reliability are critical. In the hands of developers, Rust is more than just a language, it's a way to build systems that are fast, safe, and unbreakable, the perfect companion for the future of blockchain.

Golang, or simply Go, emerges from the halls of **Google** with a quiet confidence. It's a language born for efficiency, designed to handle the complexities of server-side applications and blockchain platforms with the same calm precision. Statically typed and compiled, it moves with the speed and reliability needed in a world where every process matters. Created by Google, Go's purpose is clear from the outset: to build systems that are both scalable and secure. It's a language that doesn't get tangled in complexity. Instead, it thrives on simplicity, letting developers write clean, readable code that won't collapse under its own weight. And behind that clean syntax lies the power that supports the concurrent handling of processes, the lifeblood of blockchain nodes. Multiple processes run efficiently, side by side, without missing a beat. Go compiles fast, it executes even faster, making it an ideal choice for systems that can't afford to slow down. Go's true strength shows in its use cases. It is the foundation upon which blockchain node software is built, the language trusted to write consensus algorithms and manage transaction validation. Projects that demand stability and precision turn to Go. In the world of blockchain, **Hyperledger Fabric** stands as a testament to Go's capabilities, an enterprise-grade platform built on permissioned networks. **Cosmos SDK**, a framework designed to build interconnected blockchains, also leans on Go's strengths, ensuring that every piece of the puzzle fits together seamlessly. Go doesn't shout–it works, efficiently and quietly, its fingerprints all over the systems that drive the future of blockchain technology.

C++ stands as one of the oldest giants in the programming world, a language renowned for its raw power and relentless efficiency. It's been the backbone of countless systems, and in the realm of blockchain, it's the foundation upon which the pillars of decentralized technology are built. Created by the visionary Bjarne Stroustrup, C++ was designed to offer deep control over memory and CPU resources, making it the perfect fit for the demanding, performance-critical world of blockchain nodes. The language's true strength lies in its low-level memory control, allowing developers to extract every ounce of performance from their machines. It's the kind of control that blockchains need, where every byte, every cycle, can mean the difference between success and failure. C++ also brings multi-threading to the table, giving it the ability to handle complex operations and distributed systems, the lifeblood of blockchain infrastructure. Its use cases are as powerful as the language itself. C++ builds the very core of blockchain software, driving some of the most high-performance blockchains in existence. It's also trusted to craft the intricate cryptographic libraries and consensus mechanisms that underpin the security and reliability of decentralized networks. Some of the most iconic projects owe their existence to C++.

Python enters the scene quietly, with a simplicity and elegance that belies its power. It's a language known not for raw speed or efficiency like C++ or Rust, but for its accessibility. Developers of all levels are drawn to Python's clear, readable syntax, finding it easy to learn yet versatile enough to handle the complexities of blockchain development. Created by Guido van Rossum, Python's purpose is clear: to be a tool that anyone can pick up, a language designed for scripting, automation, and data analysis. Though Python may not race ahead in performance, it thrives in areas where speed isn't the sole focus. It plays a pivotal role in scripting, testing, and prototyping, the behind-the-scenes work that brings blockchain projects to life. Its readable syntax makes it an ideal choice for collaboration, where developers can easily share and build upon each other's work. And Python's vast array of extensive libraries, from cryptography to data science, makes it a go-to tool for a wide range of tasks, giving it a versatility that few other languages can match. In blockchain, Python finds its place. It writes testing frameworks for smart contracts, making sure everything runs smoothly before those contracts go live. It scripts automation for blockchain integration with web applications, making the complex seem effortless. Python is also the backbone for lightweight blockchain applications, where ease of development and iteration are key. Some of the most important projects in the blockchain world turn to Python for its unique strengths. **Ethereum**'s **PyEthereum**, the original Python implementation of Ethereum, was used for testing, a critical part of Ethereum's development. **Truffle**, a development framework for Ethereum smart contracts, uses Python for automation and scripting, proving that even in a space where performance is paramount, Python's simplicity and power have their own indispensable role to play. In the hands of its developers, Python becomes more than just a language, it's a bridge between ideas and execution, offering a smooth path through the complexities of blockchain development.

JavaScript, a language born for the web, finds itself woven into the fabric of the blockchain world. Its journey starts with creating interactive websites, but it evolves, expanding its reach into decentralized applications, or dApps, where users interact with the blockchain seamlessly. Brendan Eich first brought JavaScript into existence, and over time, it becomes indispensable not just for building engaging frontends, but also for shaping the architecture behind the scenes. Enter **Node.js**, the runtime that allows JavaScript to step beyond the browser. Developed by Ryan Dahl, it brings JavaScript to the backend, where it powers services that dApps rely on. Its event-driven architecture thrives in an environment where asynchronous operations are the norm. In the world of decentralized apps, where every interaction with the blockchain happens in real-time, this feature is critical. Node.js handles the complex dance of requests and responses with ease, making sure the system runs smoothly without missing a beat. Together, JavaScript and Node.js offer something unique, an ability to build both the frontend and backend of a dApp. A developer can use a single language to create the entire ecosystem, from the user interface to the backend services and APIs that interact with smart contracts on the blockchain. It's an elegant solution for a complex problem, and developers embrace the simplicity of working with a unified toolset. JavaScript's influence is felt in some of the most widely used blockchain projects. **Metamask**, the popular Ethereum wallet and dApp browser extension, is built with JavaScript, making it easy for users to interact with their digital assets. **Web3.js**, the JavaScript library that connects users to the Ethereum blockchain, allows developers to create browser-based blockchain applications, from wallets to exchanges. It's a language that has found its place not only in the world of the web but at the heart of blockchain technology, where it bridges the gap between users and the decentralized world. **JavaScript and Node.js**, once tools for web developers, now power some of the most important innovations in blockchain, shaping the way people connect with decentralized systems. Their story is one of transformation, adapting to new challenges and thriving in the fast-paced world of dApps.

Simplicity enters the blockchain world with a quiet sense of purpose, a language crafted with precision and safety at its core. It's not like the others, born from complexity and speed. Instead, Simplicity emerges with a singular focus, security, ensuring that every line of code written for smart contracts is not just functional but flawless. Created by **Blockstream**, a company known for pushing the boundaries of blockchain technology, Simplicity is designed for those who seek certainty in an uncertain digital landscape. In its essence, Simplicity offers something rare, a formal verification. This isn't just code that runs, it's code that can be mathematically proven to be correct. Developers no longer have to hope their smart contracts will work as intended, they can know. By stripping away potential pitfalls like loops and recursion, Simplicity reduces complexity and the risks that come with it. It's a language that doesn't allow for ambiguity, where every contract is crafted with exacting care. Simplicity finds its use in the realm of smart contracts where security and correctness are paramount. It is especially tailored for platforms built on the **Bitcoin blockchain**, where stability and trust are more important than fast-moving innovations. This language becomes the tool of choice for developers working on systems that need to be bulletproof, where mistakes aren't an option. One of the key projects embracing Simplicity is the **Liquid Network**, the Bitcoin sidechain platform developed by **Blockstream**. Here, Simplicity's strengths are put to the test, providing the foundation for contracts that demand absolute reliability and security. It is the language of those who prioritize safety over speed, precision over flash, building systems that can stand the test of time in the ever-evolving world of blockchain.

Haskell stands apart in the world of programming, a language defined by its mathematical precision and elegance. It isn't just built for speed or simplicity, it's crafted for those who value correctness above all. Born from the minds of academics and nurtured as an open-source project, Haskell is a functional programming language where every computation is treated with the care of a mathematical proof. For those working on blockchain projects that prioritize security and correctness, Haskell becomes the tool of choice. Its purpose is clear: Haskell offers a world of formal verification and safe code execution, making sure that every line of code behaves exactly as expected. There's no room for ambiguity. With strong static typing, Haskell ensures that the code is type-safe, catching errors before they ever reach runtime. Its use of immutable data aligns perfectly with the concept of blockchain's immutable ledger, where every transaction is etched permanently into the record. Haskell's use cases are steeped in security. It's trusted to write secure smart contracts, where a single flaw could mean the difference between success and disaster. Developers turn to Haskell when they need to build blockchain infrastructure that not only works but works flawlessly, with a focus on correctness and reliability. One of the most prominent projects leaning on Haskell's power is **Cardano**. The smart contract platform **Plutus**, built on Cardano, uses Haskell as its foundation. It's no coincidence that a blockchain project so focused on formal methods and security would choose Haskell, a language that embodies those values in every function, every immutable line of code. Haskell isn't just a tool for developers, it's a statement of intent. It says that in a world of ever-growing complexity, some things–like security and correctness, are non-negotiable.

Java steps into the scene as a versatile, object-oriented language that has made its mark across countless industries, and blockchain is no exception. Created by **Sun Microsystems**, Java carries with it a legacy of portability and scalability that makes it a reliable choice for large-scale applications. Its power lies in its ability to transcend platforms, a language that fulfills the promise of "write once, run anywhere." For blockchain developers, this portability means that nodes can operate seamlessly across different systems, a crucial feature in the world of decentralized networks. Java's purpose is clear from the outset: it's built to be platform-independent, a language designed to handle the complexities of large, distributed systems. Scalability is where Java shines, allowing developers to create expansive blockchain networks that can grow and evolve without losing stability or performance. Java's strengths find their use in the core of blockchain development, from building the very nodes that keep the network alive, to designing intricate consensus algorithms that ensure everything runs smoothly. For enterprise-level blockchain applications, where scale and reliability are key, Java provides the foundation. One of the notable projects harnessing Java's power is **IOTA**, a cryptocurrency project with its sights set on the **Internet**

of Things (IoT). In this world, where devices connect and communicate seamlessly, Java's portability and scalability prove to be invaluable, offering the stability needed to manage such an interconnected vision. Java is more than just a programming language, it's a cornerstone for developers building the future of blockchain, a tool that offers both reliability and flexibility in an ever-expanding digital landscape.

Clarity is a smart contract language designed to run on the **Stacks** blockchain, anchored to Bitcoin's immutable foundation. Unlike other languages, Clarity is built on one core principle: decidability. Every outcome is known before the code runs, ensuring certainty. Its syntax, reminiscent of **Lisp**, embraces structure, with parentheses encasing every expression. The journey begins simply: an integer variable called counter, initialized at zero. A function forms to increase its value. In Clarity, functions are called explicitly, returning a single immutable result. Once set, values remain unchanged, ensuring stability as the contract evolves. Data types like integers, booleans, lists, and tuples are precisely defined, shaping the contract's reality. For instance, a balance of one hundred units is declared and maintained throughout the contract's life.

Contracts are more than containers; they house public functions and variables, open to interaction. A public function sets the balance and returns a promise of success. Meanwhile, private functions remain hidden, essential but accessible only from within. Assertions enforce certainty at execution. If a condition fails, the contract halts. Tuples group related values, like “Alice” and her balance of one hundred, into cohesive units. When errors occur, the contract throws an error, refusing to proceed until resolved. Mapping transforms lists, applying private functions to each value, like multiplying each by ten, altering the data’s course. Conditional statements guide the flow: if the amount is greater than zero, success, if not, an error halts progress.

Transfers are central to a smart contract's role, enabling asset movement. A single command transfers tokens, as reliably as Bitcoin’s blocks. Contracts interact with one another, calling methods from other contracts and forming a web of cooperation. Finally, Clarity mandates an explicit return. Success is declared with an “Ok,” or failure with an “Err.” In Clarity, there are no loops or risks of endless execution, it always walks a straight line, knowing its end before it begins. This is Clarity: a language of certainty, predictability, and trust.

Cairo, developed by **StarkWare**, stands at the forefront of blockchain innovation, tailored for zero-knowledge proofs with a focus on scalability, privacy, and efficiency. It addresses the limitations of existing blockchains like Ethereum, where slow transactions and high gas fees are persistent challenges. As a language optimized for **STARKs (Scalable Transparent Arguments of Knowledge)**, Cairo enables developers to build decentralized applications (dApps) that operate efficiently off-chain while providing verifiable proofs on-chain.

Cairo, short for **Cairo Arithmetic Intermediate Representation for Zero-Knowledge**, is a low-level programming language resembling assembly code, designed to generate STARK proofs for verifiable computations without executing them directly on the Ethereum mainnet. It serves as a bridge between traditional blockchain constraints and the potential of Layer-2 solutions such as **StarkEx** and **StarkNet**, processing transactions off-chain to lighten Ethereum's load. Built for efficiency and transparency, Cairo bypasses the need for trusted setups by leveraging raw mathematical proofs. It powers highly scalable dApps, reducing the impact of Ethereum's gas fees and transaction delays. General-purpose and Turing-complete, Cairo is equipped to handle everything from simple financial transactions to complex decentralized applications with precision. In Layer-2 solutions like StarkEx, Cairo processes transactions in batches, converting the computational load into efficient STARK proofs that are verified on Ethereum at a fraction of the cost. StarkNet, a permissionless ZK-Rollup, further demonstrates Cairo's potential by enabling scalable smart contracts and dApps to thrive without hitting Ethereum's limitations.

Further Reading

Nakamoto, S. (2008). *Bitcoin: A peer-to-peer electronic cash system*. Reference Website:
Reference Website: https://bitcoin.org/en/

Poon, J., & Dryja, T. (2016). *The Bitcoin Lightning Network: Scalable off-chain instant payments*.
Reference Website: https://lightning.network/

Blockstream. (2015). *The Liquid Network*.
Reference Website: https://blockstream.com/liquid/

Lerner, S., & RSK Team. (2016). *RSK: Bitcoin powered smart contracts*.
Reference Website: https://rootstock.io/

Ali, M., & Nelson, J. (2017). *Stacks: A blockchain for decentralized apps and smart contracts*.
Reference Website: https://www.stacks.co/

Somsen, R. (2018). *Statechains: Sending bitcoin offline*.
Reference Website: https://bitcoinops.org/en/topics/statechains/

Willett, J. R. (2012). *OmniLayer: Distributed exchange and asset creation*.
Reference Website: https://www.omnilayer.org/

Sztorc, P. (2017). *Drivechain: Enabling multiple blockchains with bitcoin*.
Reference Website: https://www.drivechain.info/

ARK Team. (2017). *ARK: All-in-one blockchain solutions*.
Reference Website: https://ark.io/

Buterin, V. (2013). *Ethereum: A next-generation smart contract and decentralized application platform.*
Reference Website: https://ethereum.org/en/

Poon, J., & Buterin, V. (2017). *Plasma: Scalable autonomous smart contracts.*
Reference Website: https://plasma.io/

Immutable Team. (2020). *Immutable X: Scaling NFTs on Ethereum.*
Reference Website: https://www.immutable.com/

ZK-Rollups.
Reference Websites:
https://matter-labs.io/
https://starkware.co/
https://loopring.org/#/

Optimism Foundation. (2019). *Optimistic Rollups: Scaling Ethereum with optimistic layer 2.*
Reference Website: https://optimism.io/

Coleman, J., Horne, L., et al. (2015). *State Channels: Enabling instant payments on blockchains.*
Reference Website: https://statechannels.org/

Offchain Labs. (2021). *Arbitrum Orbit: A next-gen layer 2 for Ethereum.*
Reference Website: https://arbitrum.io/

Tether Limited. (2016). *Tether: Fiat currencies on the Bitcoin blockchain.*
Reference Website: https://tether.to/en/

Binance. (2019). *Binance Chain: A decentralized exchange blockchain.*
Reference Website: https://www.bnbchain.org/en/bnb-smart-chain

Yakovenko, A. (2017). *Solana: A new architecture for a high-performance blockchain.*
Reference Website: https://solana.com/

Centre Consortium. (2018). *USDC: A stablecoin backed by the U.S. dollar.*
Reference Website: https://www.usdc.com/

Ripple Labs. (2014). *Ripple: A consensus protocol for financial transactions.*
Reference Website: https://ripple.com/

Lido Team. (2020). *Lido: A decentralized staking protocol.*
Reference Website: https://lido.fi/

Markus, B., & Palmer, J. (2013). *Dogecoin: A peer-to-peer electronic currency.*
Reference Website: https://dogecoin.com/

Sun, J., & Tron Foundation. (2017). *TRON: Decentralizing the web.*
Reference Website: https://tron.network/

IOHK. (2017). *Cardano: A blockchain platform for smart contracts.*
Reference Website: https://cardano.org/

Team Rocket & Sirer, E. G. (2020). *Avalanche: Consensus protocol for high scalability.*
Reference Website: https://www.avax.network/

Ryoshi. (2020). *Shiba Inu: A decentralized ecosystem.*

Reference Website: https://shibatoken.com/

Nazarov, S., & Ellis, S. (2017). *Chainlink: Decentralized oracles for smart contracts.*
Reference Website: https://chain.link/

Bitcoin ABC Team. (2017). *Bitcoin Cash: A peer-to-peer electronic cash system.*
Reference Website: https://bitcoincash.org/

Wood, G. (2016). *Polkadot: Vision for a heterogeneous multi-chain framework.*
Reference Website: https://polkadot.com/

Maker Foundation. (2017). *Dai: A decentralized stablecoin system.*
Reference Website: http://makerdao.com/en/

Adams, H. (2018). *Uniswap: A decentralized protocol for automated liquidity provision.*
Reference Website: https://app.uniswap.org/

Lee, C. (2011). *Litecoin: A peer-to-peer electronic currency.*
Reference Website: https://litecoin.com/en/

Monero Core Team. (2014). *Monero: Privacy and decentralization on the blockchain.*
Reference Website: https://www.getmonero.org/

Stellar Foundation. (2014). *Stellar: An open network for storing and moving money.*
Reference Website: https://stellar.org/

Polygon Team. (2019). *Polygon: Layer 2 scaling solution for Ethereum.*
Reference Website: https://polygon.technology/

ETC Team. (2015). *Ethereum Classic: A blockchain for smart contracts.*
Reference Website: https://ethereumclassic.org/

Aave Team. (2020). *Aave: A decentralized lending protocol.*
Reference Website: https://aave.com/

Protocol Labs. (2017). *Filecoin: A decentralized storage network.*
Reference Website: https://filecoin.io/

VeChain Foundation. (2018). *VeChain: Building a blockchain ecosystem for businesses.*
Reference Website: https://vechain.org/

Kwon, J., & Buchman, E. (2016). *Cosmos: A network of distributed ledgers.*
Reference Website: https://cosmos.network/

Micali, S. (2019). *Algorand: A secure and scalable blockchain.*
Reference Website: https://algorandtechnologies.com/

StarkWare Team. (2021). *Starknet: Scaling Ethereum with zero-knowledge proofs.*
Reference Website: https://starkware.co/

PayPal & Paxos. (2023). *PayPal USD (PYUSD): A U.S. dollar-backed stablecoin.*
Reference Website: https://www.paypal.com/us/digital-wallet/manage-money/crypto/pyusd

Sky Mavis. (2018). *Axie Infinity: A decentralized game universe.*
Reference Website: https://whitepaper.axieinfinity.com/

Goodman, L. (2014). *Tezos: A self-amending crypto ledger.*
Reference Website: https://tezos.com/

Wormhole Team. (2020). *Wormhole: A cross-chain messaging protocol.*
Reference Website: https://wormhole.com

Sky Mavis. (2021). *Ronin: A sidechain for blockchain gaming.*
Reference Website: https://roninchain.com

Mina Foundation. (2020). *Mina Protocol: A succinct blockchain.*
Reference Website: https://minaprotocol.com/

Decentraland Team. (2017). *Decentraland: A virtual world built on blockchain.*
Reference Website: https://decentraland.org

Synthetix Team. (2018). *Synthetix: Decentralized synthetic assets on Ethereum.*
Reference Website: https://synthetix.io/

Paxos. (2019). *Paxos Gold (PAXG): A regulated digital asset backed by gold.*
Reference Website: https://paxos.com/paxgold/

PancakeSwap Team. (2020). *PancakeSwap: A decentralized exchange for BEP20 tokens.*
Reference Website: https://pancakeswap.finance/

Wilcox-O'Hearn, Z., & Green, M. (2014). *Zcash: Privacy-enhanced cryptocurrencies.*
Reference Website: https://z.cash/

Duffield, E. (2014). *Dash: Digital cash for instant transactions.*
Reference Website: https://www.dash.org/

Legal Disclaimer

No Financial Advice: The information contained in this book is for general informational and educational purposes only. It reflects the personal opinions and perspectives of the author and is not intended to constitute, and should not be construed as, financial, investment, or trading advice. The author is not a licensed financial advisor, and the content of this book should not be interpreted as a recommendation or endorsement of any particular investment strategy, financial product, or asset.

Investment Risks: The field of cryptocurrencies and digital assets is highly speculative and subject to significant volatility. Investing in digital assets involves substantial risks, including the risk of losing your entire investment. The author makes no representations or warranties regarding the accuracy, completeness, or reliability of the information presented in this book. Readers should conduct their own research and consult with a qualified financial advisor before making any investment decisions.

No Guarantees: The author does not guarantee the accuracy, completeness, or timeliness of the information provided. The views expressed in this book are based on the author's opinions and are subject to change without notice. The author shall not be held liable for any losses, damages, or expenses incurred as a result of the use or reliance on the information provided in this book.

No Endorsements: Any mention of specific cryptocurrencies, digital assets, companies, Exchanges or investment strategies is not an endorsement or recommendation of those entities or practices. The author does not receive any compensation or incentive for mentioning or discussing any particular assets or services.

Legal and Regulatory Compliance: The legal and regulatory environment surrounding cryptocurrencies and digital assets is constantly evolving. Readers are responsible for ensuring that they comply with all applicable laws and regulations in their jurisdiction. The author assumes no responsibility for any legal or regulatory issues that may arise from the use of information contained in this book.

Professional Advice: The information in this book is not intended to replace the professional advice from qualified financial, legal, or tax advisors. Readers should seek professional advice tailored to their individual circumstances before making any financial or investment decisions.

No Liability: In no event shall the author, publishers, or any affiliated parties be liable for any direct, indirect, incidental, special, or consequential damages arising from the use or inability to use the information contained in this book, even if advised of the possibility of such damages.

Forward-Looking Statements: The book may contain forward-looking statements or projections regarding future performance of cryptocurrencies or digital assets. Such statements are inherently uncertain and should not be relied upon as guarantees of future results.

By reading this book, you acknowledge that you understand and agree to this Legal Disclaimer.

Thanks!